Organization Philosophy

Organization Philosophy

Gehlen, Foucault, Deleuze

Tim Scott
Senior Lecturer in Organization, University of St Andrews

palgrave
macmillan

First published 2010 by
PALGRAVE MACMILLAN

Palgrave Macmillan in the UK is an imprint of Macmillan Publishers Limited, registered in England, company number 785998, of Houndmills, Basingstoke, Hampshire RG21 6XS.

Palgrave Macmillan in the US is a division of St Martin's Press LLC, 175 Fifth Avenue, New York, NY 10010.

Palgrave Macmillan is the global academic imprint of the above companies and has companies and representatives throughout the world.

Palgrave® and Macmillan® are registered trademarks in the United States, the United Kingdom, Europe and other countries

ISBN 978–0–230–24722–2 hardback

This book is printed on paper suitable for recycling and made from fully managed and sustained forest sources. Logging, pulping and manufacturing processes are expected to conform to the environmental regulations of the country of origin.

A catalogue record for this book is available from the British Library.

A catalog record for this book is available from the Library of Congress.

10 9 8 7 6 5 4 3 2 1
19 18 17 16 15 14 13 12 11 10

Printed and bound in Great Britain by
CPI Antony Rowe, Chippenham and Eastbourne

To Laurie and Molly

Contents

List of Figures

Preface

Work and organization are embodied practices originating in the imperative for Man to create the conditions for 'his' survival. Technical innovation arises from Man's ability to manipulate objects and ideas in the distinctive human interval between stimulus and response. The embodiment of technologies is apprehended in developments in pathological anatomy and medical instrumentation since the late eighteenth century. These combined to disclose a new model of the body as a system of organs and the body thus organized became the prototype for a model of medical organization and for social organization more widely.

But empirical methods arising from such developments lost sight of their origin in the body, and of an older, more subtle empiricism revived in the early philosophical works of Gilles Deleuze. By addressing Deleuze's works on Hume, Bergson, Nietzsche and Spinoza, we can recover the significance of organization as embodied practice. Hume explains how subject and society are organized by material forces surpassing the human. Bergson discloses an ontology of efficient difference as the positive movement underlying Hume's analysis. Nietzsche comprehends how this movement contains a will carrying within it the seminal idea of organic composition or organization. These two movements constitute an affirmative genealogy of organization which Man sadly contradicts, not only by the organizations he forms, but also by the negative ('critical') tendency of his organizational scholarship.

To become a truly active, organizing being, Man must overcome his reactive nature. Spinoza explains what we must do to realize this destiny: combat the sad passions and inadequate ideas we suffer under the natural conditions of our existence; cultivate the joyful passions and the power of action by organizing our encounters with others. This is what is meant by a post-structural revision of organization.

Foreword

This manuscript was originally researched and written between January and December 1995. It rose from the ruins of a very different book which, after four years of frustrated writing, I destroyed; an act I have rarely regretted. *Par destruens, pars construens*. Why have I waited until now to publish? Several reasons, but mainly a lack of confidence. Was it sufficiently original? Would it resonate with any reader? Another reason was that the era that would be known as *Deleuzian*, predicted by Michel Foucault, was then only just dawning. It is now full morning, with a more widespread interest in the ideas and influences referred to here.

Following its completion, I entered health services research, which I thought might benefit others more than a monograph on organizational philosophy. A practical philosophy should, I thought, be followed by applied research. But I found there was nothing especially practical about health services research. Immersed in the minutiae of randomized controlled trials, my eyes lingered on Deleuze's books, neglected on the shelf. I would reflect upon Levine's truism that the most practical thing is a good theory, Robbe-Grillet's distinction between information and meaning and Robert Cooper's trenchant remark that organizations hate one and love the other. Hence, I eventually abandoned health research to return to organization studies, more specifically to its maligned underclass of critical and post-critical marketing and consumer studies.

Another concern was that in writing the later chapters I might have drawn too much on my reading of Michael Hardt's excellent *Gilles Deleuze: An Apprenticeship in Philosophy*. Having read most of Deleuze's early works on the history of philosophy, I found that Hardt's anarchistic synthesis offered a coherent narrative on the development of Deleuze's thought, through his Bergson, Nietzsche and Spinoza studies. I adopted Hardt's basic narrative structure for my chapters four to six. I see now that my discomfort about my debt to Hardt was partly hubris. Rereading *Gilles Deleuze* as I edit this manuscript, I do not think I have overstepped the bounds of scholarly community. I have brought together lines of thought from philosophical anthropology, the history of ideas and of technology and sociology and tried to place the Bergson-Nietzsche-Spinoza narrative into a wider philosophical context. I have also added a chapter on Deleuze's Hume study at the head of the Deleuzian narrative, and expanded on the theme of Spinoza and organization considerably. These chapters are at minimum a development of the Deleuze-Hardt narrative. I set out to read Deleuze with the specific problem of organization in mind. Deleuze often refers to organization in passing; Hardt contrasts organization with order. I have taken the analysis a stage further, to read Deleuze as an organizational philosopher.

Of course originality is a problematic notion, especially by Deleuze's own mores. All the philosophical works read herein are interrelated. Gehlen refers to Nietzsche, Bergson to the Scholastics, Foucault to numerous historical and unacknowledged philosophical sources, Nietzsche to Spinoza, Spinoza to Descartes and so on in a dance of ideas that varies from courtly formality to intellectual brawling. These comments apply mainly to chapters four to six, but they prompt the question of originality more broadly. When asked when he got his most original ideas, Igor Stravinsky is said to have answered, '[w]hen I am working'. In philosophy the answer would surely be 'when I am reading'. It is in conversation with a text that the mind is most creative: if ideas are to come at all, that is when they are likely to appear. But ideas are not singularities. One has only to read authors like Heidegger or Derrida, who work with ideas as if they were Russian dolls, to see that no concept has any origin or end, for those trajectories presume thought without language.

Acknowledgements

A number of people may be surprised to learn that they have helped and encouraged me to finally bring this book to light. My special thanks to Iain Munro and John Desmond for their friendship and intellectual community; Richard Wieskopf and Bernadette Loaker for helping revive my enthusiasm for the project; Ken Munro and Roger Stapleton for technical helping retrieve the original electronic files and Paresh Raval and the volunteers in the University of St Andrews Alternative Format Suite for transforming the manuscript into an electronic document. Without the assistance of the foregoing I doubt if I would ever have got this far.

It remains to add that if I had felt it necessary to update the book in light of all the relevant literature published since 1996, then I would not have published it. I would rather it remain as it was first written. As a series of essays and commentaries on works in philosophy and philosophical anthropology, it does not contain time-sensitive data. Regrettably, of course, this means that in 2009 numerous authors go unacknowledged. I decided not to attempt to update the bibliography, as this would effectively have meant starting over.

Introduction

This book comprises of six chapters on organizational philosophy viewed from a post-structural perspective. Each chapter addresses a somatic approach to organization theory and practice. My guiding principle is materialist in the philosophical sense: that organization refers to the embodiment of a multiple of parts into a larger, more coherent and powerful complex. This perspective draws on a long but neglected tradition of materialist thought holding to the belief that nothing exists but matter, its motions and modifications. Consciousness, which has preoccupied modern scholarship in this field, is by materialist thought seen as being of secondary importance to the affections of the body.

This approach has important implications for the study of organization as a process, and of organizations as existing bodies. We shall need to address both aspects in terms of physical passions, ideas and actions. Hence, we are interested in the kind of feelings, thoughts and conduct of which both corporeal and corporate bodies are capable. This approach is not anthropomorphic since it draws on an analysis of embodiment in terms of prehuman forces and principles. Nor does it imply an objectivist approach to their study: on the contrary, I shall refer to a mode of empiricism operating in the subjective sphere of what we can know about the internal workings of our own minds and bodies; how other bodies and minds affect our own; and the implications this holds for personal and collective action.

The advantages of this approach to organizational scholarship lie in its affirmative spirit, in stark contrast to the negative spirit of the Hegelian dialectic. It is conventional in the latter tradition to address organization in oppositional terms: organization is viewed as the regulative antithesis to the thesis of personal freedom, the ideal synthesis being a model of Man as a reasonable, social being; or it is viewed as an object of mediation (the 'other') through which the ego becomes conscious of its real identity. An affirmative approach by contrast, views the organization not as opposed to Man's desires but as the necessarily oblique means to their satisfaction. Other animals live by instinct, but Man is essentially an organizational being.

This analysis depends on a theory of Man[1] as an impossible animal, one so weak and vulnerable to natural forces that we must respond in a qualitatively different way from other species. In lieu of a natural niche, Man has a special talent for constructing a cultural world (a tautology) which is our second nature. We have this ability not as an option to be exercised as the will takes us, but as the necessary foundation of our survival as a species.

If this fundamentally active second nature is so constructive, why then is our experience of organizational life in general, and as employees in particular, felt so often to be negative? Why is something conducive to our survival and enjoyment so often alienating and depressing in practice? I shall address this paradox below, but put simply I offer two main responses: first, we have not yet learned very well how to translate our species' genius for organization into existing organizations. The organizations that we have tend to be more like negative orders: we only have the organizations we deserve given our weak understanding of our culture-nature. The second response is that even where we encounter joyful organizations, we tend to interpret them negatively: we are so used to resenting perceived contradictions of our abstract and idealized notions of freedom that we are incapable of seeing even genuine examples as a viable means to express our desires.

This is not an apologia for the organizations that we have, rather an attempt to draw a fundamental distinction between our potential for

[1] By 'Man' I mean humanity dominated by men. I have used the shortest available term, which is also Gehlen's. The choice of an appropriate term to designate the human species is very problematical. How could I use 'humanity', when one of history's greatest silences concerns men's subjugation of woman? Surely it is more accurate to use the masculine when it is men who have dominated the globe, economically, politically and socially. Besides, Bergson, Deleuze, Foucault, Gehlen, Hegel, Kant, Hobbes, Hume, Nietzsche, Plato, Spinoza were all men, as I am. To think that the cause of woman is served by switching to a glib new terminology, as some sociologists might prefer, is delusory and dishonest (though most users of the term Man mean humanity, which is just as delusional). I write here about the thoughts of men, a philosophy of men, run through no doubt with silent masculine assumptions and interests. If there is an equivalent philosophy of women (there is of course), I long to read it, but cannot begin to write it.

affirmative thinking, feeling and acting (organization); and what we have historically become: passive bodies, capable of mainly negative thinking, feeling and reacting. Man's vulnerable natural condition constitutes a laborious burden, which our institutions and organizations should be designed to relieve. But we will only be able to achieve this relief consistently when we are capable of viewing organization theory and practice affirmatively.

Guide to the text

In Chapter 1, I explore philosophical, anthropological and sociological perspectives on organization as a material, embodied process. I argue that whereas animals respond instinctively to internal and external stimuli[2] the attenuation of Man's instincts allowed an interval to form between stimulus and response: by virtue of this interval Man constructs his cultural world. As culture expands, the interval between stimulus and instinctive response widens, until the immediate force of instinct is so weakened that our behaviour becomes explicable only in terms of the cultures we make for ourselves. The two basic dimensions of culture are the unique dexterity of human thought and action. Both occur in the gap between automatic stimulus and response.

I then examine how embodiment has been addressed in sociology and find that, with few important exceptions, it has been neglected and even suppressed by a prevailing objectivist approach to problems of socialization. Sociology has been concerned mainly with describing how social institutions regulate the lives of social agents. This analysis is founded on a negative conception of human nature and society: that

[2] This is an over-generalization. It may be that a chimpanzee thinks in a basic way before acting, at least more than an insect. But the cognitive gap between ape and Man is wider than between ape and insect. Recently I observed a gull stamping its feet on the turf to imitate rainfall, the pattering of which attracts earthworms to the surface. Gulls are undoubtedly intelligent for birds, but I do not jump to the conclusion that this stamping is any more than instinctive, or possibly mimetic. The gull doubtless associates the behaviour with eating worms. It may adduce from observation that to imitate the patter of rain will bring worms to the surface. To the sceptic who counters that much human behaviour directed towards consumption appears little more sophisticated than the gull's learned behaviour, I answer, 'Perhaps, but the same person who behaves in that way may in the next hour solve a complex mathematical equation'. We slide in and out of automatic and cognized behaviour constantly. As Elias (1987) observes, man differs from animals in that his learned behaviour predominates his unlearned behaviour.

we are basically driven by natural instincts and must be restrained by regimes of institutionalized regulation. A materialist analysis by contrast, does not view Man as constructed by his institutions, he is rather their creator. In addition, Man is the self-creator within the phenomenological sphere of his body. The world does not happen to Man; he is its maker, externally in an objective sphere of being, and internally in his subjective experience. By ignoring the empirical imperative that Man is first and foremost a body, sociology has tended to focus on the objective, neglecting the subjective realm.

The body is the somatic locus of our experience of the world, and also the locus of effects of which that world is cause. There is undoubtedly an external world, but our knowledge of it is internal to the body – our internal environment or ecology of passions, actions and thoughts. The social relation is therefore always an embodied relation; organized in the radical sense that it becomes part of our own corporeal organization even as our changing ideas of the latter are embodied reflexively in the corporate organization of society.

The implications of this materialist approach to organization are developed in Chapter 2 with reference to the example of medical organization. First, I describe how the human body historically came to be organ-ized (viewed as a body with organs), influenced by the science of pathology; and how the institutions of medicine and society similarly came to be organized by reference to the organs of the body, which pathological anatomy disclosed. This illustrates the simultaneous effect of organization on the personal and collective levels (corporeal and corporate, respectively). I secondly present a brief history of medical technology to illustrate how Man's inventiveness is firmly embodied in our corporeal and corporate organization(s); how the invention of the ophthalmoscope, for instance, carried the physician's glance and imagination into the interior of the body, and the effects this has had on the wider organization of medicine and of society. Medicine is exemplary in this context, as our sense of what organs are and how they interact within a body, consequently our whole sense of organization, are heavily influenced by the rise of medical science and technology over the past two centuries, or so.

The ensuing chapters describe the contribution by philosopher Gilles Deleuze to a materialist theory of organization. Chapter 3 addresses Deleuze's treatment of David Hume's theory of human nature. Hume discloses a subjective empiricist account of individual and collective organization as embodied in physical affects. Ideas are impressions of sensations; mind becomes a subject by the application of natural principles of association; and society is organized by the invention of artificial general rules. Thus, self and society are organized from what is given (mind and partial sympathies, respectively) by the application of forces that are impersonal and belong to nature. Here we see the genesis of Deleuze's philosophy expressed in his later philosophical works and in his collaborations with Felix Guattari: a theory of Man and society as organized in the material given, which is prehuman, by principles (such as causality and reason) which surpass the human. The conclusion from this is clear: organization is not a human invention per se; rather the human is a special site of nature's inventiveness, finding its most complete expression in human nature and society.

Hume is principally concerned to explain how a subject and a society are constituted in the given, that is, the sense impressions, passions and ideas from which an organization is composed. Deleuze follows a lead indicated by Hume himself: that the fundamental nature of the given (although strictly speaking the given has no nature) is differentiation. The given is different in itself. This alerts us to the idea that a rigorous materialist explanation of organization as embodiment should not confine itself to the constitutive movement of organization alone, it should rather begin from an adequate comprehension of the material to be organized. In this sense Deleuze's Bergson studies, addressed in Chapter 4, represent a fresh start – as though his work on Hume helped Deleuze clarify his own philosophical project. In his Bergson studies he addresses an ontological theory of difference as the positive movement of becoming. Deleuze rejects the Hegelian dialectic's negative analysis of difference because it is opposed to the positive distinction of life itself. Hegel does not view being as composed of distinct things, he rather sees distinction as arrived at by negation. For Hegel, therefore, being different is always being different from another thing. The problem with this definition is that difference, identity and recognition are always contingent on the other. There has arguably been no single more influential idea in twentieth-century thought than this Hegelian notion of difference as a negative oppositional dynamic.

For Bergson, by contrast, being is different from and within itself. Its speculative mediation through the Hegelian other only serves to construct an abstract notion of authentic human consciousness, which is the last thing either he or Deleuze want. The most important point that Deleuze's Bergson studies add to the argument, therefore, is that affirmative organization does not denote a process of differentiation on the way to self-conscious identity. Such an account is false insofar as the raw material of organization is already absolutely different in itself.

The dialectic leads us away from the world of concrete bodies and into the ideal and abstract realms of a transcendental philosophy which is ultimately disclosed in Hegel's work as a justification for the ruling order.[3]

With his original reading of Bergson, Deleuze arrives at a pure conception of difference as the *élan vital* or life force; and a conception of Man as having a special ability to realize that force in his world. But this leaves us with a problem: Bergson's rigorous conception of difference appears to exclude any idea of organization. If being explains itself differentially, without limit, how can it ever converge to form whole things, bodies or organizations? This is the problem addressed in Chapter 5 through a reading of Deleuze's influential book on Nietzsche.

If Nietzsche's conception of the will to power is roughly equivalent to Bergson's concept of efficient difference as the internal motor of the becoming of being, his notion of the eternal return proposes a complementary constitutive movement in the being of becoming. Deleuze's Nietzsche study develops his critique of Hegel beyond the scope of Bergson's positive ontological speculation, taking us onto the terrain of power. Nietzsche redefines the terms of critique and therefore the conditions of real organization: to organize his existence creatively is Man's material essence, but that creation must be preceded by a total destruction of order. This means that in order to be adequate to creative organizational practice, organization theory must first destroy any position from which the material existence of the body as the real locus of organization could be negated. According to Nietzsche, the only possible outcome of such a critique is a radical perspectivism.

Nietzsche shows how that perspectivism works in practice: the Platonic question, 'What is truth, justice, organization...' presupposes an ideal form of things, an end to which all concrete examples must aspire. But Nietzsche argues that this is an idealist question par excellence. It is not a philosophical question at all, but a political one; it does not want truth but rather the power of ordering what the truth will be. For Nietzsche, therefore, the properly philosophical question is rather '*Which one* is true, just, organized, etc.'. Such a question invites a plurality of answers, each one defining a specific perspective. This leads

[3] Here I acknowledge my debt to Michael Hardt's excellent study; *Gilles Deleuze: An Apprenticeship in Philosophy*, University of Minnesota (1993). This work was invaluable in checking and informing my own readings of Deleuze's writings on Bergson, Nietzsche and Spinoza. I have of course acknowledged Hardt's specific readings and ideas in the text.

to the proposition that organization cannot be defined by appealing to formal types generated by positivistic research. Such research is driven by the false idea that there is an authentic kind of organization, an authentic experience of organization, and that this longed for authenticity will eventually disclose the objective truth about what organization really is. But the point about organization is that it does not comply with the notion of a predetermined order of truth. Real organization as a process is not determined in advance of its construction. The undetermined movement of organization is its very nature.

Nietzsche defines existence in terms of impersonal forces, of which there are reactive and active qualities. The active quality of force is the affirmative will to power, the force of organization or culture. This force is the same in all of life but it has a special intensity in Man because he is ecologically undetermined. The radically open horizon of our existence determines only that we must be creative, but our historical organizations express mainly the reactive quality of force: our organizations, our cultures, our human nature are for Nietzsche, living contradictions of our active essence. For him, therefore, we have not even begun to organize; and Man as we know him historically has the outlook of the slave: he is full of resentment and guilt; and whenever he invokes ideal forms he negates life itself.

According to Deleuze's reading, Nietzsche views organization as endemic to existence: the principle of the eternal return is internal to the will to power, endowing form to the motion of becoming. If the will to power is the affirmative movement of differential becoming – becoming different in fact, the eternal return is a circular motion of composition, or being, internal to the movement of becoming. Organization is composed of these two movements: the will to power as positive vital energy, and the eternal return as the idea, the form; as organism, as organization. There was never chaos in Nietzsche's universe, never any fundamental state of disorganization. From the outset becoming has given and has taken form.

Nietzsche leaves us in another impasse: he answers the question as to the fundamental nature of organization but views human culture as a perversion of that nature. Moreover, as Zarathustra tells us, the cultural destruction that we must first undertake is so total that we cannot expect to realize our power of affirmation, enjoyment and organization until untold generations hence. To realize his active essence, Man must ultimately overcome his nature and become more than human.

This leads in Chapter 6 to Deleuze's Spinoza studies, and the culmination of the argument. Spinoza addresses Man's existence relative to universal substance, both in terms of the attributes of extension and thought, and the degree of absolute power which all living things envelop in their existence. Spinoza explains the role of reason in the formation of adequate ideas and how these can contribute to our development of joyful passions and actions, on one hand, and our renunciation of the sad passions resulting from inadequate ideas and leading to inaction, on the other. Spinoza is a philosopher of organization as embodiment in the materialist tradition: he explains how we can organize our encounters with others to form more powerful bodies and organizations, by attacking the causes of our sadness and by generating joy. Finally, Spinoza allows us to propose a new definition and approach to the project of increasing organizational effectiveness, both at the level of the corporeal body and the corporate institution: for Spinoza, a body's power to effect is equated with its power to be affected; meaning that to increase our efficacy we must first increase our power to be affected by other bodies. The only way to achieve this is to organize with other bodies, to pool and amplify our power. Above all, therefore, Spinoza explicates organization as an embodied practice of empowerment and enjoyment.

In the following text, frequent references to key works are denoted by initials, e.g., 'Deleuze (1983), *Nietzsche and Philosophy*, p. 63", becomes simply '(*NP* 63) or [*NP* 63]'. Where a citation follows a verbatim extract, square brackets are used. Abbreviations are listed in the Glossary.

Gilles Deleuze was a leading figure in the post-structuralist movement. His works have played a significant part in defining its terms: the theme of difference, the critique of the dialectic, the demystification of transcendentalism and a return to the materialist tradition. Michel Foucault predicted, 'One day, perhaps, this century will be known as Deleuzian' [Foucault, 1977]. Deleuze quite often refers to organization in his early work, implying a fundamental process wherein the consequences of his philosophical ideas need to be worked out in detail. To that task this book is a modest contribution. Gilles Deleuze died in Paris on 4 November 1995.

1
The Organized Body

> For by Art is created that great LEVIATHAN called a COMMON-WEALTH, or STATE, (in latine CIVITAS) which is but an Artificiall Man; though of greater stature and strength than the Naturell, for whose protection and defence it was intended; and in which, the *soveraignty* is an Artificiall *Soul*, as giving life and motion to the whole body.
>
> —*Leviathan* p. 81

The title page of Hobbes's *Leviathan* (1651) is engraved with an image of the sovereign state as a body composed of a multiplicity of smaller human figures. The significance of this image for me here is that Leviathan is a pragmatic constitution of and for the material bodies of the people.[1] Leviathan is an assemblage of *corporeal* parts brought under a unified relation to constitute a greater, more powerful, *corporate* body. Its power is symbolized by its massive sword and crook, secular and sacred authority invested in one entity. The constitution of individuals into a greater force is affirmed by the detail of Leviathan's head, presented as a single great 'organ'. If Leviathan's active power is constituted by the power

[1] Hobbes's political philosophy is not my concern here – I merely purloin the image of Leviathan for my purposes. As a corrective, consider Nietzsche's (1961) counter-statement: '[t]he state is the coldest of all cold monsters. Coldly it lies, too; and this lie creeps from its mouth: "I, the state, am the people"' [Zarathustra I 'Of the New Idol' p. 75]. This might seem to denounce Hobbes's Leviathan, but Zarathustra is condemning the actual state as a travesty of democracy in contrast to the positively embodied state proposed by Hobbes. Nietzsche and Hobbes are both uncompromising professors of the materialist tradition (on Nietzsche's materialism, see Deleuze's *Nietzsche and Philosophy*, 1983; and on the materialist tradition of philosophical thought more generally, see Michael Hardt's *Deleuze* (1993).

of its elemental bodies, the intellect needed to guide that power is a multiplicity of embodied minds unified into one great mind. This thesis examines the two complementary movements involved in this constitutional process: how multiple bodies are organized into larger, more powerful ones, and how sensations impinging on those bodies become thought. This double movement I invoke by the term *organization*.

This interpretation of Leviathan implies that the state is not a negation or repression of the will of a people but that both are inseparably involved in one another in a material, dynamic, affirmative relation between bodies constituted on different scales of magnitude. The corporate body is the organization of the existence and power of corporeal bodies into a greater power of existing. This thesis argues that the terms embodiment and organization are practically synonymous. Any social institution or organization can be conceived in a similar sense to Leviathan, materially constituted by those bodies whose power it constitutes into a greater force.

Power – its assemblage, concentration and amplification – is the proper purpose of organization. I offer an analysis of how the lesser power of human bodies can be organized into the greater power of the superhuman bodies that we call organizations. Through an analysis of the constitutive forces of bodies we shall explicate a positive and practically creative philosophy of organization. This approach involves a total critique of negative conceptions of power, to be replaced by an affirmative conception of organization.

Power is power to exist. Each body comprises a specific and variable power to exist which tends either towards its minimal or its maximal potential (Deleuze, 1988). In illness, which is our body's internal reaction to the invasion of an external force, its power to act is diminished (though its power to act upon the disease may increase); while a return to good health, which is the re-establishment of harmonious relations constituting the body, increases its power to act. Thus, although a given body or organization constitutes a stable relation between multiple parts, which defines its power of existing, this relation is vulnerable to encounters with other bodies whose relations tend either to increase or reduce its power (Deleuze, op. cit.).

1.1 The organic sense of organization

The terms *embodiment* and *organization* refer to similar processes. If Leviathan is the organization of a people into a state, it is also a transformation of an *assemblage* of individual parts into an integrated and dynamic *system*. This process of transformation I term organization and we shall designate any body so formed *an* organization. The embodied state *as* state is not composed of a pure heterogeneity, in the manner of an empty container ready to be filled; but is rather composed of lesser 'leviathans' which constitute its major organs. These mini-leviathans are in turn composed of yet smaller organs, and even the individual human bodies comprising the smallest organs of the state are themselves composed of organs, and so on down to the smallest possible elements.

Organization does not mean an assemblage of different parts transformed into an indifferent unity; it rather means their transformation into a new relation of difference in the sense that the organs of the body are made of different components and are also different in being functional components of that body. Organization thus means becoming *organ-ized*. It might be objected that biological and institutional organs are dissimilar by nature, the latter being organs only metaphorically. But this distinction is not robust: corporeal and corporate bodies both combine animate and inanimate parts. Perhaps, then, the real distinction lies in the fact that whereas the heart, lungs, skin, etc., depend for their existence on their composition into a biologically functioning whole, the corporate organs, by contrast, are capable of existing separate from institutions. As this thesis turns on the proposition that corporeal and corporate organs are essentially similar, let us clarify this point. Biological tissue is organic when differentiated into subsystems performing specific functions in the maintenance of a body. But this is equally true for social tissue: bodies are socially organic when differentiated to enact specific roles in the maintenance of a larger social body. In either case living tissue combines to form a greater and more powerful body than its un- or dis-organized parts.

The objection that an organic conception of organization is metaphorical (e.g., Morgan, 1986: 11–76; Turner, 1992: 17; Williams, 1976: 191) can be answered etymologically. Williams (op. cit.) refers to a metaphorical sense of organic 'to indicate certain kinds of relationship and thence certain kinds of society. In this latter sense it is an especially difficult word, and its history is in any case exceptionally complicated' [189–90]. From the early fifteenth century, *organon* was applied in English to the senses, the eye as a 'seeing instrument', the ear as a 'hearing instrument', thus describing parts of the body as organs. It is from this distinctly physical reference of *organ* that the modern usage of *organize* and *organization* is derived (190). A bifurcation of the biological and instrumental senses of organ meant that by the nineteenth century *organic* could be used in contrast with organized. Thus the nineteenth century development of the natural sciences established a distinction between the biological sense of *organic* and cultural and administrative *organization*. This indicates that the notion of biological bodies being more literally organic than social bodies is quite a recent convention.

Coleridge distinguished broadly between *organic* and *inorganic* bodies or systems: in the organic '"the whole is everything and the parts nothing", while in the *inorganic* "the whole is nothing more than a collection of the individual parts"' [Williams, op. cit.: 190]. Coleridge does not distinguish between biological and non-biological bodies in this regard – anything that constitutes a whole is organic. Thus, we need not assume that artificial bodies are necessarily inorganic, or that all natural bodies are organic. Russell argues that 'a machine is essentially organic, in the sense that it has parts which cooperate to produce a single useful result, and that the separate parts have little value on their own account' [191], a definition redolent of Coleridge's.

Although an organic definition of organization is comparable to Williams' 'old metaphor of society as a *body*, with *members*', it is not clear why, in relation to the Greek *organon* (an instrument, engine or tool), we should regard this sense as any more or less metaphorical than its biological reference. And if there is no reasonable objection to conceiving organization as embodied, there are some strong reasons in its favour. The collective social body expresses a similar organic *élan vital* as the organic individual body: both are constituted as living relations between parts. Insofar as we comprehend the *élan vital* as active power, the corporate body is more powerful and vital than the corporeal body when its constitutive being exceeds the force of its organic parts.

From another perspective, corporeal and corporate bodies are conventionally distinguished in terms of their internal communications. The former emit hormonal 'messengers' such as adrenalin into the system effecting changes in organic activity. This might seem very different from socio-technical media like postal and telecommunications systems. Yet arguably, the body's hormonal system and the telephone network are in important respects very similar and in fact interdependent: each is a medium designed to alter the status and activity of a system, and each acts upon the other system. What, if not adrenalin (and other hormones), impels one to write a note or select a telephone number? Conversely, what is it but the exchange of letters, phone calls, faxes, emails, etc., that triggers activity in offices and homes each day? Hormonal and postal systems may be conceived as one vastly extended bio-graphical system of intra and interpersonal communications: each presupposes the other to transform volition into action. The biological and the social-technological interact in practice, though they may be conceived as separate in abstraction. In the social body, languages (gestural, verbal, written, graphic), activating corporate organs, are equivalent to the corporeal hormonal system. Moreover, both systems are physically embodied in the behaviour of social organizations and in their constituent human parts.[2]

1.2 Organ-Machines

I shall argue that corporeal and corporate bodies are similar in that their existence is constituted in *extension* (body) and *thought* (mind), and both are capable of *affecting* and being *affected* by other bodies (Deleuze, 1988a; 1990). In this sense, individual organisms and social organizations embody similar vital forces but at different levels of magnitude. This conception of social organization draws on a long but neglected tradition of philosophical materialism of which Hobbes's Leviathan is one instance. Hobbes not only proposes to analyse and construct society in the shape of a gigantic body, he also addresses the relations between organic bodies and technological machines in a similarly embodied way – a subject we shall address in detail in Chapter 2. In this Hobbes adheres closely to the Greek *organon*, going so far as to explain certain similarities between the human body and society.[3]

Perceiving the common denominator of mechanical and organic bodies in their common and vital quality of motion, Hobbes is able to conceive and articulate a relation of mutual implication between machines and men. This relationship is so involved in our modern social-technological

[2]Some blind and deaf people use a language of tactile micro-gestures, traced rapidly with the fingertips on the palm of the receiver's hand. In this language the practical continuity between the organic and the social-technological is demonstrated most clearly, if only because we do not yet adequately comprehend the embodied nature of more familiar media. As we shall see later in this chapter, the hand as a key instrument of technology and communication is the cultural instrument par excellence.

[3]'Nature (the Art whereby God hath made and governes the World) is by the *Art* of Man, as in many other things, so in this also imitated, that it can make an Artificial Animal. For seeing life is but a motion of Limbs, the beginning whereof is in some principal part within; why may we not say, that all *Automata* (Engines that move themselves by springs and wheeles as doth a watch) have an artificiall life? For what is the *Heart*, but a *Spring*; and the *Nerves*, but so many *Strings*; and the *Joynts* but so many Wheeles, giving motion to the whole Body, such as was intended by the Artificer? *Art* goes yet further, imitating that Rationall and most excellent worke of Nature, *Man*' [*Leviathan*, 1651 81].

age as to hardly admit any practical distinction between men and machines.[4] The growing impact on contemporary thinking of Deleuze and Guattari's *desiring machines* (1983), *social-technological machines* and *rhizomic machines* (1987; 1986), indicates that Hobbes's perception is by no means obsolete, in fact it remains one of the most radical conceptions of material relations between human bodies and technology. To conclude our definition of organization, therefore, let us briefly address the ambivalent perception of technology as a force of destruction, on the one hand and, on the other, as a force of construction.

The contradictory status of the automobile is a prime example. From a Hobbesian materialist analysis of life as motion, our relation with the automobile is more than instrumental, it is rather a relation affecting the fundamental speed of our motion of existence. Whereas our forebears were *equestrians*, their existence organized in a practical relation with the horse and cart, our modern mode of existence is organized in conjunction with the engine and chassis.[5] Modern Man is the *automobile* animal. This is much more than a negative symbolic relation and the automobile is much more than a negative object of desire as the phallic thesis conceives it.[6] It is rather the key term of a relationship

[4]'All which qualities called *Sensible*, are in the object that causeth them, but so many several motions of the matter, by which it presseth our organs diversly. Neither in us that are pressed, are they anything else, byt divers motions; (for motion produceth nothing but motion.) But their appearance to us is Fancy, the same waking, that dreaming. And as pressing, rubbing, or striking the Eye, makes us fancy a light; and pressing the Eare, produceth a dinne; so do the bodies also we see, or hear, produce the same by their strong, though unobserved action. For if those Colours, and Sounds, were in the Bodies, or Objects that cause them, they could not bee severed from them, as by glasses, and in Ecchoes by reflection, we see they are; where we know the thing we see, is in one place; the appearance, in another' [*Leviathan*, 1651 86]. In other words, sensation is a *relation of motion* in one's body, caused by motions of the body perceived; this sensation causes impressions (ideas) in the mind. In Chapter 3 we review Hume's development of this materialist definition of mind to explain how it becomes a subject and society.

[5]By 'modern' I mean at the present time of writing. Cultural relations of modernism and postmodernism, or historical relations of modernity and postmodernity (Cf. Lyotard, 1984; Harvey 1989) are not addressed specifically here.

[6]The characterization of the automobile as a phallic substitute is a weak critique of masculinity and culture. The automobile symbolizes a lack (the negative basis of the phallic thesis) only insofar as an analysis of the individual's embodiment of social definitions of desire is grounded in a negative perception of desire. Our thesis expresses an alternative, materialist view; that a body lacks nothing and that *all desire is a positive desire for something* (Deleuze, 1988).

of mutual involvement, a *practical relation* in a strong sense to be developed in this thesis.

Hobbes expresses this practical relationship when he describes machines as bodies and bodies as machines. Viewed in terms of their common quality of motion the distinction between the organism and the machine breaks down to reveal a more fundamental and affirmative analysis of their relations. This does not mean that we should be uncritical of the practical relations that we compose with technologies, but that we should start with an adequate conception of how bodies and machines are mutually embodied in their design and applications, composing the relations of social-technological organizations. Man's relationship to his technology is ecological in the sense that it is integral to the cultural environment he constructs for himself. This raises the important question of the origins of organization: why is it that Man, unlike other animals, continually constructs and reconstructs the conditions of his existence?

1.3 Anthropology and organization: Gehlen's Man

Arnold Gehlen (1988) evokes Nietzsche's description of Man as the *not-yet-determined animal*.[7] Unlike animals, Man has no natural niche and is therefore singularly unfitted for survival. We have little natural protection against climatic extremes; no adequate organs for defence or attack; are poorly equipped for flight and the acuity of our senses is greatly inferior to most animals (*M* 26). Finding Man too radically different to accommodate the notion that he embodies a higher form of development, Gehlen rejects the evolutionary thesis: 'One envisions Man fictitiously as animal only to discover that he makes an imperfect and indeed impossible animal' [Freyer, 1948; *M* 13]. Animals are passive, they do not create their own conditions for survival; while it is Man's unique nature to be active: 'for now, as an initial definition, we will define Man as an "acting being *handelndes Wesen*"' [*M* 16].[8]

Man's capacity for creative action corresponds to his reduced capacity for instinctual behaviour. Gehlen refers to Lorenz's characterization of Man as having severed almost all connections between 'releasers' and innate, specialized patterns of movement. Through a series of original

[7] *Noch nicht festgestelltes Tier.*

[8] We shall later develop the significance of the Anglo-Saxon *hand* in the construction of terms denoting Man's dexterity. At this point we notice how *hand* conjoined with *Wesen* (essence, being) suggests that the possession of human hands is connected in an important sense with the definitive character of the human.

experiments, Lorenz established two basic types of species-preserving behaviour common to animals but generally absent in Man: *orientation response* and *instinctive movement*. Orientation response (*Taxis*) is caused by an external stimulus, as when a frog positions itself symmetrically in relation to a fly before snapping out its tongue to catch it, first by locking its eyes onto the target, then by shifting its body into alignment. Instinctive movements are precise configurations of activity executed according to an innate automatism and resulting from *internal* endogenous stimuli (*M* 17). Instinctive movements such as nest-building and courting behaviour are complex patterns of movement triggered by an appropriate *releaser*. As such they are not environmentally specific and can be released in a void. For example, Lorenz observed how a young starling could be induced to execute 'all the appropriate movements for trapping prey, including pursuing the non-existent quarry with its eyes and head, swooping down, snapping and swallowing – all this without an actual object' [*M* 18].

Man is disengaged from virtually all orientation responses and instinctive behaviour, as they are too specific and rigid to be functional. Instincts remain within us but detached from any natural context, such that purely affective 'emotional storms' may occur, accompanied by unpredictable actions, 'in response to equally unpredictable stimuli that surface in the greatly restructured perceptual world of Man' [*M* 19]. Unbound by instinctual behaviour, Man is open to opportunities for activity and learning detached from biological necessity; 'the ability of a free (for example, experimental) activity to become detached from biological needs on the one hand, and from the pressures of a reward situation on the other, makes it possible to carry out such behaviour independently of a stimulus' [*M* 21–2].

1.4 Man's burden and relief

Being thus undetermined, Man is exceptionally vulnerable to natural forces. Gehlen borrows Scheler's (1961) conception of Man as *weltoffen*, world-open. 'Man's "world", in which the perceivable is clearly not limited to what is necessary for basic survival, may at first seem to be a disadvantage. To say that Man is "world-open" means that he forgoes species adaptation to a specific environment. Our unusual receptivity to perceptions that do not have innate functions constitutes a burden that we must overcome in special ways' [*M* 27]. We can think of this burden as the basis of what we commonly refer to as *work*. Faced with the burden of being *world-open*, Man seeks *relief* (*Entlastung*), which is provided by the institutions constituting a society and culture. The sphere of culture contains the basic materials and symbols of our existence: tools, weapons, customs, laws, language. Animals are adapted to ecological niches. Man constructs cultural niches for himself. Culture is an artificial 'second nature' that we must construct to survive: 'The cultural world exists for Man in exactly the same way in which the environment exists for an animal' [*M* 29].[9] *Culture is Man's 'natural' environment.* On this point Gehlen misleads, however, as we do not only construct culture merely to survive, any more than higher mammals merely survive in nature. Given minimally favourable circumstances, many mammals experience and exhibit enjoyment and suffering, from the dog that prefers a sunny spot, or pines for its meal, to the human who delights in the arts, or suffers bereavement. There is a good deal more to living than just survival.[10]

Man relieves his indeterminate natural condition by habituation. And institutions embody Man's own determination to 'finish' his nature. Different cultures incorporate different ways of dealing with diverse environments, while each individual member of a culture embodies a personal variation of that response. Each specific culture is contingent and different, but the requirement to construct a culture is necessary and the same: given his lack of adaptation Man must create conditions for survival and more. In this necessity mothers invention, for we turn our natural vulnerability to account: 'the underlying thesis is that all the deficiencies in the human constitution, which under natural conditions would constitute grave handicaps to survival, become for Man, through

[9]It is true that some human groups lived until quite recently in conditions comparable to niches. Australian Aboriginals, for instance (a class which condenses a diversity of communities), had when Europeans arrived on their continent, minimal material culture, being 'stone-age' tribes. Yet they had and are reviving rich symbolic cultures. This demonstrates that even when well-adapted to nature Man fabricates a world for himself by his works, cf. Martin Heidegger, 'The Origin of the Work of Art' in Heidegger, *Off the Beaten Track* (Cambridge: Cambridge University Press, 2002). Despite his insistent recourse to abstract concepts, Heidegger is here quite compelling, not only as an example of idealist philosophy struggling valiantly to operate in the realm of language, without ever allowing its focus to be distracted by linguistic concerns (semiology, for example), but in its ability to tease out distinctions historically condensed, conflated and consolidated. For Heidegger, the work (whether equipment, painting, temple etc.) constructs an intelligible world while at the same time revealing the unintelligible earth upon which it draws and depends. The work reveals the earth, which was already there, but could not be seen, concealed in its unintelligible nature.

[10]'in the human context the concept of nature has to be re-defined' [Elias, 1987].

his own initiative and action, the very means of his survival; this is the foundation for Man's character as an acting being and for his unique place in the world' [*M* 28].

Institutions mediate between stimulus and response, desire and gratification; this alleviates the constant necessity to act for survival and expands the diversity of human activity. This diversity is assured by the power of habituation, traditional systems of government and division of labour (*M* xxxiv). In contrast to such relieving behaviour, 'there is the other sort of difficult and usually physical labour, which affords only a small degree of relief, which demands great efforts, and which to this extent, from the anthropological view, carries the stigma of "inhuman"' [*M* xxxiv]. When work ceases to contribute to the maintenance of an institution, when it becomes a sheer animal effort to survive, it ceases to be human work as we define it. Insofar as Man is an institutional animal, we should define all *human* work as institutional. This suggests a unification of Man's burden and its relief under the concept of organization: organization is that process by which Man transforms his natural corporeal weakness into corporate strength, by constructing cultural institutions.

1.5 Burden and relief in the organization of mind

A crucial outcome of institutionalization, as we define it here, is the development of human consciousness. 'For, in the sublimated forms of interaction with things, *in the "suspension" of direct manual activity made possible through sight*' and 'in the linguistic, and ultimately intellectual, methods of responding to the world – as well as in the higher levels of "work" (that is, all planning, organizing, and symbolic activity) – one finds ways of dealing with the world that are particular to the human being' [*M* xxxiv].[11] An important feature of Man's reduced instincts is therefore his development of *mind* into *reason*. The more human action becomes, the more it embodies relieving behaviour, rather than direct labour, and involves reasoned thought. Animals responding immediately to environmental stimuli have no need of reason; their existence is quite unconscious, without any reflective

[11]'Man alone ... is able to go beyond himself as an organism and to transform, from a centre beyond the spatio-temporal world, everything, himself included, into an object of knowledge ... The centre, however, from which Man performs the acts by means of which he objectifies body, psyche, and world in its spatial and temporal abundance, cannot itself be part of this world' [Scheler, 1961, in Gehlen, 1988: 15].

pause between stimulus and response.[12] The genesis of Man's intellect lies in his need to choose between alternatives. To exercise prudence in deciding between this or that food, to take this or that mate, how many children to rear, whether to grow maize or beans, how many pigs to keep, to take this degree or that, to work for company X or Y and so on. This intellectual dimension of Man's burden is relieved in turn by institutions, which mediate between problems and their solution. Physically and mentally, Man relates to himself and his world indirectly, through culture. Our natural indeterminacy and concomitant need to stabilize our existence lead to our practical affirmation of institutions. Paradoxically, this affirmation is also 'that "alienation" that first makes freedom possible' [*M* xxxv]. Because Man always relates through culture, 'the direct playing out of subjectivity is therefore always false. ... The human being can maintain a lasting relationship toward himself and his peers only indirectly, he must find a detour, parting from himself, and here is where institutions come in. ... At least now human beings are burned and consumed by their own creations, and not by brutal nature as animals are. *The institutions are the great orders that preserve and destroy us*' [*M* xxxv–xxxvi, emphasis added]. The origin of reason is a question to which we shall return. Presently it suffices to note how, in the context of Gehlen's thought, reason springs from Man's natural vulnerability to play a crucial role in organizing his cultural creativity.

1.6 Man's affective response to world-openness: Motivation, work and organization

Along with the origins of human action and thought we shall address a third existential force: *affectivity*. Affectivity refers to the physical and mental affects that external encounters cause in the body, the feelings involved in these encounters and their implications for our ability to act. Man's response to his burden of world-openness is his construction of institutions but this response has two affective tendencies, it can be

[12]By *unconscious* I mean here the unreflective or immediately physical. This differs from a received Freudian sense of a mental sub-system ('Ucs') obeying a different symbolic logic from conscious mind. In fact Freud's (1953) account of the conscious and unconscious systems does not exclude the possibility that the unconscious is at root a physical rather than a mental system. Irigaray (1991) uses this interpretation to contradict Lacan's (1977; 1977a) determination of the unconscious as structured like a language. According to Irigaray, women have no language. For her, the unconscious refers specifically to the female body.

predominantly *active* or *reactive*. By transforming natural weakness into cultural strength the active institution affirms Man's world-open nature and envelops it in a cultural horizon. The reactive institution, by contrast, is a negative and resentful response to Man's burden, a construction founded on a futile denial, instead of a constructive recognition of his natural condition. Nietzsche describes the active Man as positive and joyful, and reactive Man as negative, sad and full of *ressentiment* (Deleuze, 1983).[13] This point is considered in detail in Chapter 5. My present aim is to argue that Gehlen's philosophical anthropology, drawing strongly upon Nietzsche, is readily applicable to empirical work and organization. Our basic affective responses to our world-openness will determine our attitudes and feelings towards the general need to labour, to specific types of work and also to the experience of organization and organizations.

How we feel about work and organization is linked to our apprehension of their origins and purposes, on the one hand and, on the other, to our labour itself; that is, to a *speculative analysis*, and the enactment of a *practical ethics* of work and organization, respectively. World-openness is Man's natural burden, but it does not have to be carried as a burden; the purpose of the institution is to relieve the weight of that load. If, therefore, the institution itself is felt to be burdensome, something is very wrong and we might well expect this negative reaction to infuse culture with a character of *ressentiment*. It is when Man perceives his species activity as purely defensive, when he resents making the effort to oppose a seemingly cruel and indifferent nature, which fails to provide the resources and conditions for an easy life, that culture becomes a collective embodiment of *ressentiment*.[14] Just as Nietzsche views Man as shot-through with *ressentiment*, he conceives of an alternative, wholly affirmative, response to nature (Deleuze, 1983: 175–94). To be affirmative means to turn every reaction into an action, to transform Man's negative response to his natural condition into positive and creative

[13]More precisely: '... a reaction alone cannot constitute *ressentiment*. *Ressentiment* designates a type in which reactive forces prevail over active forces. But they can only prevail in one way. ... And the word *ressentiment* gives a definite clue: *reaction ceases to be acted in order to become something felt (senti)*' [Deleuze, 1983: 111].

[14]We see from this how the ahistorical appeal of Utopias and Golden Ages may spring from *ressentiment*: Cf. K. Thomas (1964) for a selection of examples relevant to work; also *Don Quixote*'s satirical evocation: 'Happy the age...' [Cervantes 1604, *Don Quixote* I, Ch. XI, pp. 85–7].

action.[15] In the context of Gehlen's analysis, affirmation entails relinquishing an idealized view of nature in *opposition* to culture in favour of embracing nature as the material given from which culture is formed.

The only nature we know is human nature, or culture. Man, in his natural condition, *has no nature* – this is what *weltoffen* means. Culture is a second nature only inasmuch as it is logically secondary to nature; but, so far as Man is concerned, culture *is* his nature as everything known to him is mediated by his institutions. This is why Hume (1738) says that the only object of science for Man is his own human nature. Far from being antithetical to nature, positive culture is the means by which Man's world-openness is affirmed by (social) organization. On this basis, culture would cease to embody the reactive Man's *ressentiment* of his natural deficiencies by becoming a joyful affirmation of both nature and of itself.

Thus far we have only rehearsed a general analysis of our two basic affective responses to the task of constructing Man's 'second nature', linking Gehlen's analysis of Man's laborious burden of world-openness (*weltoffen*) and its institutionalized relief (*Entlastung*), to empirical work and organization, respectively. Work is here conceived as the expression of that burden in day-to-day existence (the so-called life-world), organization as the construction of cultural systems for its relief. This allows us to apprehend Man's species burden as embodied in his species relief. Therefore, in referring to Gehlen's 'species activity' we should hold these conceptions of work and organization together in mind. And since there can be no empirical work that is not organized, that is, no burden of labour that is not mediated by social institutions (even that hard labour which Gehlen describes as 'inhuman'), it is reasonable to use the term 'organization' to cover both categories. Organization therefore refers to institutionalized activity of any and every kind, to the organic process of its institutionalization and to any specific body so formed. If our views and experience of work and organization are predominantly negative, expressing a generalized – and often a specific – *ressentiment*, then we would expect to find this *ressentiment* informing every worker's responses to varying degrees. Many criticisms and grievances are undoubtedly grounded in accurate analysis and genuine insult, but we must also consider the contribution of *ressentiment* to the design and functioning of organizations at every level. It might then be found that individual and

[15] This conception of work as creative transformation is of course familiar from ideas of transformation, praxis and pragmatism, developed by Fichte and Hegel, Marx and American Pragmatism, respectively (cf. Gehlen, 1988: xiii).

collective dissatisfaction is provoked by instituted working arrangements and conditions which are themselves expressive of the *ressentiment* permeating reactive social organization and society.[16]

If Man is *undetermined* by nature, he is also *over-determined* by culture in the sense that his institutions overlap and mutually reinforce one another. In which case both the Mechanistic view that Man is naturally disinclined and must be induced to work, and the Romantic view that Man is naturally inclined to realize his true nature in work, are equally polarized. If, after Gehlen, we see no unified essence of Man, it will be difficult to isolate a singular attitude towards work. As a species we have no choice but to work for our survival but how we organize that work into institutional forms of relief is culturally determined. Work and organization are both necessary but their actual expressions are unlimited. In response to Mechanistic and Romantic models of the worker, therefore, we need to reject the form of the question: '*What* is the authentic nature of the worker?' and replace it with a very different form, asking: '*Which* men and women are inclined or disinclined to work? *Which* kinds of work? Under *which* conditions?'[17] Our answers to these questions will address how our specific obligation to labour is organized into its relief or exacerbation. Hence, *insofar as it is sensible to talk of an essence of Man, that essence must refer to his organizational ability*, since it is this ability that wrests a cultural world out of his natural vulnerability; that constructs institutional organs and so organizes the culture-nature of Man. Insofar as the question of a motivation to work attempts to establish different types of worker response, these types should attend first of all to Nietzsche's fundamentally active and reactive types of force manifested in Man. From this it becomes evident that we meet the responses to work that we deserve, in the sense that we have not yet learned how to break the stranglehold of *ressentiment* in the workplace any more than in other cultural institutions.

What distinguishes Man from animals is the weakness of his instincts. His freedom from the type of automatism manifested by animals is the burden of labour. This laborious burden can be relieved only by institutions to transform the effort of labour from a direct struggle to survive, into a culture of enjoyment. The key to understanding

[16] *Ressentiment* is conceivably the dominant quality of most industrial behaviour (cf. e.g., Fox, 1985). A materialist approach to industrial relations would begin with the analysis of *ressentiment* and then advance to *the advocacy of a positive industrial ethic.*

[17] The form of the question is addressed specifically in Chapter 5.

institutions and institutionalization is the insight that the institution is designed to organize Man's encounters with the world. In this respect the role of reason as the guide of action is crucial. To this we shall return, but now let us turn our attention to a sociology of embodiment.

1.7 Embodiment and organization in sociology

A theory of organization as a process of personal and social embodiment is interested in how the discipline of sociology views the problem. Turner's (1992) analysis will help develop the argument that the mutual embodiment of the individual and the institution are two aspects of a common process of bio-cultural organization. Turner argues that a sociology of the body has been overshadowed by a social constructionist orthodoxy; consequently, the body has been curiously absent from the scene (*RB* 34).

Structuralism views Man as acted upon and constructed by external social forces: that he is not essentially creative but rather created by institutions which transcend him. I have argued after Gehlen, that Man is creative rather than created, active in the world, more than acted upon and that in constructing a world he simultaneously constructs himself. The aim is to reject a model of Man as passively determined by a social order, in favour of a model of Man's creative essence as the *élan vital* of social organization. Our historical existence has involved an excessive degree of passive determination under the influence of political, economic, religious and social orders. In this sense structuralism theorizes the problem but offers no solution. Our disagreement with structuralism is located in differing views concerning Man's real nature. Man, as he has been constructed historically, is inadequate to his real, actively constructive nature. The question that we shall ask, therefore, is whether Man's existence is adequate to his essence. If Man is in essence an active being, how is it that his existence is so reactive?

Turner asks sociology to remember the empirical ground of embodiment as the biological, physiological and organic foundation of society; and the social character of such biological processes as conception, gestation, birth, development, death and even the disintegration of the human body (*RB* 35). By thinking the social as embodiment we can begin to conceive socialization as an active accomplishment rather than a passive process. Sociology has been articulated along a continuum between agency or action, and structure or institution. This invokes an established opposition in German thought between the immediate, practical and sensual life-world, and the mediation and constraint of social systems and institutions (*RB* 3).[18] Among German sociologists Max Weber (Gerth & Mills 1948) is renowned for his analysis of the bureaucratic reduction of the individual to a cog in the administrative machine (*RB* 3). This implies that social structure and human action are hostile to one another. I shall argue that, on the contrary, structure and action are inseparably involved in one another and tend, in fact, to affirm one another. Weber's view of the transformation of Western culture from traditionalism to modernism, under the impact of rationality, is too abstract and general for Turner, who prefers to conceive of a heterogeneous transformation of the human world through a myriad of embodied practices (*RB* 76). He emphasizes that being a social agent involves being a body, that social life and organization are experiential as well as objective phenomena, inasmuch as one is before all else a physical being (*RB* 76–7).

Turner levels a similar criticism at Anthony Giddens (e.g., 1974; 1976) whose primary concern to defend the idea of knowledgeable, purposeful action, involves a tendency to oppose empiricism as a positivistic reductionism (*RB* 87). Thus the body in Giddens's, as in Weber's sociology, 'is relegated to a feature of the constraining environment; the body cannot enter action theory or structuration theory as a necessary feature of the agent or agency. The actor is essentially a thinking and choosing agent, not a feeling, a being agent' (*RB* 87).

Turner's critique of Weber and Giddens addresses a general tendency in sociology to conceive the social agent as an almost disembodied entity, with physical extension and feeling as subordinate conditions of consciousness. From a materialist perspective, by contrast, mind is embodied, the body's idea of itself and all the impressions constituting this idea, occur as effects of encounters with other bodies (Hobbes, 1651; Hume, 1888; Deleuze, 1988; 1990; 1991). We cannot therefore subordinate the physical and affective life to the dictates of reason, when reason is itself embodied and given a practical tendency by affection. Reason is neither the motor of action, nor the primary guidance system of the body, which is affection; it is rather a qualification of affection capable of seeing beyond the immediately sensual experience. Reason is practical in extending the body's horizon of interest into the social and vice versa. Unlike in classical sociology, therefore, the life of the knowledgeable agent does not start where the physical body and

[18] An abundant literature is available on the influence of German scholarship on the disciplinary structure of sociology – for example, Burrell and Morgan (1979); Game (1991); Giddens et al. (1974); Giddens (1976) and Holub (1991).

its conditions of existence come to an end: this is where it begins and where it remains. It was this criticism that led Horkheimer and Adorno (1973) to refer to the suppressed history of the body as the secret history of Western culture.

1.8 Internal and external disciplines of embodiment

Two basic epistemological elements apply to corporeal and corporate embodiment. Embodiment happens *objectively* to bodies when they come under a constitutive relation; it is also the *subjective* experience of becoming organized or embodied. Turner terms these the external and internal regulation of the body, respectively. The forces of objective external regulation of bodies were intensified and differentiated as a result of massive increases in populations involved in the Industrial Revolution. As Foucault remarks: 'The great eighteenth-century demographic upswing in Western Europe, the necessity of co-ordinating and integrating it into the apparatus of production and the urgency of controlling it with finer and more adequate power mechanisms cause "population" with its numerical variables of space and chronology, longevity and health, to emerge not only as a problem but as an object of surveillance, analysis, intervention, modification, etc.' [Foucault, 1980: 171]. But Foucault does not refer only to objective technologies designed to control the perceptions and behaviour of populations; he also invokes the organic nature of the body as a site of resistance to the forces of objectification. 'The body, required to be docile in its minutest operations, *opposes and shows the conditions of functioning proper to an organism*' [*DP* 156]. Here Foucault is far from describing the body as a passive, docile medium, acted upon by social-technological forces; he rather sees these forces resisted by the *organic* body, whose discovery is an outcome of attempts to treat it as a machine: 'A body of useful training and not of rational mechanics, *but one in which, by virtue of that very fact, a number of natural requirements and functioning restraints are beginning to emerge*' [*DP* 155]. Even as he invokes Western cultural forces of rationalization, Foucault notes the resistance which those forces meet in the individual and collective body.

Turner poses the problem of comprehending the historical evolution of objective discourses on the body, how our perspectives are the result of social constructions, while retaining an apprehension of the subjective and phenomenological nature of embodiment (*RB* 8–9). Foucault, in his early works on the birth of the clinic (1973), the insane asylum (1965) and the prison (1977), focuses on the power of disciplinary knowledge to determine structures of subjectivity. In his later work, on the history of sexuality (1978, 1985, 1988), Foucault refers to a different kind of embodied regulation or discipline, less well recognized and more relevant to a materialist approach to organization. Specifically, Foucault (1988: 18) refers to four main types of regulative technologies, the enumeration of which will help elucidate our own concerns:

> (1) technologies of production, which permit us to produce, transform, or manipulate things; (2) technologies of sign systems, which permit us to use signs, meanings, symbols, or signification; (3) technologies of power, which determine the conduct of individuals and submit them to certain ends or domination, an objectivizing of the subject; (4) technologies of the self, which permit individuals to effect by their own means or with the help of others a certain number of operations on their own bodies and souls, thoughts, conduct, and a way of being, so as to transform themselves in order to attain a certain state of happiness, purity, wisdom, perfection, or immortality.

This typology should not make us think that technologies of production, signs, power and the self, operate discretely from one another. By the terms *embodiment* and *organization* we mean to invoke all four types of technology working together, as one. A production technology is embodied in the passions, actions and thoughts of workers individually and collectively. A semiotic technology is embodied in the generation and exchange of meaning, which involves a modification of ideas, actions and feelings; such a technology is always concomitant with a production technology in that things produced are always signs as well as things, and signification is a form of production tied to other productive technologies. A technology of power (a politics) involves the production of governors and governed in the body of the state, and this also is concomitant with both a productive and a semiotic technology. Finally, a technology of the self is inseparable from the relations of production, symbolic codes and politics, which form the social and institutional context within which the subject is produced through more or less voluntary practices.

Foucault's approach to technology addresses both the constitution of the human individual and of the social institution. Instead of perceiving these two aspects as opposed, we should, like Foucault, apprehend them as twin foci of a common organizational process. Foucault emphasizes this relation as a *mutual production*; the corporeal body and the corporate body, the human organism and the human organization, do not pre-exist nor do they have any practical existence, separate from one another. Culture, embodiment and organization refer to these technologies of production, sign systems, power relations and subjectivity, which present the productive forces constituting the human and social bodies together. Therefore, 'The disciplines of the body and the regulations of the population constitute the two [theoretical] poles around which the organization of power over life was deployed' [Foucault, 1978: 139]. But we must not forget the body's tendency to resist the forces of socialization. As Nietzsche and Foucault conceive it, the body is a material site of active and passive resistance, and it is also the locus of the Dionysian principle of sensual enjoyment (Deleuze, 1988). As such, the body actively resists the forces of rationalization and control by virtue of its substantial sensual existence. It is the basic unit of the *somatic society* in which the variable capacity of the body to be active and passive constitutes the somatic principle of political and cultural activity (*RB* 12).

1.9 Examples of embodiment: (I) Sitting and walking

Some practical examples of personal and collective embodiment will help to flesh out the foregoing. Turner suggests we conceive the body 'as a potentiality which is elaborated by culture and developed in social relations. Thus we do not have to pose an absolute dichotomy between acquired and innate behaviour, between culture and nature' [*RB* 16]. Mauss (1979) develops the idea that embodied activities like sitting and walking are both physical and cultural in nature. Such everyday activities have an organic foundation elaborated into many different cultural forms. Mauss refers to these 'body techniques' as combined organic, personal and cultural phenomena. In the West we sit on chairs, whereas in many parts of the world it is usual to squat, or sit cross-legged. These techniques are natural and cultural, organic and organized: sitting techniques exemplify the cultural embodiment of natural physical attributes and abilities. Insofar as one individual sits slightly differently from another, in accordance with his or her unique physical configuration, there is also a personal dimension to such body techniques. They involve the individual in a distinct culture, which exists as a distinguishable collective body only insofar as it is enacted by individual bodies.

A similar argument applies to walking: within organic limitations, our style of walking is a cultural accomplishment, part of a wider body-culture: At its most elementary, walking is a spinal reflex, 'but it is elaborated at higher and higher levels until, finally, we can recognize a man by the way he walks, by *his* walk' [Sacks, 1981: 224; quoted in *RB* 16]. Sitting and walking are elementary examples of what we mean by a combined corporeal and corporate embodiment or organization.

But we have only addressed these examples from an objective viewpoint: there is another important aspect to sitting and walking which is their subjective experience. As I sit or walk I am aware of my body's stillness or motion and my situation in certain surroundings. My subjective experience of my body is composed of the same organic and social elements as its objective aspect but it is felt rather than perceived. This internal experience is the starting point for phenomenological thought, which attempts to understand how an apparently private experience informs a collective consciousness (Husserl, 1962; Merleau-Ponty, 1962). The objective aspect of the body is also the starting point for a positivism that seeks to formulate laws of behaviour based on simple observations.[19] As Turner argues, a social structuralism, typically based on the influence of language, ideology and epistemology, only views the objective aspect of personal and social existence; it neglects the sensual aspect of life including a phenomenology of the affections (*RB* 41). If this is true of sociology it is even more so of organization studies, where accounts of personal experience are rare by comparison with objective approaches.[20]

Plessner (1976) uses the terms *der Leib* and *der Korper* to represent two aspects of embodiment. *Der Leib* refers to the animated, living, experiential body, while *der Korper* refers to the objective, institutionalized body (*RB* 41). A related distinction thinks of the body in terms of external and internal social spaces: 'The external character of the body is concerned with the representations of bodies in social spaces and their regulation and control'; by contrast, a treatment of the body as an internal space concerns 'the internal structure, organization and maintenance of the body ... the interior problem of the body is one of restraint, that

[19] In Chapter 3, where Hume's theory of human nature is addressed, I demonstrate how empiricism, rigorously apprehended, begins at precisely the same point as phenomenology, that is, in our subjective experience of our own body as it is affected by encounters with other bodies.

[20] Notable examples of the personal dimension of organization include Kamata's (1982) personal account of working for Toyota; Bukowski's (1971) autobiographical *Post Office*; Emerson's (1970) observational study of gynaecological examinations and Game's (1991) personal account of bathing at Bondi. Since the original writing, many more must have appeared.

is of the control of desire, passion and need in the interests of social organization and stability' [*RB* 58]. I return to relations between the interior and exterior body, and their implications for corporate as well as corporeal organization in later chapters. We conclude this opening chapter with a further empirical example of embodiment to illustrate some implications of the argument for a materialist approach to organization as embodiment.

1.10 Examples of embodiment: (II) The hand

I presented the argument that human culture is Man's response to his vulnerable natural condition; a 'second nature' that makes human existence viable. There is a strong sense in which culture can be apprehended through the dynamic relationship between our hands, eyes and minds. Is it not through the precise coordination of these organs that most artistic, social, scientific and technological achievements are produced? In conventional terms, the eye perceives the object, the mind forms an intention concerning it and the hand executes that intention. But this description does not capture or explain the continuity between the organs and their motions. The eye is not passive, it selects *desired* objects (indeed it may perceive only desired objects); the precise motion of the hand can alter even as it executes an action, and the mind is quite capable of believing falsely that the modification was intended. Moreover, eye, mind and hand can compensate for one another's absence in a given situation, or even permanently. The ability to locate a light switch accurately in the dark points to the fact that the eye does not merely guide the hand, it contributes to a spatial-temporal map with co ordinates distributed throughout the body, enabling me to repeat a movement with near perfect accuracy in the absence of vision. This suggests that not only the brain but the whole body constitutes memory; that memory is embodied.[21] In the blind person (and more so in the deaf and blind person) a substitution of the hand for the eye becomes so marked that the hand may replace the eye as the body's primary organ of navigation. Insofar as they are nervous, the eye and the hand are extensions of the brain and, insofar as it develops visual and tactile related capacities, the brain is an extension of the eye and the hand. But one has only to close one's eyes to switch off vision and switch on enhanced auditory, olfactory and tactile modes. There is no

[21] Merleau-Ponty's (1962) account of amputees' continued sensation of missing limbs is relevant to this notion of embodied memory.

determinate order of sensory perception and we have little idea of our sensory capability. We may never know, as the sensory nervous system, like the rest of the body, undergoes continuous and more or less radical reorganization in response to changing internal and external environment conditions.

But it is the hand above all that is held to distinguish Man from animals. So dexterous and versatile is the hand compared to even to that of the great apes, that it is arguably Man's definitive cultural limb. Hertz (1960) makes a connection between physiological traits and cultural classification in the phenomenon of *handedness*. Handedness became a pretext for cultural distinctions between normal/abnormal and good/bad.[22] Many examples of technologies incorporate the prevalence of right-handedness (scissors are nearly always right-handed). Thus, Hertz defines the pre-eminence of the right as a social institution – in Durkheim's terms, a social fact (*RB* 109). Handedness illustrates the reciprocity between organic and social embodiment. A culture of the right embodies a natural frequency which becomes an object of social evaluation and prejudice. The irony is, of course, that a privilege of the right needs the left for comparison.

The cultural significance of the hand has been addressed by other scholars. We have already noted how Gehlen (*M* 16), in defining Man as an 'acting being' (*handelndes Wesen*), points etymologically to the hand as the primary instrument of human action. 'Acting', a translation of *handelndes*, is rooted in *hand*, the German equivalent to both act and hand in English. Thus we see a strong etymological connection between Man as an 'acting being' and as a 'handling being'. Moreover, *Wesen* means both being and essence, implying that *to act* and *to handle* are both essential to Man's being.

Heidegger (1982), and Derrida's (1988) reflections on Heidegger, relate the character of the hand to that of mind; in turn leading to a materialist conception of language. Heidegger relates the hand to thinking, technology and being. For example, 'to grasp' (*greifen*), 'to comprehend' *begreifen*) and 'term' or 'concept' (*Begriff*) all disclose a manual metaphor to evoke mental operations. A similar inspiration is found in Heidegger's reflection on *Hand, Handeln, Handwerk, Zuhandenheit*

[22]In parts of Asia, basic cultural distinctions between food and personal hygiene lead to a strict separation between the uses of the right and left hand. O'Gorman (1845) refers to an acquaintance as 'a sinister biped', meaning left-handed. Protestant Scots sometimes refer to Catholic Scots as 'left footers'. Some Catholics refer to the left as 'the Devil's side'.

(readiness-to-hand) and *Vorhandenheit* (presence-at-hand) (*RB* 110). In fact, Heidegger interprets the hand as the very territory of Man's being: '*Der Mensch "hat" nicht Hand, sondern die Hand hat das Wesen des Menschen inne, weil das Wort als der Wesenbereich der Hand der Wesengrund des Menschen ist*" ['Man "has" not the hand, but the hand has within [it] the essence of Man, because the word, as the sphere-of-essence of the hand, is the foundation-of-essence of Man"] [Heidegger, 1982: 119].

This condensed passage suggests that language and the hand are inseparably co-implicated in culture; that gesture and speech form a natural cycle of embodied expression and communication. The special role of the hand in the development of social organization 'is to reveal, to manifest and to uncover thought in handwriting, or manuscripture ... prior to mechanization, hand, gesture, speech and writing stood in a relationship of integrated unity' [*RB* 111].

A similar point is made by Deleuze and Guattari (1987: 60–1) drawing on Leroi-Gourhan's (1964) work on gesture and speech. Deleuze and Guattari argue that the *anthropomorphic epoch* is composed by '[w]hat some call the properties of human beings – technology and language, tool and symbol, free hand and supple larynx, "gesture and speech"', but that '[i]t would be difficult to maintain that the emergence of human beings marks the absolute origin of this distribution' [*TP* 60]. I take this to mean that human being is rather a property of, or dependent upon, these paired accomplishments, not the other way around. In this context the hand ceases to be an organ 'in relation to the grasping and locomotive hand of the monkey' [*TP* 61]. Rather, it becomes an encoding tool capable of reterritorialising the world, and in doing this, it reterritorializes itself from a paw to a hand as the key instrument of culture.

Leroi-Gourhan (1964) connects the hand-tool relation to the face-language relation: 'the "supple larynx" is a development corresponding to the free hand and could have arisen only in a deforested milieu where it is no longer necessary to have gigantic laryngeal sacks in order to be heard above the constant din of the forest. To articulate, to speak, is to speak softly' [*TP* 62]. The mouth becomes available for speech as the hand becomes available for technological innovation: '[w]hen men assume an upright posture, their hands are set free from the task of locomotion ... and made available for fashioning the tools with which they shape the world. ... With hands and tools for seizing prey, men no longer need muzzle-shaped jaws and mouths suitable for grabbing and tearing prey; hence, the mouth is set free from its primary hunting/eating function ... and made available for speech' [Bogue, 1989: 128].

Manual dexterity and the development of technology are related to the development of voice and speech. When we refer to cultural organization as Man's response to nature we invoke this transformation of the paw with its limited functions, to the human hand with its virtually unlimited functions and we also refer to the correlative transformation of the laryngeal grunt and howl to the complex vocalization of language. With Deleuze and Guattari, Derrida, Gehlen, Heidegger, Leroi-Gourhan and Turner, we also begin to apprehend how it is that Man, through his cultural reterritorialization of nature, also reterritorializes his own nature.

1.11 The mutual organization of hand and mind

Finally, we can appreciate the cultural organ of the hand in the development of reason. Thought occurs in the distinctively human pause between stimulus and response. Indeed we can conceive of Man in his cultural totality as fulfilling this pause occasioned by his natural vulnerability. This pause is the space within which human organization, of which a vital element is the capacity for reflective thought, is constituted. Mead (1934) perceives the pause between external stimulus and instinctual response as an opportunity for exploratory manipulation, which connects the development of manual dexterity to the development of language and thought. What distinguishes Man's behaviour from that of animals is his interruption of purely instinctual behaviour by this exploratory phase between, for instance, the presence and the consumption of food. It is in this interval that the mind can reflect on alternative courses of action even as the hands can explore alternative objects. 'Idle hands' might 'do the devil's work' but they also do experimental work; indeed the whole movement of human culture is in a sense to render the hands idle, or at least to relieve them from the continuous effort of survival, so that they and the mind become available to explore and invent.

Along with dexterity and language, mental reflection adds a further dimension to a manual genealogy of culture, and it will help think of these capacities as interrelated, not only in their origins but also in their everyday practice. When we say, '[o]n the one hand *X* and on the other hand *Y*' we demonstrate in the structure of discourse the relationship between hand and thought; both faculties engaged in a similar exploratory process, picking up one thing for inspection, then replacing it and picking up another to inspect in turn, then comparing the two. 'Mind is an emergent, even as is the hand, and there is a functional relationship between the two. We see what we handle and we handle what we see, and we know the world in "handfuls"' [Miller, 1984: 62].

Consideration of the hand as Man's primary cultural organ adds weight to the argument for an apprehension of human organization as embodied, even to the extent that the capacities for thought and language are shaped alongside our manual dexterity. In the next chapter I consider two main directions of organization (the individual embodiment of the social and the social embodiment of the individual) as it has been crucially influenced by the rise of medical technology. Important insights into the complex processes of organization can be gained by interpreting developments in medical science and technology in terms of how they have contributed to a transformation of the human body and constructions of institutionalized medical knowledge and practice. This example also addresses Man's inventive capacity, enquiring specifically into the invention, dissemination of, and resistance to, new medical instrumentation. Armed with instruments, the hand extends and elaborates its power in many ways. We shall see through these examples how the hand-held instrument becomes the primary tool of deterritorialization and reterritorialization, as it continually moves between and modifies our perceptions of our corporeal and corporate bodies.

2
Technologies of Embodiment: Pathology and the Rise of Medical Technology

In Chapter 1, I affirmed a conception of organization as a process of material embodiment, drawing on Hobbes's conception of the state, Gehlen's anthropology and Turner's sociology. All three employ an analysis of Man's need to construct culture to approach the problem of corporeal and corporate organization. The present chapter develops the argument by addressing two specific and related accounts of this process in the field of medicine.

First, I address Foucault's (1973) account of the birth of the modern hospital as an analysis of embodied organization in three senses: (1) that over the period 1780–1830, pathology developed from a study of disease as a natural genus of species, to a study of the organized body (literally, a body with organs) as the site of disease; (2) that this organization of pathology and the medicalized body transformed the institution of medicine including its corpus of knowledge, clinical practices and facilities and (3) that these developments had a profound cultural impact on ideas and practices connected to social medicine and epidemiology. The intention is to illustrate, by other means, the argument that organization concerns processes of embodiment at two analytically distinct but practically involved levels: the individual corporeal body and the collective corporate body.

Second, although Foucault addresses medical technology in terms of its techniques of perception, its knowledge, its rediscovery of dissection, and its social administration, he does not address those specific tools and instruments which played such an important and continuing role in effecting the medicalization of the body and society. Thus I turn to S. J. Reiser's (1978) history of medical technology and its contribution to clinical theory and practice.

It is partly to medicine that we owe the literal *organ*-ization of the human body. Here may be found explicit empirical evidence to support the argument that human organization and embodiment refer to a single material, isomorphic process. As Foucault (1973) says, the history of modern clinical medicine is the history of modern empiricism itself. However, I shall conclude this chapter by arguing that the positivistic brand of empiricism medical knowledge gave rise to effectively contradicts the embodied process of its own production.

2.1 A medicine of species

Foucault (1973) investigates a turning point in the history of medicine. From about 1780 to 1830, the theory and practice of medicine was transformed by a series of perceptual, intellectual and practical shifts concerning the nature of disease, the internal structures of the human body, and its complex processes of organic life, disease and death. These were accompanied by radical changes in pathological analysis and treatment. In particular, the role of sight altered isomorphically with the roles of speech, writing, memory and the use of the hands, both immediately and through instrumentation. What could be perceived of the objective body; what could be said of it; what could be learned by observation and practice; hence what actions could legitimately be performed upon it: all these practices were reorganized along similar organic lines to which the body itself was reorganized.

According to Foucault, the precise coincidence of the disease with the body of the patient is self-evident only for us, 'or rather, we are only just beginning to detach ourselves from it. The space of *configuration* of the disease and the space of *localization* of the illness in the body have been superimposed, in medical experience, for only a relatively short period of time' [*BC* 3]. The coincidence of pathological form and organic lesion (classification and topology) assumed an ability to read – at first by a slow and meticulous gaze, later 'at a glance' – the correspondences between a typology and a symptomatology of diseases, and a scientific anatomy of the human body.[1] To detach ourselves from the primacy of the visual metaphor in epistemology involves a demystification of what once seemed self-evident: to become aware of the ocular domination

[1] '[T]he illness is articulated exactly on the body, and its logical distribution is carried out at once in terms of anatomical masses. The "glance" has simply to exercise its right of origin over truth" [*BC* 4].

of nineteenth century science that persisted even at the end of the twentieth.

But how did this ability, seemingly natural to clinical medicine, to science in general, and to our everyday conduct of life, come about; what is the history of the physician's look (*regard*)? We can begin to answer this by noticing how it was preceded by a very different understanding of pathology, in which visualization was not paramount. In the second half of the eighteenth century diseases were viewed as *autonomous species* obeying a strict order of classification: '[n]ever treat a disease without first being sure of its species', [*BC* 4]. The role of clinical theory and practice was to understand 'the immanent logic of morbid forms, the principle of their decipherment and the semantic rule of their definition' [*BC* 4]. A qualitative distinction was perceived between the body as a confusion of internal masses, and the body of the disease as clearly defined by its recognizable configuration of symptoms. Diseases were thought to be structured like all of nature, according to a predetermined order of classes, genera and species.

Foucault argues that although pathologists recognized a general discrepancy between this rigid classification on the one hand and a diversity of manifestation of pathological species on the other, the basic conception of a pathology of species represented a generally held belief in an immanent 'configuration' of disease as the ontological precondition for its Linnaean taxonomy; an a priori 'perception' of the nature of disease itself (*BC* 4). This belief led classificatory medicine to regard the localization of the disease in the organism (its literal *organization*) as of secondary importance to its correct classification under a natural order of diseases.

2.2 The primary spatialization of pathology

Foucault identifies four basic principles supporting a medicine of species, combining to disclose a *primary spatialization* of disease: the *first* principle expresses a preference for 'historical' over 'philosophical' knowledge: '[t]he historical embraces whatever, *de facto* or *de jure*, sooner or later, directly or indirectly, may be offered to the gaze. A cause that can be seen, a symptom that is gradually discovered, a principle that can be deciphered from its root do not belong to the order of "philosophical knowledge", but to a "very simple" knowledge, which "must precede all others", and which situates the original form of medical experience' [*BC* 5–6]. This principle supported natural history (itself a development of natural theology) prior to the later nineteenth-century distinction between the sciences. It was supposed that nature presented herself to perception in her original truth; the observant eye requiring only to note the manifest appearance of a specimen to see that truth; the innocent eye viewed nature in her original innocence. The *knowing eye* of the philosopher, by contrast, was thought to be too sullied by experience to see what was simply present. The supposedly innocent eye is that of the painter whose influence on pathology is evident in Sauvages' quotation of Thomas Sydenham, '[h]e who writes the history of diseases must ... observe attentively the clear and natural phenomena of diseases, however uninteresting they may seem. In this he must imitate the painters who when they paint a portrait are careful to mark the smallest signs and natural things that are to be found on the face of the person they are painting' [*BC* 6]. This suggests an affinity between the eighteenth-century pathologist and the botanist; one collected diseases as the other collected plants.

The *second* principle was that diseases were classified according to degrees of formal *resemblance* (*BC* 6). The observation that apoplexy, syncope and paralysis all involve the cessation of voluntary movement and a reduction in internal and external sensory activity, caused them to be grouped together as merely different manifestations of similar functional disturbances. The modern perspective which sees in paralysis a symptom, in syncope an episode and in apoplexy an organic and functional attack, would have been foreign to the classificatory gaze (*BC* 6–7). Three diseases showing similar symptoms were reckoned to belong to the same species and classified and treated accordingly. We can hardly imagine what modern medicine would be like under this regime – if, for example, all headaches were manifestations of one disease, and the same for diarrhoea, inflammation or bleeding. The skill of the modern physician points in the opposite direction: to classify and treat meningitis in a similar manner to a migraine would now be considered a serious medical error.

The principle of similarity constituted much more than a naive empirical diagnostics, however; it disclosed the *third* principle – a rational order of disease: '[t]he veil is lifted from the principle of their creation; this is the general order of nature' [*BC* 7]. Sydenham invokes this order in the context of an already outdated natural theology: '[t]he supreme Being is not subjected to less certain laws in producing diseases or in maturing specific morbific humours, than in growing plants and animals. ... He who observes attentively the order, the time, the hour at which the attack of quart fever begins, the phenomena of shivering, of heat, in a word all the symptoms proper to it, will have as many reasons to believe that this disease is a species as he has to believe that a plant constitutes a species because it grows, flowers, and dies always in the same way' [*BC* 7]. The principle of similarity in the classification of diseases was seen to correspond to their divine ontological order. The order of diseases was part of, or perhaps isomorphic to, the order of life; governed by the same structures and divisions,'the rationality of life is identical with the rationality of that which threatens it. Their relationship is not one of nature and counter-nature; but, in a natural order common to both, they fit into one another, one superimposed upon the other' [*BC* 7].

But the *fourth* principle of classificatory medicine is that, while each disease is perceived as an autonomous species, its practical manifestation is encountered only in the body of the patient, with all the complications that this brings in terms of age, sex, disposition, strength, etc., *to disturb the pure, ideal form of the disease itself*. Thus the pathologist had to circumscribe the body of the patient in his diagnosis: 'in relation to that which he is suffering from, the patient is only an external fact; the medical reading must take him into account only to place him in parenthesis' [*BC* 8]. It should not be surprising therefore, that a knowledge of the internal structures of the body, although valued, should be held of less account than the ability to identify the species of diseases affecting it. Anatomical knowledge was required only insofar as it might enable the physician to exclude its distorting effect upon his diagnosis: '[i]t is not the pathological that functions, in relation to life, as a counter-nature, but the patient in relation to disease itself' [*BC* 8].

A similar relation applies to the physician, whose intervention was seen to interrupt the natural lifecycle of the disease, even deflecting his own accurate diagnosis, prognosis and treatment. Therefore he attends patiently as the disease unfolds to reveal its true identity to him: only when it has reached maturity will it be prudent to intervene. 'In the period of invasion, the doctor must hold his breath, for the "beginnings of disease reveal its class, its genus, and its species; when the symptoms increase and become more marked, it is enough "to diminish their violence and reduce the pains; when the disease has settled in, one must follow step by step the paths followed by nature, strengthening it if it is too weak, diminishing it if it strives too vigorously to destroy what resists it"' [*BC* 8–9].

The role of the eighteenth-century physician was to let the disease follow its natural course: to interfere was dangerous, unnatural. Disease was ascribed with a right anterior to its affection of the body: to violate that right would be to pervert the sacred order of things. The principles of natural theology, resemblance, rationality and autonomy all combined to produce an understanding of disease as a *predetermined order* of pathological possibility. The internal structures of the body were still largely unexplored in the West (with few notable exceptions, such as Leonardo da Vinci) and disease could not therefore be comprehended adequately from a perspective of the body. Such a perspective could only be acquired through a pathology based on anatomy, which in turn depended on the dissection of cadavers. Only when the body of the patient was *organized* in this way, through an exploratory disorganization of dissection; that is, when it came to be understood as a unified body of distinguishable organs and subsystems, could disease cease to be viewed as a predetermined and sacred order, and begin to be understood as a more unpredictable, organic phenomenon, in relation to which the individual physician and the institution of medicine might take a more active, interventionist role.

As long as the corporeal body was locked into a medicine of species, the role of the corporate body was similarly determined. The revolution in medical empiricism not only transformed the structures and roles of medical institutions, but its influence also spread through Western culture. The passive medical ethos of watching and waiting for the disease to take its natural and proper course, came to be replaced by a new active ethos of search and destroy, based on a theory of diseases as aggressive invaders of a highly organized body. For this change to happen the physician's impassive, observant eye had to be replaced by the active, probing eye of the modern clinician. *A new space of the visible had to be invented.*

2.3 The secondary spatialization of pathology

A medicine of species oscillated between the ideal form of a disease and its material manifestation in the body of the patient. This was an encounter between two different life forms and their different modes of spatialization; between a two-dimensional *table* of rational pathology and a three-dimensional *volume* of the organic body.[2] The physician dealt with two incommensurable figures, for how 'could the flat, homogeneous, homological space of classes become visible in a geographical system of masses differentiated by their volume and distance? How can a disease, defined by its *place* in a family, be characterized by its *seat*

[2] 'We are dealing here with those complex, derived figures by means of which the essence of the disease, with its structure of a picture, is articulated upon the thick, dense volume of the organism and becomes *embodied* within it' [*BC* 10].

in an organism?' [*BC* 10] The former defines the *primary spatialization* of, pathology; the latter defines its *secondary spatialization* in the body. Disease was conceived as a mobile entity that could appear in one part of the body, then transfer itself to another part, yet still remain identical in nature.[3] This remarkable mobility allowed a nose bleed to change into a menstrual flow or a cerebral haemorrhage and still be perceived as one and the same disease (*BC* 11).

By sympathetic relays (the diaphragm, the stomach); by diffusion (through the nervous and vascular systems); by functional correspondences (allowing the intestines to commune with the kidneys and the kidneys with the skin) or by resonance in one part of the nervous system, triggered by pains in another part, a disease tended to redistribute itself around the body; without ever losing its essential structure or identity. The doctrine of sympathies not only apprehended a body in communion with its own parts, it perceived pathways along which disease moved within the alien space of the body. It also allowed one disease to invoke another far removed in the nosological table (*BC* 11). Complications are explained in this manner, but the physician would be slow to deduce from dissimilar symptoms a unity of disease. Thus alternate episodes of lethargy and mania, which might today be diagnosed as bipolar disorder, would rather be viewed as two very different diseases triggering one another successively.[4] The movement of causality could also be reversed: '[t]he paralytic affections are a much more frequent *cause of madness* than is thought; and they are also a very common *effect of mania*' [*BC* 11–12, emphasis added].

In this pathology, duration is not of the organism: the disease follows its own temporal order of development; nor does it evolve in interaction with the body.[5] For this reason attention to the mechanics of the body

[3] 'The space of the body and the space of the disease possess enough latitude to slide away from one another' [*BC* 10].

[4] The observation that a similar metaphor for mania and depression as triggering one another, might conceivably be applied by a modern clinician, testifies to an extraordinary though wholly predictable effect: that the language and practice of medicine still carries strong traces of the species theory of disease, two centuries after it began to be overturned. Indeed it seems very likely that new theories, in medicine and elsewhere, do not substitute their discredited predecessors as neatly and completely as we might like to believe. Rather, new theory overlays old, such that they become intermingled in the minds of even the most accomplished experts. Today, I would hazard to suggest, clinicians still waver between observational and interventionist models of practice, hardly aware that in doing so they re-enact a major historical development in microcosm.

[5] 'time is integrated as a nosological constant, not as an organic variable' [*BC* 12].

was secondary to the classification and operation of diseases, as Tissot (1767) made clear, 'Physicians must confine themselves to knowing the forces of medicines and diseases by means of their operations; they must observe them with care and strive to know their laws, and be tireless in the search for physical causes' [*BC* 13]. Such physical causes might involve humorous imbalances: convulsions might be caused by a 'desiccated' nervous system, but such mechanical conditions merely provide a favourable ecology for disease to establish itself, they are not its real cause. Disease never becomes so involved in the body that it loses its essential structure and identity as an independent species in the nosological table.

In the secondary spatialization of pathology, therefore, the body is perceived more positively than in the primary mode; as the necessary medium of transfiguration by which the essence of the disease will be recognized in its visible effects upon the body. The configuration of a disease will be repeated but in a different, more concrete medium and therefore require careful interpretation. The body thus becomes 'the local, sensible presence of this order – a segment of enigmatic space that unites the nosological plane of kinships to the anatomic volume of vicinities' [*BC* 14–15]. Increasingly, the medical *look* relinquishes its systematic doctrines and begins to examine the internal structures of the body more closely. At this stage the relationship between classification and embodiment is reversed: '[t]he patient is the rediscovered portrait of the disease; he is the disease itself, with shadow and relief, modulations, nuances, depth; and when describing the disease the doctor must strive to restore this living density' [*BC* 15]. Secondary spatialization opened the interior structures of body in all their detail to the clinical gaze: '[d]octor and patient are caught up in an ever greater proximity, bound together, the doctor by an ever-more attentive, more insistent, more penetrating gaze, the patient by all the silent, irreplaceable qualities that, in him, betray – that is reveal and conceal – the clearly ordered forms of the disease' [*BC* 15–16].

It is helpful to remark about this distinction, between a two-dimensional *order* of disease on the one hand and a three-dimensional *organization* of the body on the other. The importance of secondary spatialization for our analysis is that it begins to comprehend pathology as a science of organic embodiment. Once pathology is released from its strict primary spatialization, disease becomes an organic process, deterritorialized from a fixed order of classes, genera and species and reterritorialized within the concrete organization of the body. This reterritorialization occurred simultaneously in the body of the patient, in the institutional body of medicine (its *corpus* of knowledge and its body of practice) and, in a third innovation, a new conception of public health. This in turn led to the creation of further institutions, all embodying at corporate levels the newly organized corporeal model.

2.4 The tertiary spatialization of pathology

'Let us call tertiary spatialization all the gestures by which, in a given society, a disease is circumscribed, medically invested, isolated, divided up into closed, privileged regions or distributed throughout cure centres, arranged in the most favorable way' [*BC* 16]. Foucault's *third* space of pathology addresses the impact of a transition from primary to secondary spatialization upon society at large. Changes in the status of medical knowledge and practice, its writing and teaching, and its technical innovation had a widespread impact on the political, economic and social organization of society. The newly medicalized human body was quickly matched by a medical model of the social body, a process speeded by the keen and growing interest in the social dimensions of disease. Just as the body of the patient presented resistance to disease and its treatment by virtue of its material constitution, so the greater body of society presents its own kinds of resistance. This tertiary space was/is constituted by collective responses; 'it brings into play a system of options that reveals the way in which a group, in order to protect itself, practices exclusions, establishes the forms of assistance, and reacts to poverty and to the fear of death' [*BC* 16]; it is the locus of political struggles, Utopian ideals, economic constraints and social confrontations.

The increasing complexity of society in the later eighteenth century was perceived to have a denaturing effect on disease itself. Uncomplicated cultures suffered uncomplicated diseases, whereas civilization, wealth and good living produced a diversification and cross-contamination of pathological species (*BC* 16–17). If culture provided an artificial breeding ground, the old style prisons and hospitals, in which proper segregation and quarantine were unknown, concentrated this effect, spawning their own unmanageable hybrids and syndromes – hospital or prison fevers, making diagnosis a far more difficult task. 'In fact, no hospital disease is a pure disease' [*BC* 17] and hospital medicine was therefore perceived within the medical profession to be a bastardized practice.

The natural locus of disease was the family (*BC* 17). According to their taxonomy, families of diseases were discovered by symptomatic resemblance. It would be easy for this botanic model to perceive in the hospital *an unnatural hothouse of disease* which threatened to disrupt its proper classification, diagnosis and treatment. How much better to throw open the doors of the old hospital and allow disease to escape back into its natural element, thereby regaining a simplicity and balance in the bosom of nature from whence it came. The locus of disease was the family in two senses, therefore: a disease belonged in its taxonomic family and the patient belonged in his familial setting. Therefore, medicine had only to return the patient to the bosom of the family to let disease take its natural and proper course.

For disease had flourished and taken over the hospital; it needed to be flushed out of its enclosed pestilential domain, into the transparent space of society. Like the body, society was beginning to be perceived as an open structure, whose visibility would be assured by locating the agents of a social medicine in its midst. The family doctor could apprehend disease in its natural environment, uncomplicated by the distortions and cross-breeds of the hospital. Provided with a kind of free social spatialization, disease would quickly flourish and die away, finding in the family the natural locus of its own abolition (*BC* 17–18).

A reconstruction of disease as located within a society viewed as a kind of open clinic, required considerable changes in finance and administration. Donors' intentions were reinterpreted and the old hospital foundations were dissolved in favour of a generalized system of medical care. For different reasons, economists and clinicians agreed that medicine was better administered in the family than in hospital. Separating the sick man from his family deprived the latter of the assistance dispensed to him – and assisting them both would only double the burden of cost to society. By returning him to his family, however, his benefits were shared.[6] However rationalized, this was to be a private medicine administered to private patients; but it was recognized that a general *vigilance* would be required over physicians to prevent abuse; a vigilance that could be exercised only by the *state*. The possibility of this vigilance conceived of society precisely in terms of visible manifestations; 'a homogeneous space in which no intervention is authorized except that of the gaze which is effaced as it alights' [*BC* 19].

Foucault's tripartite spatialization of pathology discloses a *progressive development of the medical imagination and look*. The table of diseases

[6] '[S]omeone will have to eat the meat from which his broth is made; and in heating his tisane, it costs no more to warm his children as well' [*BC* 19].

began to lose its ideal autonomy, as the field of pathology expanded to include the embodied nature of the disease. Then both disease and body were incorporated into a new social context which also demanded the widest possible scrutiny. What we see in this development is the depreciation of a rational order of disease (the classificatory table), a new appreciation of the body and a need (or desire) to disclose more clearly its internal structure of organs and tissues. The locus of pathology changed from the two-dimensional plane of the table to the three-dimensional volume of the body; from the precise configuration of a disease to the precise seat of the pain, lesion or discharge itself; thence to the social arrangements considered most conducive not only to the cure of specific cases, but also to their eradication from society. Disease, the body, the medical institution and society: all became *organized* in that they ceased to be seen as an immutable external *order* of things, and began instead to be understood as an unpredictable, external process of transformation, mutation and development.

2.5 The common syntax of illness and speech

All of which demanded a different way of looking at things and a new way of explaining what that look disclosed. Perhaps reacting to its former conservatism, medicine became temporarily obsessed with an extremely positivistic idea of empiricism that could see no interval between observation and recognition; to see was to know immediately: '[a]ll theory is always silent or vanishes at the patient's bedside' [*BC* 107]. The revolution in medicine in relations between the eye, the mind and the hand entailed a renunciation of mediaeval systems and a new primacy awarded to *observation*. The physician's prior knowledge of disease and the patient's narrative, previously so important to diagnosis, now came to be seen as obstructive. Disease must be given the space to 'speak' for itself in signs manifested on the body. The field must be cleared for the exercise of a silent medical gaze.

Thus, one of the remarkable aspects of the new empiricism arising early in the nineteenth century was its suppression of *recognition*; its assumption that things 'speak' for themselves; that reality is articulated as such. Foucault finds this first in clinical medicine that perceives the signs of disease as having the same structure as a discourse: '[t]he clinical gaze has the paradoxical ability to *hear a language* as soon as it *perceives a spectacle*' [*BC* 108]. The clinician had only to clear his mind of prejudice to allow disease to speak a language that he could immediately understand. This might seem a difficult concept to grasp until we recognize its residue in our own fundamental assumptions about knowledge: that the world is conveniently structured like a language.[7]

Disease becomes the origin of its own operations and truth and its observation teaches the physician this truth, provided he is ready with eye, ear and mind open only to its teaching: 'it is not enough for it [the gaze] to exercise prudence or scepticism; the immediate on which it opens states the truth only if it is at the same time its origin ... it is analytic because it restores the genesis of composition; but it is pure of all intervention insofar as this genesis is only the syntax of the language spoken by things themselves in their original silence' [*BC* 108–9].[8] What was visible to the observer was immediately connected to what was expressible about the observed: the gaze and language became two facets of the same experience.[9] The visible and the expressible shared a common syntax: 'a pure Gaze that would be a pure Language: a speaking eye' [*BC* 114]. Under the influence of this idea the clinic became the dual locus of medical practice and training, and the modern teaching hospital was born.

A golden age of the slow, searching gaze (*regard fixe*) of the clinician did not last long before its immanent limitations were perceived. The external signs of disease were too variable, too open to interpretation to provide the basis of a reliable science; besides, the practice of pathology

[7] Of course, these are also the terms used by Lacan (1977) to describe the structure of the unconscious. I have not ventured to explore the potential impact of Foucault's critique on Lacanism. To the extent that we structure the world as a language, it is so structured.

[8] Deleuze (1988) observes that Foucault's attribution of a unified gaze implies a unified medical subject or consciousness, which he regards as a 'lapse' in Foucault's thinking. Foucault's earlier works are characterised by his concern with impersonal statements which do not (unlike propositions or phrases) presuppose a speaking subject or a referential world of objects (cf. Deleuze, 1990). Deleuze suggests that Foucault's 'rarified form of positivism, which in itself is poetic, perhaps helps to rekindle a general experience in the dissemination of discursive formations or statements ... while it also reintroduces into various locations at the heart of these formations a mobile site which is still that of a doctor, clinician, diagnostician or symptomatologist of civilizations' [*BC* 13]. I take Deleuze to mean that Foucault's stratagem of invoking the gaze simulates its intense positivism and thereby evokes the experience of the gaze itself; as well, perhaps, as one who can gaze reflexively upon it.

[9] 'To describe is to follow the ordering of the manifestations, but it is also to follow the intelligible sequence of their genesis; it is to see and to know at the same time, because by saying what one sees, one integrates it spontaneously into knowledge; it is also to learn to see, because it means giving the key of a language that masters the visible' [*BC* 114].

was already moving in another direction: away from a contemplative art, to an active experimental science. The physician's ponderous gaze therefore quickly became an instantaneous *glance*.

This point tends to be overlooked by those who invoke Foucault's work to establish a theory of the body as a text (e.g., Turner, 1992; Fox, 1993): the gaze is only one brief stage in the visual development of empiricism described by Foucault. With his conception of the incisive medical glance, Foucault's analysis goes beyond the notion of the body as a text; beyond the gaze as a 'successive order of reading', which 'records and totalizes' and which 'gradually reconstitutes immanent organizations', spreading out 'over a world that is already the world of language' [*BC* 121]. The notion of reading the body like a text is still locked into a two-dimensional theory of perception, it remains on the ground of a superficial order, whereas pathology was actually getting organized into three dimensions.

2.6 The glance and the knife: Dissection and organization

Whereas the gaze has an affinity with language, the glance has an affinity with touch. The glance does not scan the body as a field, 'it strikes at one point, which is central or decisive ... the glance goes straight to its object' [*BC* 121]. The glance neither hears nor speaks a language, it is silent and tactile like a finger probing the depths of the body: '[h]ence that metaphor of "touch" (*le tact*) by which doctors ceaselessly define their glance [*BC* 122]'. The body with organs is a volume that needs to be palpitated with *knowing hands*. Under the medical glance the body becomes a *tactile body* to be handled with care, as the Latin root (*tactus*, sense of touch), of Foucault's *le tact* and the English tact implies. We return to the idea of the hand as the essential organ of culture. The physician is ready to feel his way manually over and into the body, as one might feel for toys in a bran tub. The glance is the demystifying look and its manual correlative is the hand of pathological anatomy. It is a look that slices deftly into the body, a look that is synonymous with the anatomist's knife. Thus, we find ourselves, in the first decade of the nineteenth century, on the brink of the most complete organization of the human body: '[t]he medicine of symptoms will gradually recede, until it finally disappears before the medicine of organs, sites, and causes, before a clinic wholly ordered in accordance with pathological anatomy' [*BC* 122]. The body-*with*-organs, the *organized* body, is about to become the primary focus of medicine and provide a new definition of organization itself.

The Latin *tactus* is also allied with technology (through L. *tactica* from Gk. *taktike* [*techne* art]. The glance of the eye, the technology of the knife and the tact of the physician's careful hand are all contemporaneous with the development of pathological anatomy (and, as we shall shortly argue, with medical instrumentation). According to Foucault, the conventional view that prior to the nineteenth century pathological anatomy was inhibited by religious and moral prohibitions on dissecting bodies, which was conducted covertly by a few dedicated researchers, is quite false. The dissection of cadavers was not repressed. 'Morgagni had no difficulty in the middle of the eighteenth century in carrying out his autopsies; nor did Hunter, some years later. ... From 1745 the Vienna clinic had had a dissection room; so had the clinic that Tissot had organized at Pavai; at the Hotel-Dieu in Paris, Desault was quite free "to demonstrate on the body deprived of life the alterations that had rendered art useless"' [*BC* 125]. Rather than prohibited, the provision of corpses for dissection was officially prescribed (*BC* 125).

The reason for falsifying the history of pathological anatomy was to justify, retrospectively, a strong *medical* resistance to opening corpses. Medicine had hitherto sought to identify disease in the living body, so when it was admitted that lesions could explain symptoms, and that the clinic should therefore be founded on pathological anatomy, it was found convenient to invent a false history of non-medical resistance to account for the previous lack of progress in that direction (*BC* 126).[10]

Once recognized by medical authorities, however, pathological anatomy transformed the organization of medicine, in terms of the sources and kinds of knowledge it made available, its methods of analysis, its conduct of clinical examinations and its reorganization of medical schools and hospitals (*BC* 124). In terms of embodied organization, dissection radically reorganized both the corporeal and the corporate bodies of medicine. It began to explain the physiological embodiment of disease in terms of clearly defined organs and this also became the locus of a general reorganization of medical knowledge, institutions and practices. The clinical hospital became departmentalized according to the body's major organs, subsystems and diseases.

Therefore, although the corpse had actually been a part of medical research since the Middle Ages, the possibility that it could be the point

[10] '[A] neutral gaze directed upon manifestations, frequencies, and chronologies, concerned with linking up symptoms and grasping their language, was, by its structure, foreign to the investigation of mute intemporal bodies; causes and locales did not interest it: it was interested in history, not geography. Anatomy and the clinic were not of the same mind' [*BC* 126].

of entry into an entirely new *corpus* of medical theory and a new body of medical practice was not fully realized until the nineteenth century. What seems so obvious today, but seemed so irrelevant to clinicians of the late eighteenth century, is the notion that the institution of medicine could become so powerful through a rejuvenated science of dissection. Bachat (*Anatomie Générale*, 1801, p. xcix) put the case bluntly: 'for twenty years, from morning to night, you have taken notes at patients' bedsides on affections of the heart, the lungs, and the gastric viscera, and all is confusion for you in the symptoms which, refusing to yield up their meaning, offer you a succession of incoherent phenomena. *Open up a few corpses*: you will dissipate at once the darkness that observation alone could not dissipate' [quoted in *BC* 146, emphasis added].

But opening corpses was not the only major innovation involved in the birth of the clinically organized body: the invention and development of tools and instruments were also significant. The organization of the human body was therefore achieved by a *twofold* effort: the invention of instruments, like the stethoscope and the X-ray, allowed physicians to examine the interior of the living body; this data could then be compared with lesions in the corpse. This reciprocity is clearly seen in the work of Laennec (1819; 1884), a key figure of both movements. The remainder of this chapter presents a brief account of some of the most important medical instruments invented during the nineteenth and early twentieth centuries, along with my interpretation of the respatialization which they effected on the patient's body, and on the collective medical perception and recognition of that body; its corporeal and corporate organization, respectively.

2.7 Clinical organization: The role of medical technology

Before the nineteenth century, physical contact between physician and patient was considered distasteful and avoided as far as possible (Reiser, 1978). The scene of the medical diagnosis was similar to the confessional: the patient described his symptoms and the physician administered an appropriate remedy.[11] The effusive nature of such remedies as bleeding and purging are easily equated to penance. Following a prolonged debate in the first half of the nineteenth century, however,

[11] As it remains in psychiatry and psychoanalysis. Even group therapy in its various forms seems unable or unwilling to shake off the structure of the confessional. (See Foucault's *History of Sexuality Part I* (1978) for the significance of the confessional structure in secular life.)

physical examination of the living patient became established as the key diagnostic procedure, transforming the work of the doctor and his relationship with patients (*MRT* 29). This important change was contemporaneous with the rise of dissection over the same period. Hence, autopsy (literally, to *see for oneself*) of the living and the dead body, respectively, formed two complementary movements constituting the organization of the body of the patient and of the medical institution alike.

2.8 The stethoscope

The use of manual percussion[12] in diagnosis had never attracted a wide medical following, partly because of the highly subjective nature of its process. Far greater success was realized by *mediate auscultation* (listening to the body through a stethoscope). Laennec's invention of the stethoscope (c. 1819) provided a new method of listening to internal signs of disease which, unlike percussion, was not especially difficult to learn (*MRT* 28). It had the additional advantage of interposing an instrument between physician and patient, thereby avoiding direct physical contact. Laennec's first stethoscopic examination was reputedly conducted simply by rolling some sheets of paper into a tube. Realizing its potential Laennec had a wooden version made and several other designs were published and used. His basic design continues to be improved to this day.

By comparing what he believed to be the *sounds of the disease itself* inside the living body with the evidence of lesions in the corpse, Laennec and his followers devised an accurate method by which to localize the seat of disease in the patient. It was upon this demonstrable correspondence of the living sound with the visible lesion disclosed at autopsy that the success of mediate auscultation depended (*MRT* 30). Among Laennec's followers, Irish physician Robert Graves considered anatomical lesions to be the most reliable signs of disease, 'for being immediately connected, as it were, *with* the primary cause, they prove the most useful of all symptoms, in enabling us to ascertain the seat and progress of diseased action' [*MRT* 30]. With mediate auscultation, 'the physician could, in a sense, autopsy the patient while still alive' [*MRT* 36]. However, the general approach to mediate auscultation altered as a result of Skoda's discovery that the noises heard were actually produced

[12] Striking the body and listening with the unaided ear to the quality of sound produced (after Auenbrugger).

by the affected part of the body, and were not generated by the disease itself as Laennec had thought. This indicated a variety of possible pathological causes rather than the invariable imprint of a specific disease (*MRT* 39).

When Laennec first placed a roll of papers between his ear and the patient's body, he invented not only an important new diagnostic tool, but a new tripartite medical relationship. Doctor and patient were joined by the tube to form a new unity, but this connection also separated them from one another in such a way that each gained a new organic specificity with regard to their relationship as a whole. This stethoscopic conjunction (the *mediation* of mediate auscultation) is also a new kind of sensory disjunction between patient and physician, a disjunction which opens onto a new field of relations between the hand that applies, the ear that hears and the mind that draws inferences from what is heard.[13] This is a *reorganization* of the medical relation in the literal sense that the physician's organs (hand, ear, brain) are set into a new relation compared with a percussive relation between the same organs. As an extension of the Heideggerian hand discussed in Chapter 1, the stethoscope presents a revised sphere or spatialization of Man's being. This revision constitutes a new stage in his cultural development, in the same sense that all technologies serve that development – by being embodied in culture, and into a more powerful organization of the corporeal and corporate body.

2.9 The spatialization of medical technology

Let us pursue this idea further. With mediate auscultation, doctor, patient and stethoscope are brought under a new and more powerful diagnostic relationship. The stethoscopic relation creates a new spatialization of the movement of life itself; a 'glance' into the living body by another living body. In this sense the stethoscope re-embodies the medical gaze in such a way that the interior of the patient's body undergoes two simultaneous transformations: exteriorized, by the 'living autopsy', and interiorized in the mind of the physician who listens. The patient's body is thus deterritorialized from its own obscure, self-enclosed space, to be reterritorialized in the mental 'space' of the physician's mind; and also in the institutional space of medical knowledge, teaching and

[13] 'It is truly to the tact of the observer, and not to the medium applied to the chest that we owe precision in auscultation'. James E. Pollock (1856), 'On a Self-Adjusting Double Stethoscope' *Lancet*, vol. 1, p. 398 [*MRT* 43].

practice. The stethoscope puts the physician *in mind* of the patient's body in a new way, and it puts the medical institution in mind of this body also. The body of the patient becomes radically organized and the actions of the doctor are altered, transformed into a revised practice and constitution of medicine.

The nature of this revision is suggested by the anomalous name of the instrument: stethoscope (Gk. *stethos-skopeo*) means to render the chest *visible*, when it was actually devised to make it *audible*. How was it that prior to the invention of an armoury of instruments designed to expose the inner workings of the body *literally* to the physician's look, we have the anomaly of the stethoscope, which did not, but was named as though it did? We can answer this by referring back to Foucault's notion of spatialization. All three modes of spatialization of pathology are metaphorical in designating and differentiating notional spaces within which a medicine of species, the body as host to disease and society as the natural locus of its distribution, are *conceivable in the imagination*. From this we hypothesize that for anything to be conceivable, a notional space is required: a certain physical distribution of phenomena must be matched by a virtual, imaginary space within which that distribution is conceivable.[14]

This points to an empirical explanation of *thought*, operating in a parallel fashion to the physical dimension of *extension* (Hobbes, 1651; Hume, 1738; Deleuze, 1990; Spinoza, 1985). It also implies that organization, as a dual process of corporeal and corporate embodiment, necessarily involves both thought and extension inasmuch as we are mind and body. The history of medical technology in general, like the specific history of pathological anatomy, should therefore be addressed in this combined fashion: as a completely *embodied* phenomenon, which means a phenomenon comprising both physical and intellectual powers and techniques. In addressing how the body of the patient is respatialized by the rise of technology, we seek to apprehend how technologies so efficacious in restructuring the body's *physical* anatomy, were equally effective in restructuring our *imaginary* construction of the body, from a two-dimensional surface on which a medicine of species

[14] This space is not prior to a distribution of elements, nor is it a context within which they occur. It is the field composed by such a distribution, as there is never empty conceptual space. As Descartes proposed a Cosmic plenum, and Spinoza an affective plenum, we perceive a mental plenum: the field of consciousness is always fulfilled by concepts. Hume (1738) said that mind is no more than its constituent assemblage of ideas.

was and perhaps still is inscribed, to the three-dimensional volume of anatomy, with which it coexists in the field of modern medicine.

I argue in following chapters that the physical and the imaginary act in a strictly parallel fashion – they do not act upon one another as cause and effect. The assumption of a naive empiricism, which medicine developed at the turn of the nineteenth century, tended to blur the irreducible difference between thought and extension. This allowed the clinician to discount his own thoughts, affections and actions in the knowledge process; it allowed the rise of a passive conception of knowledge as an immediate effect of vision. This is one of Foucault's (1973) key points when he refers to a look that effaces itself as soon as it alights on the body. Thus, when Foucault states that the rise of medical empiricism is the history of modern empiricism per se, he is pointing to a subtle and paradoxical effect of the medicalization of the body: the rise of a specifically *modern* empiricism, which involved a degradation of understanding of the body as locus of mind. The paradox here being that it was a closer scrutiny of bodies, both living and dead, which gave rise to the illusion of a disembodied empiricism: that is, *an empirical gaze and glance which efface, bracket-out, elide, bypass or ignore the body of the viewer*, which do not affect him physically in the least; a look that *seems* passive, though it arises from an explosion of activity in medical research and practice.

The idea that the mind is embodied, that the body is the locus of mind – that mind is primarily *a locus of physical affections* (impressions, images) was very clear to materialist thinkers of previous centuries. But as physicians scrutinized the body more and more closely, their dependency on visualization appears to have seduced them into the notion that the eye opens a direct pathway to the brain, through which external things can impress themselves 'on' the mind, as if upon an inert and impressionable medium, as immediate and self-evident facts. One of the key reasons to trace a history of medical technology, therefore, is to show how much more involved that process of turning physical technique into knowledge really was and is; how knowledge production is necessarily a part of organization and reorganization, conceived as processes of embodiment and re-embodiment.

To *reorganize*, *re-embody* or *reterritorialize* disease; all these terms refer to a topographical redistribution. But this redistribution is more than a revised order of the same parts, because in the transition from an imprecise percussion to a more exact stethoscopy, not only the arrangement but the very nature of the reorganized parts was altered. As the literal space of the body was being explored by anatomy and technology, a virtual space was constructed through their mutual information. This virtual space is that cognitional topography by which the physician and the medical institution *imagine* a distribution of elements constituting any given historical body of medical theory and practice. The clearer articulation of the sorts of internal sounds stethoscopy provided enabled a re-embodiment of disease in the medical imaginary as a visible counter to the three-dimensional distribution in the body of the patient. For a purely temporal succession of obscure noises was insufficient to invoke a detailed three-dimensional image of embodiment: the clarification of these sounds led to such an image by invoking an impression of internal space. It is doubtless significant that this new, three-dimensional perspective of pathological embodiment began by listening to the chest, the largest hollow space of the living body. This thoracic experience reverberated in the mind of the physician to form an impression of the entire body as a vessel containing organs, instead of the obscure impression of solidity which had previously reigned.

Armed with Foucault's conception of spatialization, therefore, we begin to understand medical technology as invoking new ways of respatializing the body. The result of this is that the historical body changes constantly, both in its external appearance and in the notional internal distribution of its parts. This implies, perhaps, Deleuze and Guattari's (1983) body-without-organs, a body prior to conceptual spatialization, a featureless body. We cannot say that the body-without-organs is the real body, since we neither conceive nor experience a body prior to its conception in the indices of culture. The body-without-organs is like Gehlen's natural Man, or Irigaray's (1991b) 'volume without contours',[15] a body necessary to conceive as the virtual counterpart to any actual conception of embodiment and organization.

2.10 The ophthalmoscope and ophthalmometer

Helmholtz's (1851) invention of the ophthalmoscope was another major advance towards rendering internal structures of the living body visible.[16] It disclosed causes of eye disorders in the living body that previously could be seen only during autopsy. Before its invention, the nature and extent of structural changes in the eye could be judged only

[15] By which she refers to the body of woman which has been unable to construct any virtual conception of itself under patriarchy – it defies imagination.

[16] Hermann von Helmholtz (1916), 'Description of an Ophthalmoscope for the Investigation of the Retina of the Living Eye'. Robert Hall (trans.), Chicago: Cleveland Press.

from the patient's verbal account of his symptoms. The ophthalmoscope provided an objective method of assessment by which physicians could evaluate the pathology first-hand. Diagnosis of astigmatism in a patient who could not see clearly, or of feigned near-sightedness in men attempting to avoid military service, could now be achieved independently from the patient's narrative (*MRT* 47). Thus, the ophthalmoscope enabled the state to focus more clearly on the individual and to make him the object of a more discriminating gaze; eyes literally seeing into eyes.

The ophthalmoscopic gaze led not only to a wholesale review of the corpus of ophthalmic knowledge, but also to a revision and reorganization of the medical significance of the eye relative to other organs. The ophthalmoscope yielded the structure and pathology of the eye to the physician's scrutiny; and autopsy revealed that alterations in the eye disclosed the presence of disease in other organs, notably the brain, heart and kidney (*MRT* 50–1). This inference is similar to that made possible by the stethoscope: the ophthalmoscope enabled the physician to deduce a cause and a seat of illness from symptoms in the eye remote from the site of the disease. In this sense the ophthalmoscope not only revealed the interior of the patient's eye, it effectively enabled the physician's eye-mind to rove through the body, searching for disease in places otherwise accessible only during autopsy. In this manner the patient's body became a more detailed and coherent structure in the physician's individual and collective imagination. But it was of course the images and ideas comprising this imaginary structure to which the physician most directly responded; not, as might be supposed, to his direct perception of the body of the patient. All technology mediates between actor and world, and the ophthalmoscope is no exception. It follows that all technology is information technology inasmuch as it generates, modulates and encodes messages about an object; a point easily overlooked by the monopolization of information by computer-based machines.

As new technology allowed the body to be more definitely objectified, it allowed a more detailed subjective impression to be formed in the individual and collective medical imagination. Here too the partnership between the new technology and pathological anatomy is clear: in due course, the physician could confirm or correct his judgement at the dissection table and amend his three-dimensional mental map of the body accordingly. The autopsy did not so much verify or falsify his conceptions, it rather provided a second chance to confirm his opinion or not. The corpse spread out before his glance no more spoke its truth immediately (although this was doubtless the illusion generated by the vividness of the experience) than did the technologically mediated visible interior of the living patient.

Four years after the ophthalmoscope, Helmholtz published his invention of the ophthalmometer. This measured the curvature of the cornea, thus providing an additional aid in testing and correcting vision. However, the accuracy of the ophthalmometer depended on taking 15 to 20 readings on a single patient and this, along with the mathematical calculations involved, prevented its adoption until it was simplified in the late 1880s (*MRT* 49).

Significantly, it become evident to ophthalmic physicians that the data provided by instruments were insufficient alone to inform a precise diagnosis. Following its annual meeting in 1894, the American Medical Association published a report on the fitting of eyeglasses, which recommended a two-stage approach to prescribing. The eye test should commence with an objective examination using ophthalmoscope, ophthalmometer and other instruments; after which subjective patient-centred methods, using geometric figures or numbers and trial glasses, should be employed. The test conclusions would be drawn from a comparison of both the subjective and the objective findings (*MRT* 49). In fact, subjective techniques were recognized as 'the most satisfactory agents to detect minute changes in the vision of an intelligent, cooperative patient' [*MRT* 49].[17] This is the situation that prevails to the present day.

I argued in the case of stethoscopy that medical instrumentation presents a special form of technological relationship, in which a powerful body of technique is composed by setting the doctor, instrument and patient into a new relationship. We find in ophthalmic medicine an even clearer example of how active involvement of both doctor *and* patient can produce a more accurate diagnosis. The role of the patient might appear passive; in fact the biological and social value of one's vision makes (or should make) the eye test an intensely active event. The static posture of the patient is only a necessary condition for the exercise of two different glances: the gaze of the optician who explores the eye for signs of imperfection or pathology; and the glance of the patient at the wall chart and other stimuli in an active self-diagnosis of his visual acuity or impairment.

[17] This method presents a practical example of the combination of objective and subjective techniques which Turner (1992) calls for in arguing for a combined empirical and phenomenological approach to social theory and research. In this sense the modern eye test presents a model for social science.

2.11 The laryngoscope

One of the first instruments designed to be inserted into the body was the laryngoscope. In 1855 Manuel Garcia, a London singing teacher, published an account of his experiments on his own body, to observe the motions of the vocal chords in breathing and in speech. His method was to hold a mirror in the back of his throat with one hand, which reflected the larynx onto a second mirror, held in the other hand which also reflected sunlight into the throat. Most physicians were incredulous and ignored the ingenious Garcia, but two years later Johann Czermak, a Polish professor of physiology, replicated Garcia's experiments using an instrument designed by Dr. Ludwig Tünck; as a result of this the laryngoscope was born (*MRT* 52).

Using the laryngoscope, especially Garcia's prototype, aptly illustrates our point concerning the tact, care and dexterity distinguishing the human hand as the primary instrument of culture. Indeed, early laryngoscopy was plagued by a common feature of such instruments: that their inventors so completely embody their invention in their thoughts and actions that others cannot emulate their dexterity in its application (*MRT* 54). Hence it became recognized that a new instrument did not replace skill in examination, it rather brought new skills to the scene. Skills which were not only manual, as one had to *learn to see* what could be disclosed by the instrument: 'the part may be visible, and yet not seen by an unskilled observer; so that the beginner need not wonder if he cannot see all that even ought to be seen, in his first views of the larynx. For this very reason it is equally difficult to show to another, either on oneself or in a patient what he ought to see'.[18]

How might something be visible to a trained eye and invisible to an untrained eye, at the same time? The answer has to do with the tripartite eye-brain-hand form of technological embodiment: 'to notice an object required a certain mental attitude and orientation' [*MRT* 54]. To observe a thing one has to be put in mind of it and there is no better way than to handle it with a certain tact and care, to make that thing a part of one's manual and mental dexterity by experimenting, observing and writing down one's observations. According to our eye-brain-hand relation of embodied practice or organization, to see is to recognize and this recognition is assisted by manipulating the object of recognition. Thus, the medical gaze, and the empirical gaze more generally, involve not only

[18] Eben Watson (1865), 'Laryngoscopy and its Revelations' [part 1], *Lancet*, vol. 1, p. 589 (*MRT* 54).

the eye but rather a relationship formed by an isomorphic dexterity of eye, mind and hand operating in unison. This is what we mean when we say that the medical glance is embodied in the physician and in the whole conduct of medicine as it is regulated by the medical institution.

2.12 The X-ray

Widespread interest in photography in the second half of the nineteenth century assured an enthusiastic reception of the X-ray, which earned Wilhelm Konrad Röntgen the Nobel Prize for Physics in 1901. A general public was fascinated, even infatuated, by the concept of being able to looking through the skin at the internal body. Some women were even afraid that their clothing would no longer protect them from penetrating X-ray eyes should the technique be made available to a depraved element in society. As an instrument of the medical look the X-ray effected further significant changes in diagnostic theory and practice.

Whereas the ophthalmoscope and laryngoscope could be used by only one physician at a time, and its evidence thereby subject to as many interpretations as viewers, the X-ray allowed multiple clinicians to view and evaluate a condition simultaneously (*MRT* 68). They did not even require the continuing presence of the patient, since the X-ray picture allowed them to observe, reflect and debate the patient's problems in his absence (*MRT* 68). This did not prevent multiple interpretations of the X-ray image but it did allow something previously impossible, except on the dissecting table, a collective simultaneous glance and imagining, rather than a succession of individual glances and images. The implications for medical teaching were immense: X-ray pictures could be distributed, projected in the lecture theatre and published; a verbal or written description of a pathological condition could be illustrated by a photograph of the lesion in question. The X-ray served to standardize clinical theory and practice by standardizing clinical recognition. Today there is no organ of the body not viewable using imaging techniques including conventional X-ray, computed tomography (CT) and magnetic resonance imaging (MRI).[19]

[19]CT produces a three-dimensional image synthesised from multiple two-dimensional X-ray images, taken around a single axis of rotation (Greek tomos – slice). MRI uses a powerful magnetic field to align the nuclear magnetization of hydrogen atoms in water in the body. Radiofrequency fields are used to alter the alignment of this magnetization, causing the hydrogen nuclei to produce a rotating magnetic field detectable by the scanner. This signal can be manipulated

Pathological anatomy and medical technology combined to create a new form of empirical truth: '[b]y showing itself in a repetitive form, the truth indicates the way by which it may be acquired. It offers itself to knowledge by offering itself to recognition. ... The genesis of the manifestation of truth is also the genesis of the knowledge of truth. There is therefore no difference in nature between the clinic as science and the clinic as teaching' [*BC* 110]. This is a modern form of empiricism according to which the true impression of the thing is identical with its real manifestation. Such truth is paradoxical in casting the agent of knowledge as a passive receptor, when this knowledge is actually the result of an unprecedented explosion in medical research and treatment, exemplified by the revolutions in pathological anatomy and medical technology; revolutions involving a whole new range of activities for doctors and patients respectively. This leaves us with a paradoxical legacy: we possess a great objective knowledge of the body, but apprehend this knowledge in abstract from the complex and embodied processes that produce it. We are empiricists in the modern sense, but have lost sight of the base of empiricism, which is the body itself. We have inherited an ideal of knowledge as occurring in consciousness, when this knowledge is really produced through conscious and unconscious physical encounters between bodies. It follows that a real understanding of organization must begin with a deeper understanding of pre-modern empiricism and it is this conclusion that leads us to a study of Hume.

by additional magnetic fields to build up enough information to construct an image of the body.

3
Subjective Empiricism and Organization: Deleuze on Hume's Theory of Human Nature

The status of the subject or ego has long been and remains a key issue in contemporary social theory: how is the subject organized in relation to a world? This is the question addressed in Deleuze's (1991) study of Hume. Or rather the question of the question is addressed, as Deleuze is less interested in subjectivity than in how subjectivity came to be construed as a philosophical problem. First published in 1953, *Empiricism and Subjectivity: An Essay on Hume's Theory of Human Nature* was Deleuze's first book. Hume's fundamental question is this: how does mind become human nature? His approach to the question is quite different from the Kantian and Hegelian transcendentalism which came to dominate the question in European thought. Hume was an empiricist in the Hobbesian mould; for him philosophy begins with the sensual body of experience. Hume begins by asking what is given to experience, and how the subject of experience is organized in the given. His answers to these questions are (briefly) that what is given is *mind*, and what proceeds from the given is *human nature*. How, then, is human nature organized from mind? How is the subject, the subject of passion, thought and action, embodied from the given? Hume argues that the elements and forces constituting the subject are supra-human. This transfers the question of human organization onto a field of impersonal forces, an approach congruent with Gehlen's view of natural, pre-cultural Man (technically a paradox) as the-not-yet-human. Hume explains the mutual organization of subject and society as the process by which natural instinct is socialized.

The question of human nature traditionally evokes some form of dualism between mind and body. I have argued that the corporeal individual and the corporate institution are modes of embodied organization; that both modes exist physically (in extension) and intellectually (in thought). According to Cartesian philosophy, the fact that one perceives oneself as an object of thought is the initial certainty of conscious existence.[1] This ontological priority of consciousness over body is the basis of idealism. According to a materialist ontology, by contrast, mind is necessarily embodied: *consciousness is the body's immediate awareness of itself*. Thus the way to approach mind is through the body, not vice versa as Descartes held.

For Hume, the cause of an idea is sensation. Sensation refers to a modification in one's own body affected by an encounter with another body. Ideas become a subject by the direct application of *natural principles of association* upon the mind. This empirical philosophy of impersonal material forces provides the intellectual core of all of Deleuze's later work.[2] As sensation is the cause of mind, Hume can explain how mind becomes subject without recourse to a psychology; his project is '*the substitution of a psychology of the mind by a psychology of the mind's affects*' [*ES* 21]. For Hume mind is not a proper object of science because mind is no more than a collection of ideas, an assemblage of raw material from which our subjective nature is composed.

Having explained how mind becomes a subject as the effect of the natural principles of association, Hume's next step is to explain how a subject becomes socialized by the embodiment of cultural forces or *general rules*. Human nature is more a moral and sociological problem than a psychological one (*ES* 22). In *A Treatise of Human Nature* (1738), Hume is concerned to explain how mind is affected by two kinds of forces, the *passional* and the *social*. These forces are not negatively related in terms of urge and restraint, as most theorists assume; rather, the social is constituted by the passions as *the oblique means for their satisfaction* (*ES* 21). This has revolutionary implications for a positive approach to organization theory and institutional analysis: Hume's institution is not negatively defined in opposition to the instinctive desires of the subject: rather, individual and institution coexist in an affirmative relation of positive desire and its (oblique) fulfilment. Hume refuses to characterize the social as restricting the power of instinct, or of separating power from its active expression. Thus, 'the coherence of the passional and the social in history is revealed as an internal unity, with political organization and the institutions giving history its objects' [*ES* 21–2].

[1] This is of course the significance of Descartes' (1986) *Cogito ergo sum*.

[2] 'Named or not, the intensive encounter with Hume gave Deleuze a decisive and unbending preference for empiricism against all forms of transcendental philosophy' [Boundas in Deleuze (1991) *Empiricism and Subjectivity*, p. 2].

A Humean conception of *understanding*, or reason, is crucial to a theory of mutual embodiment of subject and society. The role of the understanding is to extend the passional into the social and the social into the passional. The understanding always reflects *interest* and interest is always *partial*; therefore understanding or reason is never impartial – there can be no purely objective reasoning. This does not prevent us from addressing understanding and interest *(passion)*, as theoretically distinct, in a similar manner to physics dividing a movement into force and direction while still recognizing that it is really simple and individual (*ES* 22).[3] Even if the understanding can think of itself reflexively as a faculty detached from interest, this turn of thought is nonetheless interested. Thus we see that how *the understanding is the process of the passions on their way to socialization.*

When a passion, guided by the understanding, finds an enduring oblique means of satisfaction, a social institution results. Organization is that process by which passion and understanding are affirmed in the formation of the institution. It refers to the positive embodiment of social affection in the subject and the positive embodiment of subjective passion in the social. Thus, the role of the understanding is to free ideas from sensation alone, to produce a domain of culture.

The cultural creativity of the understanding rests on the ability to formulate *general rules* or *justice*. Hume's theory of justice forms another affirmative element to his philosophy and our theory of organization: the role of justice is not to repress the passions but to present the means by which they may be expressed, without destroying the individual or society. Thus, viewed from the perspective of the understanding, the question of the nature of organization is bound to Hume's theory of human nature. in explaining how mind becomes human nature, we simultaneously explain the correlative processes of social, political and moral organization. Through the piece, Hume adheres to a basic tenet of materialism: that the real substance of human nature and society is passion; human nature is the socialization of that passion to allow

[3] 'Human nature, being compos'd of two principle parts, which are requisite in all its actions, the affections and understanding; 'tis certain, that the blind motions of the former, without the direction of the latter, incapacitate men for society: And it may be allow'd us to consider separately the effects that result from the separate operations of these two component parts of the mind. The same liberty may be permitted to moral, which is allow'd to natural philosophers; and it is very usual with the latter to consider any motion as compounded and consisting of two parts separate from each other, tho' at the same time they acknowledge it to be in itself uncompounded and inseparable' [*T* 493].

its constructive expression. Culture has but one purpose: *to provide the necessarily oblique means for the satisfaction of desire.*

Having introduced some of the basic themes of Deleuze's Hume study, let us now address them in more detail, commencing with the question: what is *mind*?

3.1 How mind is organized into a subject by the natural principles of association

According to Hume, mind has no nature, being identical with imagination, or fancy; an assemblage of ideas arising from sensation. We must therefore ask how this assemblage or collection becomes a system, how it acquires a nature as subject. There is no preformed space to the imaginary, which is identical with the collection of ideas.[4] Nor is imagination a platform on which a spectacle of images is mounted. It is a play of ideas but '[t]he comparison of the theatre must not mislead us; nor have we the most distant notion of the place, where these scenes are represented, or of the materials, of which it is compos'd' [*T* 253].[5] The mental theatre is no more than the play of ideas.[6] Nor is there a subject prior to mind.[7] Hence the question for Hume becomes '*how does the mind become a subject*? How does the imagination become a faculty?' [*ES* 23]

Hume's approach to the question is relevant both to the organization of mind as subject, and to the organization of subjects into society. How does an assemblage of subjects become a society? This question correlates to that of how the mind becomes a subject, since the answer

[4] 'The collection of ideas is called "imagination", insofar as the collection designates not a faculty but rather an assemblage of things, in the most vague sense of the term: things are as they appear – a collection without an album, a play without a stage, a flux of perceptions' [*ES* 22–3].

[5] 'It is true, Hume constantly reiterates, that ideas are in the imagination. But the preposition here does not signify inherence in a subject; rather, the use of the preposition is metaphorical, and it means to exclude from the mind an activity which would be distinct from the movement of ideas in the mind' [*ES* 23].

[6] True, the Ancient Greek *theatron* (θέατρον) meant 'the seeing place', but could any building logically be designated as a theatre without an awareness of what Beckerman defines as what 'occurs when one or more persons, isolated in time and/or space, present themselves to another or others'? Theatre is primarily a performing art, not its containing structure. Indeed, such a structure is not necessary, but contingent upon the commercial exploitation of the art. Though it undoubtedly affects the character of the art, the theatre building is designed primarily to keep out those who have not paid to watch a performance.

[7] Readings (1991, pp. 86–7) makes a similar point relative to Lyotard's thought on the politics of representation.

to the latter also addresses the socialization of mind. The problems of subjectivity and society have to be approached simultaneously in Hume, as they are two elements of a common creation, which is human nature.

Mind becomes subject as the effect of *natural principles of association*. The principles act upon ideas but they do not belong to any particular ideas or to ideation, they are rather to be observed in the actions of nature itself. From the outset the *Treatise* looks beyond mind for principles to account for its becoming human nature. Imagination is delirious, without constancy or uniformity, a totality of the movement of ideas.[8,9] Constancy and uniformity are not characteristics of the imagination, either in the ideas that one has, or in the connections between them. Everything happens *in* the imagination, but nothing is done *by* it. Constancy and uniformity appear only in the way in which ideas are associated in the imagination by the principles (*ES* 23). Association finds in the imagination its term and its object: '[i]t is a quality which unifies ideas, not a quality of ideas themselves' [*ES* 24]. Only then does the assemblage of ideas acquire cohesion and direction; only then does it become an organization. The subject surpasses the given but only by virtue of first being formed in the given as an effect of principles external to mind.

Of the three principles of association *(contiguity*, *resemblance* and *causality)*, it is causality which forges the strongest bonds between ideas.[10] To demonstrate the point, Hume draws an analogy between ideation and familial relations: '[c]ousins in the fourth degree are connected by *causation*, if I may be allowed to use that term; but not so

[8] 'Being the place of ideas, the fancy is the collection of separate, individual items. Being the bond of ideas, it moves through the universe, engendering fire dragons, winged horses, and monstrous giants' [*ES* 23].

[9] 'Nor will this liberty of the fancy appear strange, when we consider that all our ideas are copied from our impressions, and that there are not any two impressions which are perfectly inseparable. ... Wherever the imagination perceives a difference among ideas, it can easily produce a separation' [*T* 10].

[10] 'It is plain, that, in the course of our thinking, and in the constant revolution of our ideas, our imagination runs easily from one idea to any other that *resembles* it, and that this quality alone is to the fancy a sufficient bond and association. It is likewise evident, that as the senses, in changing their objects, are necessitated to change them regularly, and take them as they lie *contiguous* to each other, the imagination must, by long custom, acquire the same method of thinking, and run along the parts of space and time in conceiving its objects. As to the connection that is made by the relation of *cause and effect* ... there is no relation, which produces a stronger connection in the fancy, and makes one idea more readily recall another, than the relation of cause and effect betwixt their objects' [*T* 11].

closely as brothers, much less as child and parent. In general, we may observe, that all relations of blood depend upon cause and effect, and are esteemed near or remote, according to the number of connecting causes interposed betwixt the persons'[*T* 11]. In drawing this analogy, Hume opens a parallel discussion of the associative principles of society which he does not pursue until much later in the *Treatise*. He prefers at the outset to approach the whole issue from the perspective of the subject as the empirical locus of experience. We will take up the parallel immediately, but we should be clear that Hume no more finds society to be the origin of the principles than is the imagination. We shall see that Hume places special emphasis on the family, but for the present let us notice that he also looks beyond the family group in postulating causality 'to be the source of all the relations of interest and duty, by which men influence each other in society, and are placed in the ties of government and subordination' [*T* 12]. Just as causality provides the strongest connection between ideas, so it forms the strongest and most extensive pre-social bonds between persons.

The principles of association act upon ideas and persons in the same way that they act in nature. Even in the case of causality, however, the bonds so formed are not as strong as physical causality itself. Hume does not propose a predetermined order of human relations: causality between physical bodies is inviolable, but causality as a subjective and familial principle is relatively fragile. For instance a child's physical cause is its parents, but its perceptions of duty towards them, or its relations with its siblings, can be unstable. Similarly, though causal relations between ideas (e.g., where an idea of the parents causes an idea of their offspring) present a robust habit of thought, one is still free to think the reverse causality, however implausible, that is, that a child is the cause of its parents.[11]

As they affect the mind, the principles of association produce a subject capable of belief both in what has and what has not been presented to our senses: '[w]e now see the special ground of empiricism: nothing in the mind transcends human nature, because it is human nature that, in its principles, transcends the mind. ... Association, far from being a product, is a rule of the imagination and a manifestation of its free exercise. It guides the imagination, gives it uniformity, and also constrains

[11] 'This uniting principle among ideas is not to be considered as an inseparable connection ... but we are only to regard it as a gentle force, which commonly prevails, and is the cause why, among other things, languages so nearly correspond to each other; Nature, in a manner, pointing out to every one those simple ideas, which are most proper to be united into a complex one' [*T* 10].

it' [*ES* 24]. A similar principle supports social organization: nothing in the assemblage of individuals transcends society, because it is society that, by virtue of its embodiment of the same principles on a larger scale, transcends the assemblage. Human nature occurs spontaneously on three levels: the mind, the family and the society; each an effect of the natural principles of association acting on the given.

We can apprehend these principles *only through their material effects*: 'Why', wonders Deleuze, '[i]s regulated imagination, rather than the rule grasped in its active power, human nature?' [*ES* 24]. His answer defers to the materialist tradition: as an unregulated movement of ideas, imagination has no nature; it becomes a system by the application of forces external to it. We know the principles of association only through the subject-nature they effect in imagination; we cannot know them in abstract, as no natural principle has abstract form. The subject marks, both in the sense of a transition and of an observation, its own concrete becoming as the qualification of mind, inferring from that process the principles which effect it. 'Association is a law of nature, and like every other law, it is defined by its effects, not by a cause' [*ES* 24–5].[12]

Analogous to the transition from mind to subject, social consistency is effected by the construction of institutions. Institutions are effects of the principles of association on a multitude of persons.[13] Institutions are the major organs of a social body; as such they are the means of expressing desire and activity in a social context. Institutions, like the subjects whose desire they express, are effects, not causes: '[t]he cause cannot be *known*; principles have neither cause nor an origin of their power. What is original is their effect' [*ES* 25]. The argument that a principle can be apprehended only in its material effects will resound throughout Deleuze's later work, as we shall see below and in subsequent chapters.[14]

By denying the existence of abstract principles on one hand and of a given subjectivity on the other, Hume avoids two extreme positions: an absolute structural exteriority, where everything is explained in terms of relations but where the concrete terms of the relations are

[12] 'Here, then, is a kind of pre-established harmony between the cause of nature and the succession of our ideas' [Hume, *An Enquiry Concerning Human Understanding*, p. 58; *ES* 138, n. 14].

[13] We will see below that institutions are also the result of artificial general rules.

[14] It is also influential in Foucault's work (e.g., 1977) where the notion of power that is specifiable only by its effects has excited both critical disapproval and acclaim.

absent; and a perfect interiority where a given subjectivity leads to a wholly subjectivist theory of human nature and an egoistic orientation to society. An extreme exteriority is idealist: it ignores the body as the site where raw materials of passion, thought and action are generated. An extreme interiority is also idealist: it posits a preformed consciousness distinct from the body and from social organization. According to Hume, the natural principles of association are actualized as they materially transform the pre-organized mind and human assemblage into the embodied organization of subject and society. Human nature does not transcend nature. Rather, culture is made ('beaten out' as Douglas and Isherwood phrase it) from materials nature provides by the action of natural principles upon them. Nor is culture opposed to nature, it is a necessary development of nature in the mind of Man and in social institutions.

3.2 Sensation and organization

'Nature cannot be studied except in terms of its effects upon the mind, yet the only true science of the mind should have nature as its object' [*ES* 26]. This is Deleuze's definition of *subjective empiricism*. Our experience is defined by sensation and the ideas arising from sensation.[15] Hume does not appeal to causes external to nature. In contrast to Descartes (1986), therefore, he does not view ideas as originating in God. *Ideas* are impressions of sensation in mind, entirely natural and mundane. And the principles of association that act upon those ideas are also natural, though they do not belong to and are very different from, ideas. Reason is the application of causality to ideas and because causality is a natural principle, reason is also natural, not human. Reason is embodied in the human subject as a modification of ideas in mind.

Hume's hypothesis is, 'Human Nature is the only science of Man' [*T* 273]. The study of human nature is always a study of nature becoming human, so the subject can no more be treated in abstract from the natural principles of association affecting the mind, than nature can be studied other than through its affects on the mind. On one hand, Hume presents a psychology of pure ideas, 'of simple elements, of minima or indivisibles', on the other hand he proposes 'a psychology of dispositions', an anthropology, and an ethics (*ES* 27).

[15] 'For there is no conception in a Man's mind, which hath not at first, totally, or by parts, been begotten upon the organs of Sense' [Hobbes, *Leviathan*, 1651: p. 85].

This is a critique of psychology whose real object is located in the external forces acting on mind as its organizing principles. Mind is an impossible object of study as it has no nature (*ES* 29). Inasmuch as a psychology treats its object as separate from physical affectivity, it treats an abstract, disembodied entity. This is why: 'all serious writers agree on the impossibility of a psychology of the mind' [*ES* 27].[16] A true psychology would therefore be a psychology of affections (*ES* 29).

Hume advocates an approach to social organization as a study of embodied affection or sensation, as this is the physical substrate from which all ideas in the mind, including social concepts, arise. Having grasped that all original ideas in and about society originate in the physical affections caused by the actions of bodies upon one another, we must try to clarify the role of the understanding or reason in organizing those ideas into a subject, and into the social equivalent of the subject, society.

From Hume's perspective, we can begin to understand a society, or any of its components (institutions, modes of production, cultural achievements, etc.), only by addressing how the physical affections of the multitude become ideas in the collective mind and how those ideas, that mind, become society. In our present state of knowledge we no more comprehend the physics of embodied affectivity at a corporate level than we do at a corporeal level. The outcome of this ignorance is that we treat ideas as if they were original causes when they are actually effects or quasi-causes.

There can be no science of mind as long as ideas are apprehended as causes. Ideas are only quasi-casual: ideas can only cause other ideas. This would not be a fatal problem if our ideas were adequate, that is, if they comprehended their own genesis in the physical affections. Such ideas cause further adequate ideas. But almost all of our ideas are inadequate because they do not comprehend their affective causality. Such ideas can only cause more of the same.

This is one of the great insights that Deleuze finds in Hume: the human is constituted from the sub-human by the supra-human. To understand human nature and social organization we must cast our attention inwards in order to have it deflected outwards. Empirical subjectivity begins with an inspection of mind, leading to a study of

[16] '"The intellect," said Comte with respect to impossible psychologies, "is almost exclusively the subject of their speculations, and the affections have been almost entirely neglected; and, moreover, always subordinated to the understanding. ... The whole of *human nature* is thus very unfaithfully represented by these futile systems"' [Comte, *The Positive Philosophy*, p. 384; *ES* 27].

sensation as the affection of my body by external bodies as the origin of mind. It leads also to a study of the external natural principles of association that organize mind into a subject. The myth of a human interiority is broken immediately this analysis begins.

3.3 The general rules: Artifice and organization

Hume presents two elements of human nature: the affects of association and of passion. 'Each one of them determines a system: the system of *understanding* and the system of *passions and ethics*' [*ES* 32, emphasis added].[17] Hume establishes a kind of parallelism between the two systems: the principles of association affect relations of resemblance, contiguity and causality between ideas, enabling the subject to form general ideas or rules underpinning theoretical knowledge. The passions provide the mind with its content, making a practical and moral activity possible (*ES* 32). In simple terms we can say that passion provides the content of mind whereas the understanding provides its organization.

These two systems (passion and understanding) form the basic constitution of human nature in its corporeal and corporate expressions. But we should not glibly identify the understanding with theory and passion with practice. Owing to their strict parallelism both systems are involved in theory and in practice. In Hume, belief is always a practice of the understanding, while the form of practical social organization and justice constitutes a theory of morality (*ES* 32).[18]

We can apprehend this parallelism by the two kinds of rules by which association affect the understanding. On the one hand are extensive rules, which increase the field of action by the logical relations they reveal; on the other hand are corrective rules which restrict the field of action that would otherwise dissipate into chaos. In the body and the institution these rules apply in similar ways. The becoming subject of mind, producing human nature; and the becoming social of an

[17] 'A passion is an original existence, or, if you will, modification of existence, and contains not any representative quality, which renders it a copy of any other existence or modification' [*T* 415].

[18] In later works, as we shall see, Deleuze distinguishes between *ethics* and *morality* in order to affirm practical reason and critique moral orders. Hume's idea of morality is best understood in a more general sense by reference to the distinction between natural and moral philosophy. All of modern philosophy qualifies as moral philosophy according to Hume's definition.

gathering, constituting a morality, require extensive and corrective rules alike (*ES* 32).

In Deleuze's Hume study we find a rigorously materialist conception of practice that will mark all his later philosophical work; its roots in the empirical tradition are traced only here. Understanding, or theory, is regulated passion; the content of intellect is desire, the social form of desire reason. Because passion or desire finds its oblique expression through the institution, reason is social in character. *Human nature is passion made social in order to be expressed.* The force of socialization precedes neither the human nor the social; it is first the result of nature acting upon nature, the principles of association acting upon the given. There is no *human* essence of human nature; culture is formed within nature, an envelope, pocket or invagination of the human, an interval between instinctive stimulus and response. Even the highest intellectual achievements do not transcendent their natural passionate content, which is why Deleuze observes, 'Reason is a kind of feeling' [*ES* 30].

Organization occurs in that interval. At a personal level organization invokes the practical embodiment of social reason to form the subject; at a social level it describes the practical embodiment of a human subject into a society. At either level what is weak – natural Man, an gathering of such men – is made more powerful. The whole movement of organization involves power's increase; bodies becoming organized into larger, more powerful bodies.

How does this account support our definition of the organized body (or the embodied organization, which amounts to the same thing)? It presents a genealogy of organization as a genealogy of practical being. What is most natural to the body is to be affected, and what is most natural to the mind is imagination; these are the two elements of passion. The impassioned mind becomes human nature, on both its individual and collective levels, by the affections of principles of association which belong to nature. Subject and society are therefore qualifications of mind, passion deflected by reason, the practical result of which is action (*ES* 33, 34).

There are two kinds of practice: a practice of understanding and a practice of ethics (*ES* 35). The practice of understanding enables the subject to view nature (including his own nature as subject) as a whole. 'Nature, the object of physics, is *partes extra partes*. This is its essence. ... Nature can no more be discovered than it can be invented' [*ES* 35]. Nature is an extensive magnitude of an infinite number of parts, an assemblage, and the role of the understanding is to determine those parts by the application of general principles of knowledge (*ES* 35). This constitutes the basic method of any physics, whether it applies to the corporeal, or to the corporate assemblage.[19]

The practice of ethics takes a different course from that of the understanding. Here the parts are mutually exclusive and cannot be associated by the action of the principles. The elements which an ethics treats resist combination into a whole, they are not extensive parts (*partielles*), they are mutually exclusive, partial (*partiales*) by nature. The challenge of an ethical practice is to divert and negotiate between partialities: as such it is an artificial and inventive endeavour (*ES* 35).[20] A *moral* society transcends its constitutive individual membership by imposing a negative order. Ethical practice, by contrast, discards transcendence for integration. Whereas the understanding composes wholes, proceeding from one part to another, an ethics responds to the mutually exclusive tendency of immediate wholes (*ES* 36): it constructs but does not assimilate.

At this point we shall have to revise the common assumption that the individual is the basic component of social organization, along with our preconceptions of the processes of organizing those components into a greater social body. For Hume, the natural individual is not the person but the family, tribe or clan. Being coherent already the family, tribe or clan resists organization into a larger unity. For this reason Hume's ethics does not present a synthesis of undifferentiated parts, but the positive integration of partialities already differentiated and resistant to further differentiation. The implications of this for organization theory are profound: the basic elements of the organization are not personal, but familial and tribal (a phenomenon that marketing experts well understand), not the individual as person but as social group. 'But', the student of organization protests, '[h]as social psychology not already told us this and demonstrated its validity through the work of Elton Mayo and others in the human relations school?' Yes, but not in the fundamental sense Hume describes. We pay lip service to the socially mediated nature of human behaviour, but still habitually use the language, and concepts of individualism, even as we criticize its assumptions. We still *believe* in the sovereign individual, the subject or ego and this belief informs our whole mode of conduct. Therefore, we need to address the axiomatic ego or self-concept driving individualism.

[19] 'I answer that the uniting of these parts into a whole ... is performed merely by an arbitrary act of mind, and has no influence on the nature of things' [David Hume, *Dialogues Concerning Natural Religion*, pp. 78–9].

[20] '[M]an is an inventive species' [*T* 484].

3.4 Hume's critique of egoism: Partial sympathy, the natural unit of society

Egoism claims that the main challenge to socialization is the ego. Egoism is the basis of contractarian and utilitarian philosophies. But, according to Hume, egoism fails to understand the essentially positive constitution of human nature and society. If all men act out of self-interest, society is defined negatively in terms of voluntary or involuntary restraint (*ES* 39). From a constructionist perspective, egoism is not a practical theory. According to egoism our task is not so much to construct a society as to conserve it by socializing inherently destructive tendencies. We achieve this, it is thought, by applying principles nowadays generally known as control systems. Our problem then is to pose a practical alternative to egoism. Hume provides this alternative in his theory of partial sympathies.

Hume shows us that the problem of human nature is indeed answerable only in terms of passion informed by reason, of interest made social. But interest was never the expression of the individual ego. According to Hume, egoism mistakenly focuses on a supposed interiority of mind. This supposition is destroyed as soon as we accept that the subject is constituted 'in' the mind by principles transcending it. As for the constitution of society, Hume has never said that the social unit is actually the individual, indeed his theory of the subject only serves to deconstruct the individual as ego.

'One of Hume's simplest but most important ideas is this: human beings are much less egoistic than they are *partial*' [*ES* 38].[21] Men do not naturally act out of self-interest but nor do they naturally act for the good of society: egoism and altruism are equally implausible theories of socialization. The partial nature of human action is orientated towards the group; invariably, the individual belongs to a family, clan or community before belonging to the types of communities Tönnies (1957) describes. The natural determinants of sympathy in Hume's philosophy are family, friendship and neighbourliness (*ES* 38). It is *sympathy*, a process of positive investment in the group, rather than restraint of the ego, which produces the partial tendency of our actions. Altruism is indiscriminate, it cannot recognize the difference between friend and enemy, poor or rich man. Partial sympathy, by contrast, is

[21] '[T]here are few that do not bestow the largest part of their fortunes on the pleasures of their wives, and the education of their children, reserving the smallest portion for their own proper use and entertainment' [*T* 487]. It is unclear whether Hume speaks here as a true Scot or a philosopher.

discriminating: '[s]o noble an affection, instead of fitting men for large societies, is almost as contrary to them, as the most narrow selfishness' [*T* 487].

Hume's theory of partial sympathies disrupts the whole ground of the dialectic of structure and agency in social organization: action is neither self-determined nor other-determined, but invested by sympathies whose natural horizon is the family, tribe or clan. This changes our whole idea of the structure of society, regardless of whether we considered it previously from a liberal, communitarian or socialist viewpoint.[22] Egos need to be limited by laws, but sympathies obey their own organic rules and can only be *integrated* into a larger system. Hume's critique of contractarianism and utilitarianism is directed at their false and abstract models of society. They can define justice only in negative terms, as a set of limitations on personal interest '*instead of understanding society as a positive system of invented endeavors*' [*ES* 39, emphasis added].

The concept of society as a positive constitution of mutually exclusive sympathies, rather than a negative set of constraints on egos, releases organization theory from the depressing burden of a repetitive and negative task. No longer is analysis restricted to polarized oppositions between freedom and restraint, individual and organization, organization and environment, etc. A very different project is opened: to address organization as a project of positive integration. According to Hume, 'the state of nature is always already more than a simple state of nature' [*ES* 39]. Society finds both its parts and its obstacles in naturally limited sympathies rather than in voracious egos; each individual is sympathetically orientated to his own family or tribe.

The family does not readily relinquish its partial sympathies or group identity; it is even more robust in this sense than in its relation of causality under the principles of association. Family members might entertain subversive ideas of their relations, they may play with the rules of reason, but the passionate sympathy that binds them is strong enough to defy reason. What keeps the family or clan together, though its members may be physically apart, is the natural sympathy that binds them to *that* tribe, *that* family and to that one alone. Families, clans and tribes are the real social units, 'but the characteristic of these units is that they are not added to one another. Rather, they exclude one another' [*ES* 39].[23]

[22] It is more nearly related to anarchism or anarcho-syndicalism.

[23] Of course Hume here ignores external causes of family disintegration. This is not surprising in a period of strong state, social, religious and economic sanctions

Partial sympathies cannot be subsumed under a totality. Nature, as Hume tells us, is not a whole, one can only invent a whole (e.g., *culture, justice*): indeed wholes are the only possible inventions. *Organization is this inventive process; a positive, artificial integration of heterogeneous parts*: '[j]ustice is not a principle of nature; it is rather a rule, or law of construction, and its role is to organize, within the whole, the elements, including the principles of nature' [*ES* 40]. The individual's primary relation is not to society but to the family or tribe; which is in turn related to a wider community (society) by means of rules of justice, which Hume terms *general rules*. General rules function to articulate partial interests into an organized social body.

3.5 The rule of property

The fundamental general rule is that of property. Property is invented to transform mere possession into a stable relation which does not permit of accidental violation. For Hume, property is the first artificial principle of social organization. It is more profound than contractarian or utilitarian concepts as it does not presuppose a society which, having a certain distribution of property, proceeds to legislate after the fact. Property convenes the social relation per se; it is the artifice by which the actions of each person or tribe are related to those of others: '[r]eason presents itself here as the conversation of proprietors' [*ES* 42]. When Hume states, 'I observe, that it will be for my interest to leave another in the possession of his goods, *provided* he will act in the same manner with regard to me' [*T* 490], he presents a basic principle by which a partial interest becomes related to a more general interest (*ES* 42).

Thus, for Hume, the concept of property is not based on a negative requirement to restrict greed, it is the very ground on which a set of social relations is demarcated. Property articulates mutually exclusive partial interests into a meta-system of common or at least broadly compatible interests. Its rule stabilizes possession and enables the construction of a territorial map as the constitutive ground of culture. In the artifice of the general rule 'Hume proposes an entire concept of the relation between nature and culture, tendency and institution' [*ES* 43]. Partial sympathies cannot be synthesized, 'they must either

---

on divorce. Our consumer culture has significantly displaced those values. Even when estranged, however, few would deny the partial sympathies which, if nothing else, may make estrangement so poignant.

be satisfied artificially and obliquely or be snubbed out by violence' [*ES* 43].[24] *'Passions are not limited by justice, they are enlarged and extended'* [*ES* 43].

The rule of property also effectuates another dimension of reason and of any general rule. In addition to providing for the *extension* of partial sympathies, the general rule also provides for their *correction*. It is extensive in providing the oblique artificial conditions for their expression; corrective in that it restrains their natural partiality in the *form* of their extension. In the rule of property, therefore, we see the close material relation between expression and restraint very clearly. When, for example, my neighbour and I affirm the boundary between our lands, we express our partial sympathies and restrain them at a single stroke. This is what allows Hume to construe the understanding and the passions in a relation of mutual affirmation.

Contractarian theories of justice conceive of property as negating possession and reason as negating passion. But Hume's general rule does not work in this way: 'we must understand that justice is not a reflection *on* interest, but a reflection *of* interest, a kind of twisting of the passion itself in the mind affected by it' [*ES* 43].[25] The idea that reason reflects on passion, or that sympathy presents the structure of a subject who feels passion and subsequently thinks about it, treats reason as an abstract rule, when it is actually a modality of embodied passion. 'Reflection is an operation of the tendency which restrains itself' [*ES* 43].[26] *Reason is a kind of feeling*. We refuse to split the subject into a thinking being and a feeling being, mind from body, because this contradicts a materialist foundation. Justice is the social form of reason, it allows desire to be extended and corrected simultaneously through the artifice of the general rule. The general rule is therefore a highly practical principle of social organization.

[24] 'As Bentham will explain later on even more precisely, need is natural, but there is no satisfaction of need, or at least no constant and enduring satisfaction which is not made possible through artifice, industry, and culture' [*ES* 43].
[25] 'There is no passion, therefore, capable of controlling the interested affection, but the very affection itself, by an alteration of its direction. Now this alteration must necessarily take place upon the least reflection' [*T* 492].
[26] 'The remedy, then, is not derived from nature, but from artifice; or more properly speaking, nature provides a remedy in the judgement and understanding, for what is irregular and incommodious in the affections' [*T* 489].

3.6 The institution as the social embodiment of practical reason

The relation between the subject's passion and understanding, and between his partial sympathies and the general rule, allows us to formulate a clearer apprehension of the institution: *the institution constitutes practical reason.* On the side of the subject, reason calms and guides the passions. By the application of artificial general rules, sympathy is deflected into practical expression in society. The general rules, along with the sympathies they extend and correct, constitute social institutions, or culture. Justice, grounded in property is the most fundamental institution, the ground of culture. The term *practical,* in this context, carries a strong sense of *practicable,* since the institution is necessary for any lasting satisfaction of desire.

The institution of justice provides a necessary framework to construct a post feudal society. The mutual exclusivity of partial interests would, in the absence of justice, limit all practical action to feuds and skirmishes. But with the general rules a far wider cultural experience is opened. In this manner an enrichment of the social body is made possible not by negating partial sympathies but by providing an artificial medium, a social context in fact, for their differential expression. Just as the natural principles of association act upon the mind to produce the subject, so the artificial general rules act upon the sympathies to organize a culture.

Justice modulates the passions but has no other end than their satisfaction, nor any origin but their natural determination. The role of justice is to satisfy the passions obliquely, obliquity being their only practicable route to lasting satisfaction.[27] While it is true that justice is an artifice and not a principle of nature, 'to the extent that humanity is an *inventive species*, even the artifice is nature; the stability of possession is a natural law' [*ES* 44]. Human nature is not definable by reference to particular general rules but by the propensity to embrace such rules.[28] Human nature finds its practical expression only through culture; tendency is satisfied only through the institution (*ES* 44).[29]

[27] '[T]each us that we can better satisfy our appetites in an oblique and artificial manner, than by their headlong and impetuous motion' [*T* 521].
[28] 'As Bergson said, habits are not themselves natural, but what is natural is the habit to take up habits' [*ES* 44].
[29] 'All birds of the same species, in every age and country, build their nest alike: in this we see the force of instinct. Men, in different times and places, frame their houses differently: here we perceive the influence of reason and custom' [Hume, *An Enquiry Concerning the Principles of Morals*, 1748, pp. 32–3].

Hume proposes a strong theory of society as the embodiment of practical reason.[30] Recalling our earlier discussion of Gehlen, we can now articulate more clearly what it means to invoke culture as Man's 'second nature'. To construct culture is the nature of Man, it is his species activity; but it is an activity capable of taking shape only in the act of its construction. Nature is given, even to the extent that mind, and the principles of association forming the ground of reason are given, but Man's becoming human, in the sense of an *active being*, is indeed a becoming in the sense that the outcome is not predetermined. Hume offers a dynamic theory of organization that refuses any determinate beginning or end: '[h]e presents us with a critique of the social contract which not only the utilitarians but also the majority of the jurists opposed to "natural law" would have to take up again. The main idea is this: the essence of society is not the law but rather the institution' [*ES* 45]. To focus on the law is to focus on negative restraints and to overlook positive principles of social constitution. The weakness of contractarian theories is a model of society whose essence is the law; they take away anything positive from the social and burden it with negativity, limitation and alienation (*ES* 45).

Hume's institutional theory focuses rather on the positive and creative relation between the subject and social organization as a relation of desires and the means for their satisfaction. To focus on the law places the negative inside the social. Hume reverses the problem; the negative, the lack, the non-specific need, all this lies outside the social. The social is positive, it is practical reason (*ES* 45–6).

3.7 Hume's theory of power and organizational implications

In his study of Hume we find an early expression of the materialist approach to power which Deleuze subsequently develops in his studies of Bergson, Nietzsche and Spinoza. This conception of power is determined by the relation between sensation and imagination: 'everything, which is agreeable to the senses, is also in some measure agreeable to the fancy, and conveys to the thought an image of that satisfaction, which it gives by its real application to the bodily organs' [*T* 358]. These

[30] 'Whatever restraint they may impose on the passions of men, they are the real offspring of those passions, and are only a more artful and more refin'd way of satisfying them. Nothing is more vigilant and inventive than our passions' [*T* 526].

images of satisfaction are impressions of sensation, or passions. Once lodged in the imagination, however, these images are reproduced as impressions of reflection, where they acquire autonomy in the subject: 'being reflected, the passions are found before an enlarged reproduction of themselves, and see themselves liberated from the limits and conditions of their own actuality. They see, therefore, an entire artificial domain opening up, that is the world of culture' [*ES* 56].[31]

The ability of the imagination to project ideas beyond the particular affective situation accounts for the formation of general rules and institutions. This affects our conceptions of power. Through reflection, imagination is able to separate an image from the bodily motions which caused it. This means that it is able to conceive an idea of power apart from its exercise. The formation of any rule depends on a false distinction between power and its exercise. Only the imagination can make this distinction. As it reflects the passions and their objects it detaches them from their actuality and installs them in the mind as possibilities (*ES* 57).

The falsity of distinction between the idea of power and its exercise does not prevent its affecting the passions.[32] The influence of this confusion is pronounced in those who worry excessively about future or past actions. But Hume does not denounce this false practice, this *theoretical power*; his point is rather that through a critique of imaginary power we are better able to understand the nature of imagination's positive qualities – its own peculiar power. It is only by virtue of the mind's ability to reflect affection, and for affection to resound inside the mind that mind ceases to be mere fancy and becomes organized into human nature. Imagination is able to reflect on its own organization by the principles, and even to liberate itself from them (as we saw in the case of the child who imagines its parents to be its children). 'This means that it makes the limit an object of the fancy, it plays with the limit by presenting the accidental as necessary, and separates power from its

[31] Thus the imagination has 'a set of passions belonging to it' [*T* 585]. Deleuze (1990) expands on the quasi-autonomy of ideas in *The Logic of Sense*.

[32] 'It has been observ'd in treating of the understanding, that the distinction, which we sometimes make betwixt a *power* and the *exercise* of it is entirely frivolous, and that neither Man nor any other being ought ever to be thought possest of any ability, unless it be exerted and put into action. But tho' this be strictly true in a just and *philosophical* way of thinking, 'tis certain it is not *the philosophy* of our passions; but that many things operate upon them by means of the idea and supposition of power, independent of its actual exercise' [*T* 311–12].

actual exercise. This illusion, says Hume, is an illusion of the fancy. The power of the imagination is to imagine power' [*ES* 59].

It is this unique ability of imagination to fancy a disjunction between power and the exercise of power which provides Man with his ability to construct culture. The natural principles of causality, resemblance and contiguity are commandeered by the imagination to dissolve their limits, and to organize new ones to be dissolved in turn, endlessly. In other words, once the subject is formed by the principles in the imagination *the principles no longer rigidly apply*. They still support the constancy of the subject but the subject is free to play with their limits. Only when this play becomes involuntary do we begin to see a degeneration of personality and socialization, as the mind reverts to pure fancy and loses the basic organization provided by the principles of causality, resemblance and contiguity, acting upon its ideas.

For Hume it is important to learn to distinguish between the beneficent and the malevolent power of the imagination, a distinction which turns on the quality of thoughts and actions produced. Reflections which paralyse the subject by invoking imaginary powers are malevolent and life-hating, whereas those that increase the efficient power of the mind and body are benevolent and life-enhancing. The implications of this materialist treatment of power come under close scrutiny in Deleuze's Nietzsche and Spinoza studies. We raise the issue here both to make the point that it appears very early in Deleuze's thought, and that it has profound implications for a Deleuzian approach to organization. In any organization the imaginary separation of power from its exercise plays an important role in determining the affections, thoughts and actions of its members. One might even suggest that this is the source of all organizational fear.

Wherever perceptions of power are detached from its actuality, our actions are liable to be misguided due to confused ideas about the wishes and directions of those around us. We shall tend to live too much in an imaginary world of power rather than an actual one. If this kind of thing is widespread then the sum total of affections, thoughts and actions constituting the organization will also be largely composed of imaginary doubts and fears, arising from a false notion of power. This must hinder the effectiveness of the organization in terms of its ability to apprehend its environment. The body or the organization which acts on the basis of imaginary encounters deprives itself of its real power to be affected by external bodies; it also deprives itself of its real power to affect its own passions, thoughts and actions on the basis of an adequate comprehension of that power. In practical terms the way to reduce this effect is by demystification; by reducing the 'distance' between bosses and subordinates, between departments, between the firm and its customers and so on. Only by getting closer to power as it is expressed in action, in the office or in the market, will this malevolent effect be addressed. Only then might the positive inventiveness of the power of imagination be liberated for practically creative work.

3.8 Some further implications of Hume's empiricism: Relations and difference as the bases of organization

In *Empiricism and Subjectivity*, Deleuze raises certain other themes which proved to be of seminal influence in his own philosophy and consequently in post-structuralist thought. One such theme is that *relations are always external to their terms*. Association is not a quality of objects or of the ideas; it forms relations of objects and of ideas which are extrinsic to the terms they relate.[33] Hume means that the principles of human nature act upon the mind autonomously; mind is only the material, it is not in itself human (*ES* 66). The subject is the qualification or affection of a collection of ideas; after which the idea of subjectivity is 'the reflection of the affection in the imagination *and the general rule itself'* [*ES* 64]. Hence, the partial nature of the subject is transcended by the idea of subjectivity, which includes 'the principle and the rule of a possible agreement between subjects. Thus, the problem of the self, insoluble at the level of the understanding, finds uniquely within culture, a moral and political solution. ... Practical reason is the establishment of a whole culture and morality' [*ES* 64]. A phenomenological theme is evident here. In his reading of Hume, Deleuze goes some way towards addressing the well recognized omission in Husserl's phenomenology. Husserl never really explains how the 'phenomenological reduction' of subjective consciousness comes to be a collective experience; the implication being that it involves a kind of *leap of faith*, or similar obscure step. Hume's theory of the artificial rule offers a possible solution, but it is less suggestive of a collective consciousness, than a space of culture within which the desires of partial subjects are extended into action and restrained from mutual violation. In fact Deleuze is not interested

[33] 'Let us consider, that since equality is a relation, it is not, strictly speaking, a property in the figures themselves, but arises merely from the comparison, which the mind makes betwixt them' [*T* 46].

in a theory of consciousness at any level, so he never attempts to revise phenomenology.[34]

Rather than a paranoid contraction into the self, therefore, subjective empiricism is more of a schizoid expansion leading beyond subjectivity *immediately*. Hume explodes the idea of a human interiority: the subject is not given, it is constituted in the given by a natural causality external to the given. Moreover, only by constructing artificial general rules can the subject solve the problem of its own partial sympathies, and thereby organize the cultural conditions for its own survival. Later Deleuze will develop with Félix Guattari (1983; 1990), a schizo-analysis of the subject and society that will attack some of the most influential ideas of twentieth-century thought. Deleuze's reading of Hume is one of the silent references in these important works and, on that basis alone, it deserves wider recognition.

But there is something even more fundamentally materialist in Hume's approach to the problems of subject and society. The whole of empirical thought rests on a principle of difference. The ability to feel sensation, to think and to act, depends on a basic ability to distinguish between different sensations, ideas and actions. 'For how is it possible we can separate what is not distinguishable, or distinguish what is not different?' [*T* 18]. At first our ability to characterize the given as a collection of parts might seem to be the first level of experience. But in order to experience an assemblage we must already be aware that it is divided into parts, already differentiated. Indeed, we experience the given as different within itself. Perception is perception of difference; only after the experience of difference are we able to invent a whole, such as a world. Hence nature is different, but 'Nature' is a cultural construct, a unification of difference into a world. 'Therefore experience is succession, or the movement of separable ideas, insofar as they are different, and different, insofar as they are separable. We must begin with *this* experience because it is *the* experience. It does not presuppose anything else and nothing else precedes it' [*ES* 88].

Organization begins in difference. A subject and a society are different before they are anything else. The ability to detect difference might

[34] As Deleuze remarked, unlike most of his contemporaries, he was not influenced by Heidegger. Hardt reiterates and supplements this point: 'the most general facts of Deleuze's biography, particularly the things that he did not do, indicate his difference from nearly all other major French philosophical voices to emerge from his generation: He was never a member of the French Communist Party, he did not attend the exclusive Ecole Normale Supérieure, and he was never fascinated by the work of Heidegger' [*GD* 136, n. 6].

seem to presuppose a subject capable of its perception, but this is an illusion; the perception of difference and the one who perceives differences emerge together in a mutual becoming. The 'I' that perceives a difference between myself and another has already distinguished many previous things, but with each new distinction both I and my world 'take on the differences' [Cooper, 1983] perceived spontaneously.[35] This perception and these differences make possible the sort of passions, ideas and actions that my body experiences. Of course perception presupposes a body capable of perceiving: 'we might say that the given is at least given to the senses and that it presupposes organs and even a brain. This is true, but one must always avoid endowing, in the beginning, the organism with an organization. An organization will occur only when the subject itself comes to mind, an organization that depends on the same principles as the subject' [*ES* 89]. These principles, of resemblance, contiguity and causality are the basic operations of difference.

The theme of difference, so characteristic of Deleuze's work and of post-structuralist thought more widely, arguably begins with his rediscovery of its pure expression in Hume's empiricism as a characteristic of *duration*. The subject comes to mind during perception and is stabilized by habituation and anticipation. Habit and anticipation are seen by Deleuze as dynamic determinations '– the thrust of the past and the élan toward the future' [*ES* 92]. In this respect his reading of Hume anticipates his treatment of Bergson, addressed in the next chapter. 'Habit is the constitutive root of the subject, and the subject, at root, is the synthesis of the present and the past in light of the future' [*ES* 92–3].

3.9 Conclusions: Hume and organization

The problem of the subject is the first philosophical problem.[36] Interest in the problems of subjective and social organization remained constant in the second half of the twentieth century, but the terms of the debate shifted, partly as a result of Deleuze's work. The shift is quite small by

[35] 'We use the term "spontaneity" in view of the following idea: the principles constitute the subject in the mind at the same time that this subject establishes relations among ideas' [*ES* 150, n. 60].

[36] 'It is necessary, in fact, to know upon what other causes these relations depend, that is, how the subject is constituted in the collection of ideas. Relations are external to their terms. When James calls himself a pluralist, he does not say, in principle, anything else. This is also the case when Russell calls himself a realist. We see in this statement the point in common to all empiricisms' [*ES* 98–9].

comparison to Deleuze's own vision and even smaller compared to its implications for how we live. What Deleuze finds in Hume is a way out of the impasse created by Kantian transcendentalism, a way that he does not cease to widen and improve over his career. Deleuze finds in Hume a way of shifting the problem of human nature away from humanism and structuralism altogether.

Subjectivity and organization are two sides of an empirical process of socialization. Human nature is constituted in the given by principles which transcend it; and social organization involves a positive integration of mutually exclusive sympathies by the invention of artificial rules. In neither case is Hume's empiricism reducible to a simple theory of sensation; which only accounts for Man's natural animation of body and mind as incoherent and unorganized series of physical and mental impressions. Human nature and human culture actually occur in imagination: the effect of the principles discloses to the subject the possibility of forming an artificial rule that imitates but is not constrained by nature. Human reality is a sector of the imagination (Lyotard, 1988). Hume explains how sensation becomes civilization.

'To speak like Bergson, let us say that the subject is an imprint, or an impression, left by principles, that it progressively turns into a machine capable of using this impression' [*ES* 113]. This machine is a passionate social machine, a complex desiring machine (Deleuze and Guattari, 1983). The subject is machined from its own desires, which it satisfies through artificial institutions.

4
Organization and Becoming

The previous chapter postulated organization as a process by which the given is articulated into a nature, an assemblage into an organization. It was argued that the given (ideas, bodies) is different, a pure multiplicity. But where does the given come from and how is it generated? What is difference and how are things different? We need to address these fundamental questions as part of a materialist approach to organization in order to ground it in a materialist ontology. To understand Bergson's ontology of difference, we first need to understand something about the position Bergson writes against, which is Hegel's legacy of the negative dialectic.

4.1 Hegel's logic of determination

Although Deleuze's (1991 [1953]) Hume study introduces many of the distinctive themes to be developed in his later work, it is not until his first Bergson study ('La conception de la differénce chez Bergson', 1956) that he gives full voice to his critique of the Hegelian dialectic.[1] It is arguably from this point on that Deleuze recognizes the breadth and depth of his own philosophical project (*GD* xviii). In 'La conception de la differénce chez Bergson' Deleuze develops the concept of efficient difference which first appeared in *Empiricism and Subjectivity*.[2] Bergson presents efficient difference as the internal dynamic of being. Deleuze

[1] 'What I detested above all was Hegelianism and the dialectic' ['Lettre a Michel Cressole' 1977], p. 110; quoted in Hardt (1993) *Gilles Deleuze*, p. x.
[2] I have relied upon Hardt's (1993) translations from 'La conception de la difference chez Bergson'. Although Hardt locates the inception of Deleuze's theory of difference in this work, it is in fact traceable to his earlier (1953) Hume study, as I have argued. For other developments of the theme of difference, see e.g., Derrida, *Speech and Phenomena* (1973); and Irigaray, 'Equal or different?' (1991a).

mobilizes this conception of difference against the Hegelian negative dialectic to argue for an affirmative and materialist ontology. In *Bergsonism* (1988 [1966]) Deleuze returns to the attack on the dialectic with a renewed vigour, but whereas his earlier essay chiefly addresses Hegel's conception of ontological determination, *Bergsonism* widens the attack to address Hegel's dialectic analysis of the One and the Multiple. This development allows Deleuze to explore the implications of Bergson's work for a positive theory of organization.

Hegel's approach to the question of being has been a dominant influence in modern continental thought. It is, paradoxically, based on his reading of Spinoza. Hegel takes a phrase from one of Spinoza's letters, 'Omnis determinatio est negatio' [Hegel, *Science of Logic*, 113], all determination is negative.[3] Turning the meaning of this phrase against Spinoza's own philosophy, Hegel adopts it as the central maxim of his logic. Deleuze does not take issue with the negative character of determination, he rather disputes Hegel's apprehension of being as *needing to be determined* at all. Hegel's *Logic* apprehends being as undifferentiated in itself, having no immediate qualities or distinctions. In this immediate state, being is equivalent to nothingness. In order to become different, being must first distinguish itself from nothingness. For Hegel, therefore, the difference between being and nothingness defines the real differences and qualities that constitute determinate being in its reality.

Hegel's ontological determinism has two aspects: a static *contrast* between finite qualities, and a dynamic *conflict* or antagonism between differences (*GD* 3). A static contrast refers to a passive negation of one limited quality by another: the quality of red negates the quality of blue because they are mutually exclusive; each marks the limit of the other by their difference. A dynamic conflict refers to an *active negation* between things which interact with one another. Active negation means that the prevalence of one thing over another is never permanent but requires continual confirmation, as for example in the sense that a dominant class, sex or race must continually assert its dominance over a subordinate class, sex or race in order to maintain its privileged position. For Hegel, therefore, being has no intrinsically positive qualities (differences): for him (in contradiction to Spinoza), being is qualified only by its active negation of nothingness, otherwise it remains in an indifferent and indistinguishable state equivalent to nothingness (*GD* 3–4).

[3] Letter 50 from Spinoza to Jarig Jelles. The part in question reads: '*Quia ergo figura non aliud, quàm determinatio, & determinatio negatio est; non poterit, ut dictum, aliud quid, quàm negatio, esse*'. [cf. *GD* 125, n. 1].

Hegel illustrates the principle of dialectical determination by invoking the relationship between a lord and his bondsman.[4] Lord and bondsman must each affirm his identity through their unequal relation; each therefore stands in need of the other. Their respective identities are mediated by the bondsman's servile role which is in turn mediated by the objects of his labour. This process of mediation proceeds by a *negation of a negation*; the bondsman perceives the objects of his labour as negating him; however, by transforming the objects through his labour, by partially overcoming their objective resistance, the bondsman finds the true nature of his consciousness. The lord, having no obligation to labour, is destined never to find his true identity; he can only consume the objective products of his bondsman's labour (he perceives the bondsman as another object) and this pure consumption leaves behind no residue of self-consciousness.

In contrast to a Cartesian conception of identity, Hegel recognizes no simple subject of knowledge, no knowing 'I'. For Hegel, knowledge is necessarily intersubjective, self-consciousness is mediated and independence is dependent on a relation to an other.[5] Self-consciousness knows itself, therefore, only as a structure of mediation (Butler, 1987: 7).[6] While Butler captures Hegel's meaning succinctly, her advocacy of the dialectic is open to a Deleuzian critique: (1) knowledge is indeed relational but, inasmuch as all relations are external to their terms (in this case, subjects), knowledge cannot be *intersubjective*. Knowledge does not occur *between* subjects; on the contrary, subjects per se occur within a certain knowledgeable relation. According to Hume (1738), as we have seen, subjectivity (human nature) is produced by the action of the natural principles of association on the given (mind) which is different in itself. (2) Independence is only dependent on a relation to another if dependency is assumed as the primary condition. We have seen that the given and the principles are *autonomous*, their original *independence*

[4] The section of Hegel's *Phenomenology of Spirit* referred to here is 'Independence and Dependence of Self-consciousness: Lordship and Bondage'. For a concise summary see e.g., Game (1991) *Undoing the Social*, pp. 65–89; or Singer (1983) *Hegel*, pp. 59–62.

[5] Sartre addressed Hegel's dialectic in *Being and Nothingness* (1956), describing it as 'the fundamental existential problem': one's continuing sense of subject identity involves a visual objectification of the other (cf. Weinstein and Weinstein, 1984). Foucault (esp. 1977) develops this analysis in a non-dialectical way, to explicate the importance of vision in Bentham's (1843) architectural principle of the Panopticon.

[6] Cited in Game, 1991, p. 67.

is unconditional. We shall return to this point in the next chapter. (3) From a materialist perspective, self-consciousness (subjectivity, human nature) is not a structure of mediation; it is positive desire that has become aware of its material form and its concrete objects. These critical points illustrate what is at stake in Deleuze's critique of the dialectic: the need to break out of obsessions with human consciousness and identity. The material forces of existence (e.g., difference, association, power) are impersonal; the human is only a phase.

Hegel does conceive of knowledge and consciousness in terms of embodied desire, as Game explains: '[t]he process of knowledge is motivated by desire: what moves the show along is the relation of self to other, and the desire to be desired, the desire for recognition and a mirroring of the self by the other. In this sense knowledge *is* desire' [*ES* 67]. Or as Hegel put it, 'self-consciousness is *Desire* in general' [*PS* 167]. However, from a Deleuzian perspective this is a false definition of desire, an intellectual negation of material life force itself. For Deleuze desire is always positive, always *a desire for something*.

Hegel presents the negative dialectic as a model of ontological determination. Deleuze is critical of this whole approach to the question of being. Specifically, he questions whether determination presents a true account (a) of the process by which being becomes differentiated and (b) of the dynamic movement (*becoming*) of being. Far from establishing a robust ontology, Deleuze thinks that determination only serves to undermine real being by invoking a false conception of difference (*GD* 4). However, Deleuze avoids a direct confrontation with Hegel, preferring to mount an oblique critique. Through Bergson, he first addresses the deficiencies of Mechanism and Platonism and only then proceeds to show how, when viewed from a Bergsonian perspective, the faults of both these doctrines are found in Hegelianism in their most extreme forms. By this strategy Deleuze avoids the folly of attacking Hegel on his own ground. To oppose the dialectic directly is to risk recuperation into its vortex of oppositional relations: to be effective the critique must precisely avoid being cast as antithetical to the dialectical thesis, otherwise it is destined to be synthesized by the dialectical machine. To oppose Hegel is to yield to him.

4.2 Bergson's critique of the dialectic: Contingency and abstraction

Deleuze's critique of Mechanism turns on the real nature of difference. Mechanism proposes an evolutionary theory to account for the differences in being: differences are the effects of external causes. According to Darwin, species evolve by a process of environmental selection: species are effects of external causes. Mechanistic difference is therefore contingent and accidental (*GD* 4). Deleuze's first criterion is that being must be shown to be necessary, which means that difference must be apprehended as *internal* to being.[7] In common with the dialectic, Mechanism views a cause of difference as external to its effect, the effect always depending on an 'other' as its cause. The appeal to an 'other' in Mechanism introduces an accidental quality into being. Mechanism's conception of being as a *subsistent exteriority* implies that the material causes of difference *transcend material being itself*. Bergsonian difference, by contrast, evokes the movement of being itself where the cause of difference is internal to the effect and being is a *substantial interiority*.

Mechanistic approaches to organization are evident in population ecology theory (e.g., Hannan and Freeman, 1979) and new institutional theory (Powell and DiMaggio, 1991). From the perspective of a Bergsonian critique, both theories conceive of organization as radically determined by extrinsic forces, as a subsistent exteriority. This conception locates the power to organize in environmental conditions and in the rise and fall of populations. This effect, it is claimed, is confirmed by *isomorphism*: organizational structures and processes converge as they respond to shared environmental forces. But this is a platitude: even if such isomorphism were proven, to what *depth*? To which *degree* do organizations in the same sector converge; and would it not be more relevant to ask, '[w]hat are the forces of *differentiation*, generated both by endogenous organizational influences and by interactions within specific ecologies? In other words, what are the creative forces at work to overcome the grip of isomorphism; what is the '*élan vital*?' The whole thrust of Deleuze's reading of Bergson is that power to organize comes from within: it is immanent to the organizational process; a virtual which actualizes itself, creatively.[8]

[7]'Bergson shows that vital difference is *internal* difference. But also, that internal difference cannot be conceived as a simple *determination*: a determination can be accidental, at least it can only sustain its being through a cause, an end, or a chance, and it therefore implies a subsistent exteriority' ['La conception de la difference chez Bergson' 92].

[8]In other, related terms, the question becomes whether organization is an enfolding or an unfolding process, or both, alternately or simultaneously. But these terms lead in a different direction which we cannot follow in this work.

Deleuze's critique of Platonism also turns on the real nature of difference.[9] For Plato, the cause of difference in being is not viewed in evolutionary terms. In Platonism the cause is the perfect Form, the final end to which the effect aspires: '[t]he difference of the thing can only be accounted for by its destination, the Good" [*GD* 6]. According to Plato, difference is not *in* the thing, the thing becomes different by aspiring to the perfection of an ideal quality, or end. It is the teleology in Plato which Deleuze challenges: from a Bergsonian perspective, the distinction between the thing and its destiny is false: '[t]he thing and the corresponding end are in fact one and the same. ... There is no longer any room to talk about an end: When difference has become the thing itself, there is no longer room to say that the thing receives its difference from an end' [*CDB* 96]. In common with Mechanism, Platonism presents being as a subsistent exteriority; its distinction of being is contingent upon the final cause, a cause wholly external to the movement of being.

'What Bergson essentially reproaches his predecessors for is not having seen the real differences of nature, they only recognized differences of degree' [*CDB* 79]. By 'differences of nature' Deleuze refers to necessary and substantial differences, which the Scholastics denote by *causae per se*; by 'differences of degree' he refers to accidental differences, *causae per accidens* (*GD* 6–7). 'Thinking internal difference as such, as pure internal difference, arriving at a pure concept of difference, raising difference to the absolute – that is the sense of Bergson's effort' [*CDB* 90]. Mechanism and Platonism succeed in thinking difference only as effects of *causae per accidens*. Bergson conceives of internal difference as necessary and concrete effects of *causae per se*.

In Hegelian thought the exteriority of difference is raised to an absolute principle. Whereas Mechanism and Platonism conceive difference as contingent upon *limited* external causes (physical and final qualities respectively), Hegel takes the externality of difference to the nth degree: his dialectical determinism depends on an *unlimited* external cause in the mediation of the other. As such his dialectic is vulnerable to a Scholastic response: a theory of being founded on external causality cannot account for the necessity or substantiality of being, as a cause external to its effect cannot be a necessary cause (*GD* 7–8). In determination,

[9] Deleuze presents an extended critique of Platonism in 'Reversing Platonism', *Revue de Metaphysiques et de Morale*, 1967; 2. This essay appears in English as an appendix to *The Logic of Sense* (Deleuze, 1990).

being differs from the other; its whole power of differentiation depends on its negation of nothingness, and this negation of negation is enacted in every subsequent difference. Before the thing can differ with itself it must first differ with all that it is not.

By contrast, '[i]n Bergson ... the thing differs with itself *first, immediately*' [*CDB* 96]. By presenting a real alternative, Bergson releases the intellectualist trap of the negative dialectic: Hegel tells us that mediation through the other is necessary to distinguish being (personal being, or any other kind); but Bergson tells us that Hegel is wrong: mediation is not necessary to being; the difference in being is immediate; the dialectic merely serves to obscure the real articulations in nature.

4.3 Difference as the internal movement of being: *Causa sui*

Deleuze reverses the Hegelian relation between being and difference. Hegel perceives a state of being prior to difference, an original being that is immediate, simple, empty and indifferent. Deleuze rejects the notion that being could ever lack difference, particularity and distinction: being is different in itself, composed by particular and distinct things. Just as Hume's materialist definition of mind as an assemblage of ideas specifically refutes the notion of mind as a pre-existent container, so does Deleuze argue that material being is constituted entirely by its own internal differences. Therefore the problem is 'not how being can sustain its difference, but rather *how difference "can sustain its being"* [*GD* 5, emphasis added]. The movement of efficient difference provides the necessary and substantial ground of being, not vice versa.

In his Bergson and Spinoza studies, as well as in his own philosophical thought (e.g., 1990), Deleuze mobilizes a Scholastic conception of causality.[10] We can more easily grasp the basis of this conception in its original, theological context: if God is the cause of all things, what is the cause of God? The Scholastic reply is that God is the cause of Himself (*causa sui*) and the cause of all things (cf. *GD* 125–6). Indeed, God is the cause of all things *in the same way* as he is the cause of Himself: this is the doctrine of *univocity*; the essence of universal substance is also the

[10] In his obituary, Macey (1995) claims that Deleuze 'would later dismiss his early enthusiasms as evincing a scholasticism worse than that of the Middle Ages'. This interpretation is completely opposite to Hardt's (1993), and ignores the rhizomic proliferation of philosophical questions, concepts and themes in Deleuze's later work that reflect his earlier investigations in the history of philosophy.

essence of all things. In an ontological context, the importance of *causa sui* is that the cause of being is *internal* to being itself. Hence, being does not need to negate nothingness in order to become differentiated; it sustains itself through its own internal movement of difference, its self-differentiation. The efficient cause is the internal cause that makes efficient difference the internal motor of being (*GD* 5).[11] Deleuze extends the positive theological doctrine of *causa sui* to support a materialist comprehension of being. Every real cause is *internal* to its effect.

'Now, if the objection that Bergson could raise against Platonism was that it remained a conception of *difference that is still external,* the objection that he makes to a dialectic of contradictions is that it remains a conception of *difference that is only abstract*' [*CDB* 96–7]. In addition to a critique of contingency, therefore, Bergson also accuses the dialectic of failing to mark the concrete specificity of being (*GD* 8). Deleuze draws upon Bergson's reflection on the logic of perception to support this charge: '[i]t is hardly concrete reality on which one can take at the same time two opposing views, and subsume consequently the two antagonistic concepts. ... This combination (of two contradictory concepts) cannot present either a diversity of degree or a variety of forms: It is or it is not' [*B* 96–7].[12] Bergson's argument is twofold: he points first to a *vacillation* in using two opposing terms to describe a thing; this indicates that one has failed to mark the real distinctions constituting its singularity. This imprecision is increased by the external nature of difference between the two terms. Second, Bergson claims that a combination of abstract concepts cannot invoke the concrete diversity of things. This objection is based on another plank of Scholastic logic: no effect can have more reality than its cause. The result of the dialectical synthesis cannot be any more real than the abstract movement of the dialectic itself. The dialectic swings from one concept to another without ever invoking the material object. It involves the supersession of one imprecise term by another equally inadequate approximation, a regressive compounding of errors rather than their progressive correction.

[11] This pure ontological productivity also informs Deleuze and Guattari's work, not least in their positive conception of desire and desiring machines in *Anti-Oedipus* (1983). Pasi Falk (1994) offers a clear explanation of the distinction between a negative (dialectical) conception of desire as lack (as elaborated by Lacan) and the positive conception of desire informing Deleuze and Guattari's work. Here again we see the latters' affirmative philosophy to be fundamentally antagonistic to the influence of the Hegelian dialectic in twentieth century continental thought.
[12] Cited from Henri Bergson, *La Pensee et le Mouvant* (1941: 198, 207).

According to Scholasticism a cause must be internal to its effect: difference, therefore, must be internal to being and not, as Hegel asserts, externally located in the other. If, moreover, an effect cannot have more reality than its cause, the ideal development of the dialectic cannot produce anything more substantial than its own speculative movement.[13] In his Bergsonian critique, Deleuze shows how Bergson's conception of internal difference as efficient causality successfully engages the real and substantial differences in nature – the concrete and different nature of the real (*GD* 8–9).

Hegel charges Spinoza's positive conception of being as remaining undifferentiated and abstract. Deleuze counters this with the argument that the dialectic negates the real differences of nature (*GD* 9).[14] From this perspective 'not only is vital difference not a determination, but rather the contrary – given the choice it would be indetermination itself' [*CDB* 92]. Deleuze does not mean that being is indeterminate; he rather means that the differentiation of being is an internal dynamic, undetermined by external causality; it is non-contingent, *necessary*. *Difference is the internal necessary cause in being.* In this context Bergson 'does not invite us to abandon reason, but to arrive at the true reason of the thing in the process of making itself' [Deleuze, 1956: 299].

4.4 Organization is unforeseeable

Both Hegel and Bergson invoke being as movement and becoming; each presents an ontological movement grounded in duration, 'in which no effective distinction can be made between state and process' [*GD* 126, n. 7]. But whereas Hegel's is a negative movement of determination, Bergson's is an absolutely positive movement of non-dialectical difference. Bergson invites us to apprehend being as open-ended, undetermined and unlimited by any external causality; a fundamentally creative process of '*l'emprévisible*', the unforeseeable (*GD* 10).

We have dwelt on this point at some length for good reason: Bergson's positive movement of being provides Deleuze with an alternative ground to Hegelianism, a ground on which he can begin to construct a constitutive philosophy, a ground in fact upon which we can begin to think of organization as *l'emprévisible*, the unforeseeable,

[13] 'That which carries neither degrees nor nuances is an abstraction' [*CDB* 97; *GD* 9].

[14] 'One has substituted for difference the *game* of determination' [*CDB* 96, emphasis added].

the unpredictable and always improvized and provisional. As soon as organization loses this positive, open-ended movement it atrophies into a determined order. *L'emprévisible* alerts us to a connection in English between unforeseeable and *improvisable*, which is another way of saying that organization is information, and that the opposite of organization, which Hardt terms *order*, is the opposite of information, which is *meaning*. This definition of organization disagrees with scholars who look for semiotic processes in the generation of organization: organization is the opposite of semiosis; it is a more dynamic phenomenon, or practice, of the *surprising*, the *original turn*, the *unexpected*, whatever contradicts a system by a constitutional act. Organization is what moves the semiotic along faster than it can assimilate new terms.

We can also connect the undetermined nature of organization to the principle of univocity. If prediction foretells a future, univocal being refers to the multiple actualization of the simple virtual. If the virtual transforms itself through its actualization, as Bergson argues, if it has to create the terms of its actualization, then it follows that the actual is unforeseen even by the virtual. A specific organizational form or process is always unexpected, and yet all forms are expressed in the same voice: it is one process with infinitely different expressions. This relation between unpredictability and univocity means that being is expressed as it is actualized in a specific language that is invented in the act of its expression.

It is impossible to predict how a business venture, for example, will fare in the actual. From a Bergsonian perspective, this unpredictability, or 'risk', is not due to the number or quality of variables which might affect the venture (external causes) per se. It is rather because organization is creative; it must continually invent the terms of its own actualization. If it does not do this, if it behaves reactively in the face of its environment, then it is not an active organization. Organization as an immanent, productive process is capable of turning passive reaction into creative re-action (Deleuze, 1983); it does not *suffer* variables, it consumes them in its creative process of production, as information. Thus, instead of a population ecology of organization, which seeks to articulate the transcendental forces determining the form of organization from the outside, as in a passive order (Hardt, 1993), what we seek is an internal, embodied ecology that will articulate the immanent variables of organization, which transform the effects of its encounters with other bodies into a radical theory of production. We seek a theory of the efficient force constituting the organization as a body capable of mobilizing the powers of action, passion and intellect. Population ecology, isomorphism, and their many offspring, present a myth of environmental determinism disguised as adaptation; they reduce the complex and concrete *pre-Hegelian* dialectic between organization and environment to a moral tale of intellectual surrender. We will never approach the problem of human organization by placing human creativity in parenthesis.

According to Hardt, what distinguishes organization from order is that the former involves the active transformation of the virtual in the process of its actualization. Order, by contrast, involves only the realization of preformed possibilities. In practical terms this means that an authoritarian organization is not organization in Bergson's terms, it is order. In democratic organization, the involvement of those who implement decisions in making those decisions, necessarily means that organization's ends and/or the means to their achievement cannot be determined by an elite who are effectively external to it (senior executives, major shareholders, consultants). Given the complexities and instabilities of markets and demand, along with the fact that those at the top of an organization are remote from the point of delivery, the democratic organization would, *ceteris paribus*, seem to offer a better chance of survival. In Chapter 6 I shall take up the problem of organizational effectiveness in more detail. Presently, we need only appreciate the Bergsonian principle that the transformation of the virtual is identical with actual organization. [15]

[15] If we dissect the term actual, we find all the dynamic senses that we need to describe organization: it is the emergence of what is enacted, currently; what is real and true; it is that which emerges as an artefact of that process, which is always lost to the present, a memory trace which influences the current actualization. Organization as verb is the process of actualization, therefore; and it is also, as a noun, the set of memory traces that impresses us with the idea that there is a durable thing called an organization. Recourse to Heidegger's (2002) meditations on the nature of things should show us immediately that to award that impression the status of a thing or a work is ludicrous. The process of organization is in both thought and extension, but the organizational 'object' is a figment of mind only. True there is a circular logic here: whatever is a thing is not organization and vice versa. But this is because we are here trying to forge a principle behind a definition, not a definition per se: whatever you say about an organization is untrue. And if one prefers to take a more quantitative approach, one will find that the closer one looks, the further the mirage of the organization recedes. At first it may seem massive; then it divides into divisions and departments; then into sections and groups; finally into individuals who, as we have seen, can only be regarded as parts of those groups. With each step into the organization, it vanishes; we search and search but are left examining parts and wondering how they ever fitted together. The organization, because it was only ever in the cracks between its parts, can never be located as such. This is the grand joke, or paradox, of organization studies.

On a mundane level, organization is unforeseeable and creative in the sense that its actual form is always different from its virtual intention (where there is any). Strategy and planning are therefore only preliminary phases of creative organization: interpreting and actualizing strategy are intrinsically more creative phases. Writing for example, benefits from creative planning, but its actualization from that virtual stage necessarily *involves* creation, *en acte*. Writing is good a example of organization: each phrase suggests future phrases and other directions for thought which could not be predicted before that phrase was written.[16] As in Hume's theory of human nature, the question is: how does the *given* (ideas or words) become unified into a *nature* (a phrase or text)? An appropriate answer would refer to the application of rules of language which transcend any given language. These rules of association, grammar and syntax, present the virtual relations for the construction of texts but they do not negatively determine any single text, any more than the rules of association forming human nature negatively determine any particular subject. What determines the specific text, or the specific subject, is a positive application of principles to localized differences (the given), influenced by the specific circumstances.

The notion of the internal efficient cause invokes Bergson's *qualitative multiplicity of organization*, where each organized body is an expression of its internal difference. The external contingent cause, by contrast, invokes Bergson's *quantitative multiplicity of order*, in compliance with which each instance is a degree of the same (Deleuze, 1988).

Thus, Bergson provides an important distinction between a conception of social relations as a closed and negatively determined *order*, on the one hand, and as an open-ended and positively constituted project of *organization*, on the other. Whereas order entails compliance with negative laws and it is an effect of an external causality, organization involves an immanent causality, an efficient cause internal to the effect. Deleuze's reading of Bergson argues for a conception of being as actively, positively and differently constituted; the construction of social relations presents a practical project of organization rather than passive participation in a rigid logic of being.

[16] As Cooper (1989) has suggested, we should turn our attention from writing about organization, to the organization of writing. Deleuze and Guattari (1983; 1986; 1987) refer to the rhizome and the burrow as a good model of writing, with particular reference to Kafka's work.

4.5 Bergson's critique of the One and the Multiple

Deleuze's main object of critique in *Bergsonism* (1988) is Hegel's dialectical relationship between the One and the Multiple. As we have seen, Bergson distinguishes between two multiplicities: the *qualitative multiplicity of duration* and the *quantitative multiplicity of space*. Duration is a mode of division that alters in kind as it divides; in Bergson's terms duration is the *subjective* or *virtual*. The virtual is actualized through a process of differentiation along divergent lines, or series; a movement which creates differences in kind (*B* 42–3).[17] As an internal movement, the process of differentiation qualitatively alters the virtual 'in kind'. Deleuze claims that Bergson's conception of multiplicity dispenses with the need to think in terms of the One and the Multiple. Many philosophies claim to combine the one and the multiple by reconstructing the real with general ideas (*B* 43–4), but it is Hegel's conception of relations between the One and the Multiple that Bergson has foremost in mind: '[w]e are told that the Self is one (thesis) and it is multiple (antithesis), then it is the unity of the multiple (synthesis)' [*B* 44]. Bergson rejects this dialectical approach: its concepts are too abstract and general, 'like baggy clothes ... much too big' [*B* 44]. Deleuze supplements Bergson's metaphor of the good tailor and the well fitted suit, with Plato's metaphor of the good cook and the well carved joint (*B* 44–5). The philosopher-craftsman should cut his concepts along the natural articulations of the real. Here, as we saw in the case of determination, a dialectical vacillation between badly formed concepts will never approximate to the concrete.[18] From Bergson's perspective, interaction between real bodies is not a contradiction between opposites; opposition is a false, conceptual polarization of things and its negative movement is therefore extrinsic to the real.

Deleuze finds a precedent to Bergson's critique of the dialectic in Plato's *Philebus*: in response to those who assert, 'the One is Multiple, and the Multiple is One; Being is nonBeing' etc., Plato demands to know *which one, how many, when and where*? Plato here scorns grandiose theories, he wants specific cases: '[t]he combination of opposites tells us nothing; it forms a net so slack that everything slips through' [*B* 44–5]. Bergson locates the problem of contradiction in a natural pairing of

[17] For Bergson duration is the element of memory, while space is the element of matter; the process of becoming is the actualization of the virtual, the point where memory concentrates on matter (cf. *B* 51–72).

[18] 'The concrete will never be attained by combining the inadequacy of one concept with the inadequacy of its opposite' [*B* 44].

concepts which leads only to an illusion of knowledge: concise thought must avoid analysing material things into ready-made concepts (*B* 45).[19] Against a generalized dialectic of opposites, Bergson calls for an acute perception of the nuance: the 'what?' and the 'how many?'[20]

Kant and Hegel revolutionized philosophy by substituting the negative dynamic of opposition for the static negation of simple limitation, but Bergson rejects both forms of negation on the grounds that each evinces an ignorance of *differences in kind*. Bergson affirms differences in kind independently of all forms of negation: being is positively different, therefore nothing real is negative (*B* 46). Negation begins with a general idea of being or order that can only be thought in opposition to an equally general idea of non-being or disorder. We should rather begin with a difference in kind between two specific beings or orders and *resist* the tendency to subsume their specific differences under an abstract synthesis. All the critical elements in Bergson's philosophy contribute to this rejection of the negative limitation, of the negative opposition and of general ideas [*B* 46–7].

Is Hegel really vulnerable to this critique, or does Deleuze oversimplify the dialectic in order to use Hegel as a straw man (*GD* 11)? It would certainly be wrong to think of Hegel's relation between the One and the Multiple as a static opposition: '[t]his truth is to be grasped and expressed only as a becoming, as a process, a repulsion and attraction – not as being, which in a proposition has the character of a stable unity' [Hegel, *Science of Logic*, 172]. Reference to the oppositional structure of concepts might give the impression that the dialectic describes a mechanical interaction between stable states. As Bergson observes, this impression is due to the reifying effect of language; what the propositions really invoke is a *passage*, or *becoming*. But the main thrust of Deleuze's study is not that Hegel presents being as a static opposition, it is rather that his movement of becoming is a *falsely negative movement*. Deleuze's *Bergsonism* demonstrates how the dialectic falls prey to its own negative origin; how it can never *affirm* anything about concrete existence.[21]

[19] Deleuze and Guattari (1994) will argue that real philosophy involves the invention of new concepts.

[20] '[T]he One and the Multiple in general only coincide on condition that they are grasped at the extreme point of their generalization, empty of all "measure" and of real substance' [*B* 45–6].

[21] Working on a draft of *Capital*, Marx wrote in a letter to Engels: 'the fact that by mere accident I again glanced through Hegel's *Logic* has been of great service

4.6 Against state philosophy: Order v. organization

How is the foregoing relevant to organization theory? Hegel himself indicates the context in which to address this question by his analogy between physical atomism and a theory of the State: '[p]hysics with its molecules and particles suffers from the atom ... just as much as does the theory of the State which starts from the particular will of individuals" [*Science of Logic* 167]. Hegel's dialectic between the One and the Many carries a political antagonism towards the ancient atomistic view of the State as the combined will of the people: his relation between the One and the Multiple provides an ontological foundation for his theory of political organization (*GD* 13). The ancient atomists proposed a theory of the state as the combined will of individual wills, a theory congruent with our reference to Hobbes's Leviathan as the embodiment of the people. But Hegel's dialectical relationship of the One and the Multiple is determined to *subsume* the collective will or embodiment in the synthesis of the Unity of the Multiple. The crucial change here is the elevation of the State (the Unity of the Multiple) to a superior level, granting the State primacy over the collective. For the atomists, the State brings a collection of bodies under a new more powerful relation, yet still remains grounded in those wills because it is literally composed by them. But for Hegel, the State is raised above that mundane level, acquiring a power *over and above* the collective will of the people. It does not enlarge their collective will; it replaces it with a new, totalizing will. Thus, the State alienates the political will of the people; it is a synthesis of the One and the Multiple which turns to dominate them.

Bergson's critique rejects the supersession of material society by the ideal State, affirming the real plurality of the social (*GD* 13). Because this plurality refers to *partial* rather than to personal interests, it is able to invoke the different sectional, class and institutional forces which express these partial interests and constitute the principle organs of

to me. ... If there should ever be time for such work again, I would greatly like to make accessible to the ordinary human intelligence, in two or three printer's sheets, what is *rational* in the method [the dialectic] which Hegel discovered but at the same time enveloped in mysticism' [Singer, 1983: 77]. Regrettably, Marx never did find the time but, in the light of his own treatment of the dialectic, we can be fairly sure that the two objections disclosed by Deleuze would also have been emphasized by Marx. Hegel's 'mysticism' arguably refers to the idealism and *abstraction* of his dialectical method and its consequent failure to address the world of living bodies.

society. Bergson's quantitative multiplicity of space recognizes differences of degree, 'of *order*', while his qualitative multiplicity of duration recognizes differences in kind, 'of *organization*' [*B* 38, emphasis added]. By granting primacy to the State Hegel, by contrast, recognizes neither multiplicities of quality nor of degree; by positing the synthetic Unity of the Multiple he is rendered unable to think multiplicity at all (*GD* 13).

Bergson's recognition of two types of multiplicity allows Deleuze to propose an alternative to the Hegelian dialectic, founded on the real differences in nature: 'a pluralism of organization against a pluralism of order ... far removed from Hegel's State philosophy of the One and the Multiple' [*GD* 13]. Deleuze's *Bergsonism* discloses a positive ontology of social organization as the embodiment and expression of Hume's (1738) incompatible *partial interests*. It is not a question of the State taking control and snubbing out conflicting partial interests, but of cultivating the institutional conditions for their oblique social expression and integration.

4.7 Organization as the actualization of the virtual

Deleuze's critique of Hegel's negative movement of being is the precursor to his articulation of an affirmative ontology, not only in his Bergson studies but also in his later work. The terms of this alternative are by now familiar from the critique. Being is *causa sui*, an internal movement of differentiation. Bergson presents being as a positive movement from the *virtual* to the *actual*. The virtual is the concentration of being in pure recollection or memory, and the passage from the virtual to the actual is being's qualification and differentiation of itself in a pure expansive movement.[22] One can think of this positive movement by analogy to the processes of mitosis: a zygote begins with all the necessary genetic information to divide and differentiate itself into a complete organism. The mature organism is contained in the original cell in its virtual form (genetic code). Here, as elsewhere, virtual being is never abstract nor is its actualization determined by an external cause; its cause is internal, efficient difference, its life-force, or *élan vital*.[23] Bergson's movement of being is absolutely positive, not needing to be

[22] 'The essence of a vital tendency [*élan vital*] is to develop fan-wise, creating by the mere fact of its growth, divergent directions, each of which will receive a certain proportion of the impetus' [Henri Bergson (1935 [1932]), *The Two Sources of Morality and Religion* 282, in *B* 132, n. 4].

[23] 'Difference is not a determination but, in this essential relationship with life, a differentiation ... the explosive internal force that life carries within itself' [*CDB* 93].

determined, mechanically, teleologically or dialectically; its cause is its efficient force of internal differentiation.[24] This is also the primary force of organization, the *élan vital*, the internal movement of differentiation, the efficient cause. The actualization of DNA into the organism is a primary form of organization.

This analysis turns on the crucial difference theorized by Bergson between time and space: '[t]he division occurs between (1) duration, which "tends" for its part to take on or bear all the differences in kind (because it is endowed with the power of qualitatively varying with itself) and (2) space, which never presents anything but difference of degree (since it is quantitative homogeneity)' [*B* 31].[25] Bergson argues for an identity between duration, memory, consciousness and freedom (*B* 51). Memory preserves the past in the present, while the present contains the expanding image of the past: hence, memory covers 'with a cloak of recollections a core of immediate perception' [*B* 51].[26] The real differential nature of duration, which distinguishes it from mere repetition of the same, lies in the mutual information of the present by the past: 'the following moment always contains, over and above the preceding one, the memory the latter has left it' [*B* 51].[27] As no clear break occurs between one moment and the next, 'the two moments contract or condense into each other since one has not disappeared when another appears' [*B* 51]. Thus, the differentiation of perception is not the effect of the external object, but rather the quality given to perception by memory (*B* 52–3). It is one of Bergson's most important discoveries that memory always precedes perception and the distinction of matter. In this sense we can understand organization, as fundamentally the application of memory to matter.[28]

Real difference is in duration. Duration involves a multiplicity of qualitative differences, a real movement of differentiation in time. Matter, by contrast, presents a quantitative difference between abstract,

[24] 'Differentiation is the movement of a virtuality that is actualizing itself' [*CDB* 93].

[25] In this sense *Bergsonism* develops Deleuze's reading of Hume. In Hume mind is transformed into subject. In Bergson the subject is constituted in duration by Memory, the object is presented in space as Matter.

[26] The actualization of the virtual occurs *in* duration, this is the full sense of Bergson's 'actualisation' which in French relies on the sense of *actuel* as 'contemporary' (*GD* 16).

[27] Henri Bergson, *The Creative Mind* (1946), p. 193.

[28] Bergson's distinction between memory and matter anticipates *the body without organs* in Deleuze and Guattari's work: pure matter, prior to memory, perception or distinction.

static points. Being homogeneous, matter is only differentiated by the external application of differences of degree (e.g., the geometrical division of the globe into degrees of latitude and longitude), which ignores the real differences of topography, climate, population, etc. 'Space reveals a multiplicity of exteriority, a numerical multiplicity of quantitative differentiation, a multiplicity of *order*: pure duration presents an internal multiplicity, a heterogeneity of qualitative differentiation, a multiplicity of *organization*' [*GD* 15, emphasis added]. In mitosis, real differentiation refers to the information of each cell division by genetic memory: this is how a biological body is organized; cells duplicate and specialize to form different organs according to their genetic coding and regulatory pathways. The institutional body depends on a similar efficient production, whereby partial interests (social cells) differentiate and integrate to form the social organs which actualize their memory obliquely through viable expressions of desire.

4.8 Bergson's critique of possibility and realization as the locus of order: Virtuality and actualization as the locus of organization

One reason to emphasize the relation between the virtual and the actual as the basic movement of organization is to distinguish it from a false conception of becoming as a passage from the *possible* to the *real*: 'the process of realization is subject to two essential rules, one of resemblance and another of limitation. For the real is supposed to be in the image of the possible that it realizes. (It simply has existence or reality added to it...)' [*B* 97]. Since every realized possibility occurs at the expense of the other possibles, 'realization involves a limitation by which some possibles are supposed to be repulsed or thwarted, while others "pass" into the real' [*B* 97]. Deleuze regards this as confused thinking. Bergson views being as creating the terms of its own differentiation in the process of its actualization, it does not respond to any external abstract determination which the possible implies: 'in short, the characteristic of virtuality is to exist in such a way that it is actualized by being differentiated and is forced to differentiate itself, to create its own lines of differentiation in order to be actualized' [*B* 97].[29]

[29] 'The possible has no reality (although it may have an actuality); conversely, the virtual is not actual, but *as such possesses a reality*. Here again Proust's formula best defines the states of virtuality: "real without being actual, ideal without being abstract"' [*B* 96].

If we view the productive movement of being as the realization of the possible, we violate the Scholastic principle that an effect cannot have more reality than its cause. In Scholastic theology, God is the Virtual, the *ens realissimum*, the essence of being, the most real thing (*GD* 17). If God were merely the sphere of the possible, creatures would possess more reality than God, their cause – yet nothing created can be *more real* than its creator. The same logic applies to (secular) ontology: if the virtual and the actual are both real, it is logical to perceive becoming as the actualization of the virtual by a process of internal differentiation. There is nothing *from* which being can be differentiated, so it can only differentiate *itself* and this provides further support for the argument that actualization is a temporal succession: being can only be different from itself by a series of presents becoming past.[30]

Deleuze illustrates Bergson's ontological distinction between the realization of the possible and the actualization of the virtual in evolutionary terms: '[e]volution takes place from the virtual to actuals. Evolution is actualization, actualization is creation' [*B* 98]. When speaking of organic evolution, therefore, we should be careful to avoid two misconceptions: the first obviously appears in preformism, contrary to which, evolutionism adequately demonstrates that 'life is production, creation of differences' [*B* 98]. The second misconception appears in the opposite to preformism: if differences are merely accidental, then there are no necessary relations between them, and there would be no reason why they should link up and add together in the same direction; nor any reason for sudden and simultaneous variations to be coordinated into a livable whole (*B* 99).[31]

4.9 The limits of Bergsonism: Differentiation is only the first part of organization

The organizational implications of Deleuze's Bergsonism arise from its radical productionism: the virtual produces the terms of its actualization. Whereas the real resembles the possible it realizes, 'the actual ... does

[30] Hardt marks the valuable nuance, 'actualization' also invokes 'the Aristotelian passage from the virtual into act' [*GD* 17], a sense which helps us to understand the significance of Bergson's analysis in terms of the practical embodiment of the virtual in the temporal plane of action.

[31] 'How could an external physical energy, light for example, have "converted an impression left by it into a machine capable of using it?"' [Henri Bergson (1944 [1907]), *Creative Evolution* 80] [*B* 132, n. 11]. Deleuze and Guattari develop this notion of the organic machine in *Anti-Oedipus* (1983) and *A Thousand Plateaus* (1987).

not resemble the virtuality that it embodies' [*B* 97]. This is connected to Bergson's distinction between a preformed multiplicity of *order* and an unforeseeable multiplicity of *organization* (*B* 38). A conception of being as the realization of the possible gives rise to an order in which the possibilities of life are given in advance in limited and mutually exclusive forms. By contrast, a conception of being as the actualization of the virtual evokes a creative organizational dynamic wherein internal differentiation of being simultaneously creates the terms of its own embodiment. Organization is that embodiment of actualized differences; it is not the primary productive life-force but a secondary force, which is perhaps contained or even contains the primary form, a power that shapes and composes even as differences are manifested.

Through his Bergson studies Deleuze articulates a positive ontology capable of grounding organization in a principle of efficient difference. But we should be clear that this only presents the raw material of organization in the form of a heterogeneous multiplicity, as opposed to a homogeneous multiplicity of order. All that we have really sought to establish in this chapter is *a positive ontological foundation. This foundation or ground is not organization per se, it is what happens before organization, what is given to the organizational process.* In Bergson's philosophy the problem of being rests at this point: being is an explosion of material differentiation, an infinite expansion of becoming; nature is the positive movement of the virtual *explaining* itself in the *actual*.[32] This addresses the creative impulse in nature, the *élan vital*, but it does not address the problem of constitution: by what method does the expansion of heterogeneous multiplicities cohere into wholes? Bergson's rigorous establishment of positive difference in life is one thing, but it is quite another thing to demonstrate how those differences are integrated into living bodies.

Hegel derides Spinoza's positive movement of being as emanationism.[33] Hegel's critique is twofold: first, an ontology of emanation entails a progressive loss of being; second, it cannot demonstrate any principle of coherence between productions. As to the first point, Hegel has in

[32] In Scholastic thought *explanation* has an ontological sense: '[e]ach line of differentiation or actualization thus constitutes a "plane" (*plan*) of nature' [*B* 133, n. 13]. Here actualization refers to the ex-plan-ation of the virtual. A link exists here between intellect and organization; reason explains the virtual concept into trajectories of thought. Thus, an adequate explanation of knowledge parallels an explanation of being.

[33] 'In the oriental conception of *emanation* the absolute is the light which illumines itself. Only, it not only illumines itself but also *emanates*. Its emanations are *distancings* from its undimmed clarity; the successive productions are less perfect than

mind a notion of being as a fixed quantity of energy that diminishes with expansion. Both Spinoza and Bergson would deny this conception: the creative force does not diminish, it is rejuvenated within each articulation of difference (*GD* 19). Nature preserves its creativity through the differentiation of the species, its vitality is its heterogeneity. As to the second point, Hegel recognizes how a positive ontological movement can account for the *becoming of being*, but can it account for the *being of becoming*? (*GD* 19): how can the explanation of being be a *coherent* explanation; what makes the differences relate to one another, instead of expanding without limit, *partes extra partes*? Hegel's analogy between physics and politics emphasizes the practical importance of this objection: like the ancient atomists, Spinoza and Bergson reject the unitary order of the State in favour of a multiplicity of organization but, so far, we see only multiplicity and no organization. The question remains, therefore, as to how Bergson's philosophy can be applied to the socio-political sphere: what distinguishes his positive movement of being from anarchy?

4.10 Difference and univocity: Towards an organizational logic

Responding to Bergson's explanation of becoming as a raw heterogeneous multiplicity, a radical productivity, we need to find a complementary movement of convergence, capable of accounting for how differences become constituted into wholes; how the given becomes a nature while still preserving its heterogeneity and avoiding the imposition of an external order.[34] Deleuze reads an incipient logic of convergence in Bergson: '[t]he real is not only that which is cut out *(se découpe)* according to natural articulations or differences in kind; *it is also that which intersects again (se récouped) along paths converging toward the same ideal or virtual point*' [*B* 29]. Thus, it is possible to retrace the divergent lines of becoming back to their source, as if they left a recording, a trace or inscription which can be read like a genealogy.

---

the preceding ones from which they arise. The process of emanation is taken only as a *happening*, the becoming only as a progressive loss. Thus being increasingly obscures itself and night, the negative, is the final term of the series, which does not return to the primal light'. [Hegel, *Science of Logic* (1969), 538–9; quoted in *GD* 19].

[34] Since writing this I have read Theweleit's *Male Fantasies*, congruent with the equation: fascism = order; democracy = organization. Theweleit argues that fascism is an extreme type of patriarchy based on a morbid fear of women. It may follow that Man = order; female = organization. This is hardly new to feminists and I merely note it here.

Each line of divergence corresponds to a particular facet of the virtual whole. Because each of these facets coexists in the virtual, each line of divergence carries with it the principle of coexistence with all the other lines. Although each divergent line is unique in actual existence, its formal articulation is identical to every other by virtue of their common expression of the virtual (*B* 103). This is the Scholastic principle of *univocity*, once again: actualized differences diverge from a common, virtual, univocal plane. Becoming is expressed 'fan-wise' along divergent lines, but it is univocal, it is everywhere said in the same voice and, furthermore, it is always said in the same way.

Deleuze does not elaborate on the ancient axiom of univocity until his later studies of Nietzsche and Spinoza. The resounding message of his Bergson studies is that life proceeds by division and divergence impelled by the *élan vital*, the internal efficient force. Life is divided into plant and animal, the animal into various instincts, particular instincts are divided according to species. These lines do not merely reproduce the virtual: what coexisted virtually ceases to coexist actually; the lines of differentiation are creative, they actualize only by inventing in existence the ontological level they embody (*B* 101). According to Bergson, each limited embodiment presents a concrete problem for the *élan vital* to solve. Man *is* the closest thing to a living solution and, in this sense, 'the purpose of the entire process of evolution' [Bergson, 1935: 200]. In Spinozian terms, the actual line of Man is the one that is most nearly adequate to the virtual (*B* 106). This is because Man alone is capable of tracing the open direction of becoming, of reconstructing the career of an absolutely positive movement of being, becoming conscious of the entire process which in every species is purely unconscious.[35] For this reason the human line alone can harness the *élan vital*, the creative differentiation that is valid for the Whole. By expressing his open direction he is able to express a whole that is itself open. Other directions are fixed planes, closed orbits, but 'Man is capable of scrambling the planes, of going beyond his own plane as his own condition. ... On Man's line of differentiation, the *élan vital* was able to use matter to create an instrument of freedom, "to make a machine which should triumph over mechanism"' [*B* 107].

This is a nice speculation but it is unclear why Bergson should exalt Man's abilities in empirical terms. Undoubtedly the answer lies in

[35] Bergson evidently did not see Man as a species. His view agrees with a Gehlenian-Nietzschean definition of Man as the *not-yet-determined-animal*. In a sense there are as many human 'species' as there are divergent cultures but really Man's reduced instincts despecify him. Man is the *non-specific* animal, *the body without instincts*.

culture, but culture is both more and less than a direct expression of human intelligence. One of the foundations of society is obligation, yet taken as a whole obligation has no rational grounds: '[e]ach particular obligation is conventional and can border on the absurd; the only thing that is grounded is the obligation to have obligations' [*B* 108]. In fact we have no concept to explain obligation, it can't be grounded in reason or nature; it is more than natural and less than reasonable. Bergson thinks of obligation as 'virtual instinct' [*B* 108] which, according to Deleuze, is nature's supplement of Man's partial intelligence by partial instincts. The result Bergson terms the 'story-telling function' [*B* 108], the creator of gods, the inventor of religion. Each god is contingent and absurd in itself, 'but what is natural, necessary and grounded is *having* gods; it is the pantheon of gods' [*B* 108]. Deleuze implies that human sociability is a kind of pantheon containing many gods – none of them necessary but each an expression of necessity. To tell stories, to share gods, is a basic form of human intelligence. Thus defined, sociability can only occur in intelligent beings, but it is not grounded in their intelligence (*B* 108). Conventional obligations do not disclose Man's necessarily creative condition, they rather enclose it in specific, unnecessary forms 'and Man goes round in circles in his society just as much as the species do in theirs or ants in their domain. Nothing here seems to be capable of giving Man the previously mentioned exceptional opening, as power of going beyond his "plane" (*plan*) and his condition' [*B* 109].

The social institution is no more constituted by regulation than by free will. In *Empiricism and Subjectivity* Deleuze affirms Hume's conception of the institution as a positive integration of partial interests and, in the closing pages of *Bergsonism*, he expresses a similar view. Man's creativity is that which appears in the slight interval 'between the pressure of society and the resistance of intelligence' [*B* 110]. What appears in this interval is *creative emotion*: '[o]nly emotion differs in nature from both intelligence and instinct, from intelligent individual egoism and quasi-instinctive social pressure' [*B* 111]. We are thrown back into the rigorous empirical machine of Hobbes or Hume, in which reason and action are always analysed with an eye to the practical interest, the passion, which drives them. Bergson's *intuition* or creative emotion, is that which ensures that stories are never related in exactly the same way; something is always altered in the telling: 'it has only made use of their circular play in order to break the circle, just as Memory uses the circular play of excitation and reaction to embody recollections in images' [*B* 111]. Intuition, creative emotion or passion, is the impetus or power internal to action. It occurs in the interval between social obligation and individual response: it is what occurs *first* in the interval, before thought or action. Intuition or passion is what invests thought and action with a new idea to renew its vital energy. It is this realization, along with its incipient plan 'of an *open* society, a society of creators'[36] that carries Deleuze beyond the scope of Bergsonian ontology and inexorably towards a practical philosophy.

Bergson's positive ontology is the expression of a creative emotion that breaks the circle of the dialectic and dismisses the concept of negative organization. At the end of his Bergson studies, therefore, Deleuze arrives at an insight previously articulated in *Empiricism and Subjectivity*; what moves being along is emotion, passion or affect. Passion invests reason with a content and testifies to the embodied nature of ideas. Hegel reduces all passions to the sombre motive of negative desire. Hegel's conception of desire is no more or less than fear of death, his 'Ultimate Lord'. The mutual negation between Hegel's lord and bondsman is a model of this life and death struggle in the everyday world: '[e]ach must seek the death of the other' [*PS* 187]. So far as Bergson and Deleuze are concerned, death wins the struggle only so long as we continue to view life – through Hegel's eyes – as needing to be mediated by death. As Nietzsche perceives, a desire for life is the most futile desire of all: what is the use of wishing for what we already have? What we have, what we *are*, is being which is positively different in itself. To desire being, to want it, is to negate it, to negate the being that we are and to look for some other 'place' in which to find it – which is to invent nothingness. Hegel's legacy is a philosophy grounded in this negation of life: *this* is what Deleuze despises in Hegel's dialectic. Man, to be adequate to Bergson's open and positive movement of being, must begin by affirming that movement.

Being is positive, on this point all philosophers agree: disputed is the nature of an adequate response to being. Addressing Deleuze's Nietzsche study in the next chapter, we learn what it means to affirm being to the nth degree and, in considering this affirmation, we come very much closer to an adequate and affirmative theory of organization. If Bergson's positive movement of being helps us grasp its efficient vitality, Nietzsche helps us understand why the only adequate response to that vitality is to return its affirmation to itself: we shall see that this return is the *constitutive movement* of organization.

[36]'If Man accedes to the open creative totality, it is therefore by acting, by creating rather than by contemplating' [*B* 111].

5
Organization and Affirmation

Nietzsche and Philosophy carries Deleuze's positive ontology into political territory. His analysis of Nietzsche's will to power and the eternal return provides a development of an ontology of difference to an ethical affirmation of being: Nietzschean organization is comprised of these two movements.

5.1 Nietzsche and critique

Nietzsche's work is 'an absolute anti-dialectics' [*NP* 195], anti-Hegelianism is its 'cutting edge' [*NP* 8]: '[w]e will misunderstand the whole of Nietzsche's work if we do not see "against whom" its principle concepts are directed. Hegelian themes are present in this work as the enemy against which it fights' [*NP* 162] (*GD* 27). This anti-dialectics is not directed solely at Hegel but constitutes a wholesale critique of the transcendentalism Nietzsche locates at the centre of philosophical idealism. Thus, Deleuze uses Nietzsche against Kant as well as Hegel, partly to avoid the sort of oppositional confrontation upon which the dialectic thrives. Nietzsche's relation to Kant is paradoxical; it was Kant who first understood the necessity for critique to be total and positive. Real critique must be uncompromising, admit no exceptions (*NP* 89): its positivity depends on its ruthlessness; only on the basis of a total destruction can new knowledge be created. Deleuze found, however, that Kant confused the positivity of a total critique with a humble acknowledgement of the rights of the criticized. Kant's own critique is weakened by his conciliatory and respectful attitude (*NP* 89). Kant compromised his vision of a total critique by granting immunity to the transcendental terrain of truth and justice from which philosophy itself operates. Thus, in the *Critique of Judgment* 'we learn ... what we had known from the start, that the only object of Kant's critique is justification, it begins by believing in what it criticises' [*NP* 89–90].

Hegel compounds the Kantian compromise by a partial and negative critique *par excellence*. Thus, Hegel's state philosophy may be traced to Kant's humble recognition of established values and the ruling order: '[w]hen we stop obeying God, the state, our parents, reason appears and persuades us to continue being docile' [*NP* 92]. Hegel installs a politics of compromise as the axiom of the dialectic; a suprasensible essence is recuperated in each synthesis and, ultimately, we discover just what this mysterious essence really is: the secret agenda of a philosophy enslaved by the ruling order.

Nietzsche understood that a total critique must destroy all such suprasensible grounds, obliterating metaphysics, and this turns out to be the most difficult intellectual task for one brought up in the shadow of platonic thought. Thus, Deleuze reads Nietzsche as more Kantian than Kant himself. Philosophy for Nietzsche does not begin with ideal absolutes like truth and justice, it rather begins with physical bodies and what they can do. Nietzsche creates a very different role for the philosopher, as a destroyer of values supporting the ruling order: order is the enemy; values its instruments of oppression: *truth*, *morality* and *religion* – these are the main targets of Nietzsche's total critique. Such a critique has unlimited force, it is a work of annihilation leaving nothing standing in its wake. This is the uncompromising non-dialectical negation that Deleuze's reading of Nietzsche develops (*GD* 28).

5.2 Total critique as re-evaluation: *Pars Destruens, Pars Construens*

Kant could not achieve a total critique because he did not conceive it as the destruction and creation of values (*NP* 1). There are two moments of a total critique: the negative destructive moment (*pars destruens*) which attacks not only evaluations but also the fundamental values which they presume, and a positive constructive moment (*pars construens*) which replaces the destroyed values with newly created ones. If critique addresses true or moral propositions but leaves intact the values of truth or morality, then it is only partial: by sparing established values, critique fails to prepare the ground for value-creation (*GD* 29–30).[1]

[1] 'In fact, the notion of value implies a *critical* reversal. On the one hand, values appear or are given as principles [e.g., *justice*]: and evaluation presupposes values on the basis of which phenomena are appraised. But, on the other hand and

From a Nietzschean perspective, organization must be value-creating. Bittner (1965) recognizes this in his critique of those who merely adopt the terms of analysis presented by managers: researchers who take on the values of the ruling order and do not question the presenting problem. Concepts like 'employee' and 'efficiency' are used as if their meanings were unproblematic, when they are ideological and presuppose a whole background of values and mythologies which they serve to mobilize. Even where the intention is to elucidate the perspectives of organizational actors more widely, as it is in Weber's (Gerth and Mills, 1948) work on bureaucracy, to the extent the researcher adopts actors' common-sense terms, he fails to criticize their values and, inasmuch as he refines and purifies their terms into an operational language, he distorts and corrupts those values.

Bittner refers to three ways of dealing with this problem: the researcher can simply adopt the common sense meanings as adequate for the analysis; or he can assign arbitrary meanings to the terms in the manner of a scientific operational language or, finally, he can set about discovering how such terms are used in the practical lives of those who use them. Only in the last strategy will the meaning of such terms as 'employee' and 'efficiency' be apprehended adequately: by studying how the terms of actors' discourses are assigned to real objects and states of affairs by 'competent' social actors (Bittner, 1965). Bittner's point is that terms like 'employee' and 'efficiency' have no natural meaning; their sense is to be discovered only by interpreting the perspectives of those who use them to evoke a world of objects and events. In this sense, every term carries with it an entire context of evaluations, each of which presupposes a covert value. There are no natural employees, or standards of efficiency; to describe an individual or a group in these terms is to participate in a cultural world wherein certain mythical relations of *employment* and *productivity* serve to inform actors' everyday lives. A rigorous research should address these covert values and this is possible only by addressing the evaluations they inform.

A Nietzschean approach to the problem of organization operates on this level of interpretation and value creation. By destroying established values and creating new ones, the researcher becomes a *legislator*, a creator

more profoundly, it is values which presuppose evaluations, "perspectives of appraisal", from which their own value is derived. ... Evaluations, in essence, are not values but ways of being, modes of existence of those who judge and evaluate, serving as principles for the values on the basis of which they judge. This is why we always have the beliefs, feelings and thoughts that we deserve given our way of being or our style of life' [*NP* 1].

of values.[2] This is the role of a Nietzschean 'active science' of organizational theory and practice. Such a science has three main elements: a *symptomatology*, which interprets phenomena as signs, whose meaning must be sought in the forces that produce them; a *typology*, which interprets forces by their active or reactive quality and a *genealogy*, which evaluates the origin of forces by their nobility or baseness according to their genealogy in a quality of the will to power (*NP* 75).

A Nietzschean active science does not substitute true values and true knowledge for false values and false knowledge; it is precisely *true* knowledge, *true* morality, *true* religion that make Zarathustra shudder at Man in general (*Ecce Homo IV* 330–1). It is the baseness of such *authentic* values and the notions of virtue they inform, that Nietzsche attacks (*NP* 90).

5.3 Nietzsche's perspectivism

When all transcendental values are destroyed there remains for Nietzsche only one adequate approach to critique: 'perspectivism' (*NP* 90). Perspectivism consists of isolating and destroying moral values ascribed to phenomena: '[t]here are no moral phenomena at all, only a moral interpretation of phenomena' [*BGE* 108]. Contrary to the claims of social rationalists like Habermas (1987) and Rorty (1991), a Nietzschean interpretivism does not imply a vortex of relativism or the nihilism they claim such relativism portends. Such reformists want to retain the good and discard the evil in Man, whereas perspectivism perceives how even the good in Man, *especially the good*, is a manifestation of base (reactive, negative) forces. Reformism is dialectical, a partial critique that fails to recognize the need for Man to overcome himself, to overcome his own nature, dominated as it is by reactive forces.[3]

[2] '*Actual philosophers ... are commanders and law givers*: they say "*thus* it *shall* be!" ... they reach for the future with creative hand.... Their "knowing" is *creating*, their creating is a lawgiving, their will to truth is – *will to power*' [Nietzsche (1973 [1886]), *Beyond Good and Evil*, p. 211].

[3] 'The development of perspective [in the visual arts] ... is the triumph of an artificial view of things, an illusion built upon a specific preconception, a way of seeing that is more the work of the brain than of the eye. As Lippe tells us, "[t]he unity that serves to encompass diversity is that of a geometrically reconstituted perception on the part of a fictitious eye". Today, after the experiences of colonialism – the European subjugation of the world's peoples from the perspective of a European center – we can finally see that anyone who talks about *perspective* is really talking about a *focal point*, an *ego* to which everything else becomes subordinate. In the last analysis, that person is talking about subjugation and imperialism.' [Klaus Theweleit (1987), *Male Fantasies*, Minneapolis: University of Minnesota].

Interpretivism invokes an immanent critique: in the absence of transcendental ground external to the moral values an object discourse mobilizes and conserves, the critique can only engage its immanent morality. It must disclose the masked core-values in discourse and unmask them *as if it were unmasking itself*.[4]

Let us consider the organizational implications of perspectivism by invoking an empirical example from medical sociology. Fox (1993) presents a series of interactions between surgeons and their patients. In his evaluation of each case the surgeon tends to attribute satisfactory progress to his own intervention and, by implication, to the value of surgery in general. By contrast, he tends to attribute unsatisfactory progress to other causes: the tenacity of the disease, the patient's weak condition or low morale. Why, asks Fox, when the operation is often more life-threatening than the affliction, does the surgeon never ascribe a slow recovery to the trauma of his own intervention? Fox claims there are certain compelling reasons for the surgeon's partiality in this respect: if he admits any doubt concerning the wisdom of his actions he might be open to litigation, and the value of surgery in general would be questioned. Thus the surgeon's evaluation of progress or otherwise, invariably contains a justification of his own actions and of surgery. In ascribing success to the value of surgery, the surgeon's evaluations presuppose that value and, more profoundly, that value presupposes those evaluations. In Nietzschean terms, surgery for the surgeon is always *good value*.

It may be hasty to accuse surgeons of not properly weighing the risks of surgery against its likely outcome.[5] Besides, a frank admission of

[4] This is also the deconstructive method of Derrida: an immanent critique that seeks those nuances of a discourse betraying the hidden evaluation at its core (Cf. Derrida 1981, *Positions*; Norris 1987).

[5] Perhaps not so hasty. As I was writing this, it came to light that at least 29 and possibly more than 100 children had died at Bristol Royal Infirmary at the hands of incompetent and unscrupulous heart surgeons, and a chief executive who refused to intervene.

The BRI tragedy was revealed by a more junior physician, anaesthetist Dr Stephen Bolsin. Five years earlier Bolsin had written to the head of the district health authority, (later to be BRI chief executive), to raise his concerns about a higher than average death rate among newly born babies. His allegations against the head of his cardiac unit, James Wisheart, were dismissed. Bolsin claimed that Wisheart threatened to ruin his career prospects should he pursue the matter. Bolsin then carried out his own audit of results, which confirmed that for one heart procedure nine out of 12 of Wisheart's patients had died – a figure far higher than the national average. He was also very concerned about the other surgeon Janardan Dhasmana's record for a complex operation known as 'the switch'. Over the period in question Dhasmana had carried out 38 operations with 20 deaths.

risk, combined with a patient's legal consent, may ward off litigation more effectively than blind faith in the value of surgery. Even so, the example illustrates a strong tendency to preserve certain values and to

---

The last switch took place in January 1995 on Joshua Loveday from Gloucester. The night before his death an extraordinary meeting of the cardiac team took place. Every doctor, except Dr Bolsin, agreed that the operation should proceed. But concerns about the whole switch programme had spread outside the hospital, as Dr Bolsin had contacted a key official from the Department of Health. That evening Dr John Roylance, by then chief executive of BRI, was contacted by Department of Health official Dr Peter Doyle. Doyle expressed concern about the operation proceeding. Roylance replied that as chief executive although he was a doctor, he could not override the clinical judgement of the doctors directly involved. Meanwhile, Joshua's parents knew nothing about the debate. Joshua died the next day during the operation. Joshua's death was the catalyst that made Bolsin risk his career by talking to BBC West of England Health correspondent Matthew Hill.

Hill then met the Chairman of the hospital and told him he had enough information to break the story and could do it with or without their co-operation. To his surprise, Roylance handed over a report, into the crisis, carried out by one of the country's leading heart surgeons, Mr Marc De Leval of Great Ormond Street. Hill exposed the scandal in a piece on the Close Up West regional news magazine programme in April 1995. Three years later, after the longest disciplinary hearing in the history of the General Medical Council, Wisheart and Roylance were banned for life from practising medicine. Dhasmana was also found guilty of serious professional misconduct and, although he was not struck off, his position became untenable and he was later sacked.

Any organizational scholar should immediately ask whether the BRI scandal was a unique situation, or evidence of systemic malpractice in the NHS. I have little doubt that the latter was and remains the case. My own daughter underwent open-heart surgery at four-months-old. She was originally misdiagnosed by Leeds cardiac surgeon Mr Dickenson as having a much less serious condition (atrial septal defect) than she actually had (atrio-*ventricular* septal defect). Fortunately, the diagnosis was corrected by cardiologist Dr Giovanni at Birmingham Children's Hospital. She was urgently and successfully operated on by Mr Babulal Sethia and she continues to thrive.

What became of Dr Stephen Bolsin, the whistle-blower of Bristol Royal Infirmary? He was virtually driven out of medicine in this country, an outcome he anticipated. But he had the courage to do the right thing: '[i]n the end I just couldn't go on putting those children to sleep, with their parents present in the anaesthetic room, knowing that it was almost certain to be the last time they would see their sons or daughters alive'. Thanks to Bolsin, whistle-blowing in the NHS became officially encouraged. But can one seriously believe many have the courage, or even confidence in their observations and knowledge, to expose themselves to the ostracism of more powerful doctors and surgeons? Or that one or two scandals changes everything?

Years ago I concluded that moral courage, of the sort shown by Stephen Bolsin, and in lesser degrees, is the rarest type of organizational behaviour one is ever likely to encounter. Its rarity is a depressing indictment of organizational life.

exclude alternatives. It also suggests that the surgeon who is more open to alternative interventions, and to the values they presuppose, would be led to re-evaluate the value of surgery by its location in the wider context of his professional knowledge and experience.[6] The difference between a preformed *order* and an undetermined *organization* of surgical medicine is that the former tends to protect its established values, whereas the latter tends rather to question those values with a view to their eventual substitution by new ones. One has only to consider the re-evaluation of pregnancy and childbirth occurring over the last 20 years, its change in status from a medical condition requiring routine surgical intervention (still the predominant view in the USA) to a natural process requiring minimal intervention, to apprehend how one value can be substituted for another in empirical terms. This example also serves to illustrate the embodied nature of values and evaluations in the thoughts, feelings and actions of patients, medical personnel and institutions. Here is a concrete example of how an established order, presenting a fixed horizon of possibilities, has been altered into an open organization, an organic horizon of evolving evaluations and values.[7]

5.4 The form of the question in Nietzsche

Deleuze addresses Nietzsche's perspectivism by invoking a distinction between two basic forms of questioning. In this respect his critique of Kantian transcendentalism is linked to his critique of Platonic teleology. We are accustomed to phrasing questions in the form, '[w]hat is...?' ('Qu'est-ce que?'): '[w]hat is beauty? What is justice? What is *organization*?' This formulation is due to Plato, who frequently presents Socrates as posing '[w]hat is?' type questions to his interlocutors, who typically reply by giving specific examples: '*the one that* is just, *the one that* is beautiful: a young virgin, a mare, a cooking pot' [*NP* 76]. Whereupon Socrates declares that they have mistaken his question – he does not ask *which one* has beauty but rather *what is* beauty in itself, in *essence*.[8]

[6] I know of one example: a paediatric surgeon at a Glasgow hospital who was also a leading practioner on homeopathic medicine.

[7] Countering phallocentrism with a labial motif, Irigaray (1991b; 1991c) argues that the concept of order or closure is alien to the female body, which is essentially *entrouvert* – neither wide open, nor completely closed, but rather slightly open, not quite closed. This is significant in returning the language of the subject to the organic body.

[8] Cf. my earlier comment on the German *Wesen*.

But it Socrates who is asking the wrong question (*NP* 76). Nietzsche says that the correct question is not 'Qu'est-ce que?' but rather 'Qui?' *which one* is beautiful, *which one* is just? By changing or restoring the proper form of the question Nietzsche attacks the transcendental system of values '[w]hat is?' presupposes – the Platonic theory of essences and appearances. For Nietzsche, there is no abstract quality of truth, beauty, justice, etc. These are only value judgements of concrete things. For him an essence always refers to an evaluation.

By demanding to know '[w]hich one?' and correlating each answer with the perspective of the observer, Nietzsche transforms an idealist into a materialist conception of essence, and demonstrates the falsity of the distinction between ontology and politics. The Platonic question '[w]hat is being' is transformed into a sophistic enquiry into the movements of power and desire: '[w]ho wants this version of being?' Plato shows Socrates putting his '[w]hat is?' question to very young men, stubborn old men and famous sophists. By association the sophists are also made to appear naive and stubborn (*NP* 76), suggesting that Plato's indictment of them is not so much an attack on false logic, as an attempt to discredit a whole system of sophistic thought hostile to his own. The famous sophist Hippias does not mistake the bias in Socrates' question, or fall into his trap; he holds that the question 'Which one?' is actually the best form of questioning. This implies an alternative systematic doctrine: 'an original conception of essence and a whole sophistic art which was opposed to the dialectic: An empirical and pluralist art' [*NP* 76].

The question: '[w]hich one?' (*qui*) seeks to disclose the forces that take hold of a given thing, the will that possesses it. Which force is expressed, manifested, even hidden in it? We are led to a materialist 'essence' only by the question: '[w]hich one?' 'For *essence is merely the sense and value of the thing*' [*NP* 77]. 'Qu'est-ce que?' is the definitive transcendental question, it implies a perfect suprasensible form to which all material instantiations must aspire and be judged by. 'Qui?' by contrast, is a materialist question, it looks to the movement of real forces from an identifiable perspective. The two questions invoke entirely different spheres of being (*GD* 30): abstract thought and concrete desire, respectively.

Nietzsche's attack on the Platonic form of philosophical enquiry is a total epistemological critique: he does not criticize the substantive answers to '[w]hat is?' type questions, he rather destroys their assumed field of possibility. 'What is?' implicitly devalues physical things as inferior copies of perfect ideas. This is what Nietzsche and Deleuze find so despicable and absurd: that material life should be judged inferior to imaginary ideals; the grand fallacy at the heart of idealism.

The alternative form of the question: '[w]hich is?' transforms the horizon of enquiry by inviting a plural response: '[b]eauty is this and this and this: it is a delightful person, a fine horse, a well turned pot, etc.'. 'Which one is?' releases the interlocutor from the tyranny of the essential Form or Idea of beauty, justice or organization. The tyrant is Plato, whose ontology of essences and appearances still limits the horizon of modern thought (Deleuze, 1990 [1969]).

Thus, as Nietzsche shows, '[w]*hat is* organization?' is the wrong question. We should rather be asking, '[w]*hich* organization *in particular*?', '[w]hose will possesses and guides its embodiment of forces?' and also '[w]ho *wants* organization, and *which one* do they want?' Perspectivism does not deny essence, it recognizes essence as perspectival: '[f]undamentally it is always the question "What is it *for me*" (for us, for everyone that sees etc.). ... The essence of a thing is discovered in the force which possesses it and which is expressed in it' [*NP* 77]. We have already begun to think in this pluralist way by distinguishing between a negatively determined order as a closed singularity, a closed system; and to think of immanent organization as an open plurality.

Having addressed Deleuze's Nietzschean critiques of Kant and Plato, we return to his critique of Hegel. Deleuze begins by renewing his Bergsonian position that the dialectic presents an abstract conception of being.[9] Again, Deleuze counters the abstract determination of being with a conception of material difference, but here difference has a more practical function.[10] This is the direction hinted at in the closing pages of *Bergsonism*, where Deleuze raised the question of creative emotion. He is now able to revise Bergson's *positive movement* of becoming into a Nietzschean *affirmation* of being (*GD* 32). We can begin to understand the implications of this shift from ontology to practice by addressing Nietzsche's characterization of the dialectic as *slave logic*.

5.5 Nietzsche's slave logic and master logic: Who wills organization?

Nietzsche argues that the form of the question 'Qui?' discovers the key method in the history of philosophy, the method of *dramatization*.

[9] 'The being of Hegelian logic is merely "thought" being, pure and empty, that affirms itself by passing into its own opposite. But this being was never different from its opposite, it never had to pass into what it already was. Hegelian being is pure and simple nothingness' [*NP* 183].

[10] 'For the speculative element of negation, opposition and contradiction, Nietzsche substitutes the practical element of *difference*' [*NP* 9].

Although this mobilizes the '[w]ho?' in addition to the '[w]hich? in 'Qui?', we must be careful not to confuse the actors in Nietzsche's dramatization with specific persons: they are properly apprehended as impersonal forces or wills (*NP* 207, n. 3).[11]

Nietzsche presents the dialectic as the logic of the slave, the 'speculation of the pleb', in which the abstract thought of contradiction prevails over the concrete feeling of positive difference (*NP* 10). Nietzsche counters with a master logic. He demonstrates the power of perspectivism by commandeering Hegel's own allegorical characters of lord and bondsman, turning them against their narrator to refute his dialectical logic. Nietzsche understands that being is not spontaneous but *willed*. Thus the question becomes: '[w]ho *wills* being as a negative or a positive movement?' This marks a decisive shift from the terrain of a speculative ontology, to the practical terrain of volition, will or power.

'You are evil; therefore I am good' is the slave's logic of self-affirmation. It contrasts with that of the master: 'I am good; therefore you are evil' [*NP* 119]. These two formulae might be thought to be equivalent but they could not be more different in terms of their senses and values. The master's logic *begins* with an active affirmation. Contrary to the dialectic, it does not seek identity in another. If 'I am good', if I affirm my existence immediately, then 'you', who do not do so, 'are evil'. Here the conclusion is not denigratory but merely a logical consequence of the affirmation: 'it is only an accessory, a complementary nuance' [*GM* I 11].[12] All that is not affirmative (noble) is necessarily negative (base).[13] The master's affirmation is creative because it is an absolute, value-creating beginning.

Slave logic operates quite differently, it is reactive: 'you are evil; therefore I am good' begins with a negative evaluation of the other, so that the affirmation which follows is really a negation of a negation, a *false* affirmation. In this case the function of 'therefore' is inverted from a logical nuance to a negative determination (*NP* 120). In slave logic my existence

[11] 'Thus, when we ask: "what does the one who thinks this want?" we do not abandon the fundamental question "which one?" we merely give it a rule and a methodological development. We are demanding that the question be answered not by *examples* but by the determination of a type' [*NP* 78–9].

[12] 'In the master logic everything positive is in the premises. He must have premises of action and affirmation, and the enjoyment of these premises in order to conclude with something negative which is not the main point and has scarcely any importance' [*NP* 120].

[13] For the moral distinction between good and evil Nietzsche substitutes nobility and baseness. Good and evil are human inventions; Nobility and baseness refer to impersonal qualities of force.

is *your* responsibility; whereas in master logic I am responsible for *myself*. The slave's negation of the master is partial, external and recuperative, he is really saying that the value of my existence depends upon my devaluation of yours.[14] In which case the value of my existence must be negative: '[t]his is the strange syllogism of the slave: he needs two negations in order to produce an appearance of affirmation. We already sense the form in which the syllogism of the slave has been so successful in philosophy: *the dialectic*. The dialectic, as the ideology of *ressentiment*' [*NP* 21]. The slave's negation of negation is dialectical; Hegel's method is the logic of the slave, Nietzsche's the logic of the master.[15]

We should understand that the slave does not resent the master's strength as such, what he resents is the master's failure to restrain his strength. What Nietzsche terms *ressentiment* is '*the fiction of a force separated from what it can do*' [*NP* 123].[16] When the slave begins: '[y]ou are evil' he projects an abstract notion of force, the idea of a force as a cause that is separate from its effects. Such a force will be vicious if it acts, and virtuous, on the contrary, if it does not (*NP* 123). It is in the interval between a fictional force and actual (real) force, that the moral distinctions between vice and virtue appear: *vicious* is one who acts when he could have restrained himself from acting; *virtuous* is one who could have acted but restrained himself from doing so. Nietzsche argues that this is all fictional: under a materialist conception, there is no abstract power, only power *en acte*.

Deleuze analyzes the slave's paralogism into three moments. First, the force is split in two so that the manifestation 'is turned into an effect which is referred to the force as if it were a distinct and separated cause' [*NP* 123]. We can easily grasp this fictional relation in the idea of gravity as a force, and the motion of bodies as effects. If gravity is a quality of bodies, it is illogical to put them in a relation of cause and effect.[17]

[14] 'We ask: who is it that *begins* by saying "I am good"? It is certainly not the one who compares himself to others, nor the one who compares his actions and his works to superior and transcendent values: such a one could not begin. ... The one who says "I am good", does not wait to be called good. He refers to himself in this way, he names himself and describes himself thus to the extent that he acts, affirms and enjoys' [*NP* 119]. NB. 'Enjoy' is everywhere defined as taking joy from, whereas etymologically the prefix en- denotes to put joy into or to add joy. The former suits a consumer culture, the latter is the nobler form.

[15] In terms of Scholastic causality, the logic of the slave is contingent, *causa per accidens*, whereas the logic of the master invokes a wholly internal *causa sui*.

[16] This is reminiscent of Hume's (1738) conception of imaginary power (see Chapter 3).

[17] 'The same event is posited first as cause and then a second time as its effect. Scientists do no better when they say "force moves", "force causes" and the like' [*GM* I 13, p. 45].

Second, a force so divided 'is projected into a substrate, into a subject which is free to manifest it or not. Force is neutralised, it is made the act of a subject which could just as easily not act' [*NP* 123]. Nietzsche exposes this subject as a fictional correlative of the separation of forces from what they can do: the summoning of a moral distinction between vice and virtue projects a cast of moral subjects whom Nietzsche terms 'little imaginary incubuses' [*GM* I 13, 141). The third and final moment is the reciprocal determination which constitutes the essential contradiction of morality: if I conceive of a force able to restrain itself from manifesting the force that it 'has', it is no more absurd to conceive of a force that does not manifest the force that it does not actually have (*NP* 124). Virtue, according to slave logic therefore consists in falsely attributing necessary inaction to voluntary restraint.[18]

It is not difficult to locate a practical organizational example of slave logic to illustrate Nietzsche's point. It is considered that imprisonment is a just punishment for many crimes, and that the criminal who has served his sentence has 'repaid' a moral debt to society. But this repayment is entirely passive, enforced by external causes. A prisoner *might* not have committed any more crimes during his incarceration, but that is hardly to his credit. His honesty was imposed and enforced, rather than due to voluntary restraint: imprisonment conforms to slave logic.[19] This example applies not only to imprisonment per se, but also to incarceration as a model for social organization (cf. Foucault, 1977). If justice and morality are all about restraining bodies from what they can do, then they embody the law of the slave in the reactive cultural institution.

The thrust of Deleuze's reading of this part of Nietzsche's *Genealogy of Morals* is that morality is not a positive or creative human achievement, it rather embodies the *ressentiment* of the weak and effectively transforms that weakness into a perverse, negative power. For the power of *ressentiment* does not attack power directly, it rather introduces a moral distinction between good and evil in order to transform the exercise of power into a culpable practice. This dichotomy is effectuated by distinguishing fictitiously between agent and act, by separating the force from its

[18] 'Just as if the weakness of the weak – that is to say their *essence*, their effects, their sole ineluctable, irremovable reality – were a voluntary achievement, willed, chosen, a *deed, a meritorious act*' [*GM* 1 13, p. 46].

[19] The converse also applies: a prisoner may commit many more crimes in gaol (sexual, violent, narcotic) than he otherwise would have done, had he not been incarcerated and constrained to fall in with prison culture. In this case morality finds him blameworthy for acting when he should have restrained himself – even when he could not do so due to force of circumstance.

exercise, the cause from the effect. The artificial vacuum thus formed sucks in morality to fill the gap[20]: it is not culpable to be strong or powerful: it is culpable to carry that power into action. For Nietzsche, power is always efficient force, *en acte*. The power of a specific person, machine or institution is materially expressed in how it acts, not how it could act.[21] It does not refer to intentions or to latent forces.

If the aim of slave logic or *ressentiment* is to deprive active force of its material conditions of operation and to separate it from what it can do fictitiously, it is also true that something real happens to active force as a result of this fiction (*NP* 127). It becomes reactive and is internalized, turned back against itself (*NP* 128). Active force that becomes reactive is interiorized to become *bad conscience*.[22]

Nietzsche's analysis of slave logic is his analysis of the human condition – dominated by *ressentiment* and bad conscience, all the active force of Man's nature turned reactive, corrrupted. For Nietzsche, all historical cultures have been slave cultures.[23] Yet Nietzsche distinguishes between two kinds of force: on the one hand are specific cultural forms or laws 'which are obeyed, which are always historical, arbitrary, grotesque, stupid and limited; this usually represents the worst *reactive* forces' [*NP* 133]. On the other hand, there is the generic *active* force of law-making in Man common to all cultures. In this Nietzsche perceives the active essence of Man: 'culture is generic activity; "the labour performed by Man upon himself during the greater part of the existence of the human race, his entire *prehistoric* labour ... notwithstanding the severity, tyranny, stupidity and idiocy involved in it"' [*NP* 133].

Each law is arbitrary: what is not arbitrary is the law of making laws (*NP* 133). We encountered this rule previously in Gehlen's (1988) Nietzschean evocation of Man as a radically active being. Hume (1738)

[20] Thus, the notion of 'moral vacuum' is well founded but only inasmuch as morality subsists in the fictional interval between a force and what it can do, between agent and act.

[21] Foucault recognizes this when he rigorously defines the prison organization in terms of what it really produces, which is *recidivism*. For Foucault the prison is a concrete form of an abstract machine (Panopticism); the school, workshop and factory are similar forms (Cf. Deleuze, 1988, pp. 31–51).

[22] 'All instincts that do not discharge themselves outwardly *turn inward* – that is what I call the *internalisation* ... that is the origin of "bad conscience"' [*GM* II 16, pp. 84–85; Quoted in *NP* 128].

[23] 'Culture means training and selection. Nietzsche calls the movement of culture the "morality of customs" (...); this latter is inseparable from iron collars, from torture, from the atrocious means which are used to train man' [*NP* 133].

and Bergson (Deleuze, 1988) make similar statements. The relation between Man's generic cultural urge and his extant or historical cultures is the same as that between organization and order, respectively. Man must positively organize his existence but has historically succeeded in establishing mainly negative cultural orders – which contradict and are corruptions of the active principle of their genesis. Far from relieving his burden of world openness by creating *active organizations*, Man has tended instead to construct *reactive orders*: new burdens to pile on old.

Nietzsche distinguishes between the slave's negation of life and the master's affirmation of life. The slave's initial negation represents the basic dynamic of transcendentalism: whenever a suprasensible power is invoked organic life itself is negated. Whether this power is God, the State, a system of abstract forces or a moral order, the effect is the same: organization is separated from what it can do.[24] Transcendentalism begins with Plato and we can read its influence throughout history and in our everyday lives; we continually judge material things by ideal standards. When confronted by a greater force than ourselves we react by neutralizing that force, by invoking a fictional cause external to the effect, interposing a morality between the two. Reactive forces do not triumph by getting together to compose a greater active force; they triumph by decomposing active force, separating it from what it can do, taking away part or almost all of its power (*NP* 57). Reactive force negates difference, turning it into opposition, making it an object of *ressentiment* and bad conscience. By contrast, *active force makes difference an object of affirmation and enjoyment* (*NP* 55–6).

Active force is separated from what it can do by a potent fiction: Nietzsche uses the terms 'vile', 'ignoble' and 'slave' to designate those reactive forces that exalt themselves and lure active forces into their fiction, 'replacing masters with slaves who do not stop being slaves' [*NP* 58]. Reactive force is the force of the weak but the triumph of reactive force has made the weak dominate throughout history: '[t]he strong always have to be defended against the weak' [*VP* I 395]. Zarathustra's snake is base but no less strong than his noble eagle (*NP* 61).

[24] 'the fiction of a super-sensible world in opposition to this world, the fiction of a God in contradiction to life. ... In and through this fiction reactive forces *represent themselves as superior*' [*NP* 125]. 'To be able to reject all that represents the ascending movement of life, well-constitutedness, power, beauty, self-affirmation on earth, the instinct of *ressentiment* here become genius had to invent another world from which that life-affirmation would appear evil, reprehensible as such' [*AC* 24, p. 135].

5.6 Nietzsche's critique of humanism

Deleuze refers to the discussion between Callicles and Socrates (Plato, *Gorgias*, 1979, 481–527). Callicles distinguishes law from nature: everything that separates a force from what it can do he calls law. Thus, law expresses the triumph of the weak over the strong – according to Nietzsche, the triumph of reaction over action. Everything that separates a force from its action is reactive, as is the quality of a force separated from what it can do. By contrast, every force which goes to the limit of its power is active, hence: '[i]t is not a law that every force goes to the limit, it is even the opposite of law' [*NP* 59]. But Socrates admits no distinction between nature and law, he replies that the strong who prevail by law are simply the weak banded together. He does not see that to be strong and to prevail are two different things.

Callicles tries again: the slave does not cease being a slave by triumphing over the master; the weak triumph only by separating force from what it can do, by rendering active force reactive (*NP* 59). Only by abstracting force from nature can the slave prevail. From a materialist viewpoint, forces cannot properly be conceived in abstract: 'from the point of view of nature concrete force is that which goes to its ultimate consequences, to the limit of power or desire' [*NP* 59]. This time Socrates blusters: 'what matters for you Callicles is pleasure. ... You define all good in terms of pleasure' [*NP* 59]. Socrates' ideas of nature, strength and desire are all premised on slave logic: he interprets each one as something which is always already separated from what it can do. He does not recognize that desire has less to do with pleasure or pain than with active force which goes to its limit (*NP* 59).[25]

Nietzsche reads Socrates' legacy in modern positivism which claims to rid thought of all the old transcendental values of religion, morality and the state. Yet by embracing humanism positivism confuses law and nature. Nietzsche scornfully invokes positivistic humanism in the type of the 'free thinker'. The free thinker wants to recuperate the content of religion without considering that religion might contain Man's basest (*reactive*) forces; forces we might want to discard: its fatalistic belief in revealed truths (positivism's love of facts), its interpretive impotence (positivism's failure to account for the perspective dependency

[25] Nietzsche cites the example of chemistry, in which each element extends its power without reserve: '[t]here is no law: every power draws its ultimate consequences at every moment' [*WP* 634]. 'I beware of speaking of chemical "laws": that savours of morality. It is far rather a question of the absolute establishment of power relationships' [*WP* 630].

of knowledge) and its ignorance of the qualities of force (positivism's inadequate grasp of causality) (*NP* 60).

Consider the example of the market: suppliers claim to provide what buyers 'want' to fulfill their 'needs'; but this is a fatalistic conception of relations between supply and demand, ignoring the structural conditions of a market generating specific patterns of production and consumption. There are no biological needs not socially informed, shaped and modified. By ignoring the role of the producer in shaping desire, the 'free thinker' absolves himself of any responsibility for the market, however cruel or corrupt: he does not ask himself whether the supply or consumption of intensively cultivated food expresses noble or base forces; he interprets this as a moral question and denies a role for morality in the free market. But noble and base have nothing to do with morality in Nietzsche, they are not equivalent to good and evil. They refer to impersonal active and reactive qualities of force, to an ethics of supply and demand of which the free thinker has little understanding because he can only think in humanist terms. He maintains a system of production founded on the separation of active forces from what they can do: breeding and keeping animals in stalls and cages; growing plants by monoculture; steadily reducing the variety in nature into a few 'useful' species.

The free thinker is fatalistic because he accepts whatever the market dictates: the market is God. Thus, all that the free thinker really achieves is to install the transcendental qualities once attributed to God, into Man (omniscience, omnipotence). Who therefore is the less deceived: the free thinking humanist, deluded by the belief that he has successfully banished all transcendental values from his mind, or the one who locates those values in God and is at least capable of recognizing their transcendental status?

To the free thinker Nietzsche opposes the *free spirit*: 'the spirit of interpretation itself which judges forces from the standpoint of their origin and quality' [*NP* 60]. The free spirit understands the fatalistic trope in humanism, its blind positivistic faith in facts, passed off as empiricism. The free spirit is the spirit of interpretivism: '[t]here are no facts, nothing but interpretations' [*VP* II 113]. In the type of the free thinker Nietzsche 'discloses a perspective from which many different ideologies can be attacked at once; positivism, humanism, the dialectic – positivism's taste for facts, humanism's exaltation of the human fact and the dialectic's mania for recovering human contents' [*NP* 60]. Nietzsche locates the error common to all these doctrines: they have not understood that in order to mount a genuine total critique of transcendental values we must avoid the positivistic humanism that has taken over from religion, for this route will always lead back to a false origin of impersonal forces *in* the human. We must also recognize that law is human, outside nature, and belongs to culture – but only to the basest type of culture, that of the slave. The law is negative, it hates difference and loves order, it is not an instrument of organization – it is even the opposite of organization. From a Nietzschean perspective, organizational analysis is dominated by free thinkers who seek to discover lawful behaviour.

Nietzsche conceives a *hierarchy* between active and reactive forces in two senses: first, it marks the absolute difference between and the superiority of active over reactive forces (*NP* 60). But hierarchy also marks *the triumph of reactive over active forces*: 'the contagion of reactive forces and the complex organization which results – where the weak have conquered, where the strong are contaminated, where the slave who has not stopped being a slave prevails over the master who has stopped being one: the reign of law and of virtue' [*NP* 60–1]. This is Nietzsche's assessment of human organization. If the prevalent quality of force expressed in culture is reactive rather than active, then its organizing principle is the consciousness of the slave. This means that it does not compose the differences in being in order to bring them under a greater, more powerful embodied relation. On the contrary, it decomposes existing bodies by separating their active quality of force from what it can do. This is not organization as embodiment, it is disorganization, disembodiment; the institution of a culture founded on *ressentiment* and bad conscience. From a Nietzschean perspective, organization as we know it is a reactive process designed to divest active being of its creative power. That is to say that organizations are dominated by slaves whose primary function is to alienate members from their creative productivity; to maintain their false integrity at the cost of the real integrity of their 'human resources'.

5.7 Organization: Consciousness and the body

How is this comprehensive disempowerment achieved? Mainly through a culture of *consciousness*. Hardt approaches this problem by addressing Houlgate's critique of Deleuze. Houlgate (1986) accuses Deleuze of not really understanding Hegel: he claims that Deleuze does not grasp the necessity of negation for determination, and Deleuze's own conception of self-affirmation fails to meet Hegel's criteria for genuine interiority. Houlgate reminds us that if we want determination, we must have negation: 'nis determinatio est negatio'. But Deleuze does not *want* determination: as an absolutely external movement it cannot provide a necessary foundation to being (*GD* 37–8). Thus, Houlgate's first criticism backfires, he has not read Deleuze properly. His second criticism confirms this impression: 'Deleuze thus rules out the possibility that true, concrete selfhood is to be understood in terms of the negation of, or mediation by the other' [Houlgate, 1986: 7]; and: '[i]n contrast to Hegel, Deleuze does not believe that genuine self-consciousness requires consciousness of the other's recognition of oneself' [Houlgate, 1986: 8]. Now Houlgate thinks that Deleuze is trying to establish the grounds for a genuine interiority of self-consciousness, but Deleuze specifically refutes this: he wants to *destroy* the culture of self-consciousness and egoism.[26] Nietzsche shows that self-consciousness is the accumulation of *ressentiment* and bad conscience. Furthermore, he disputes the assumption that consciousness is an issue of interiority or exteriority; it is rather one of *inferiority* and *superiority*. 'In Nietzsche consciousness is always the consciousness of an inferior relative to a superior to which he is subordinated or into which he is "incorporated". Consciousness is never self-consciousness, but the consciousness of an ego relative to a self not itself conscious' [*NP* 39].[27] Consciousness arises in an encounter between two unequal forces, it is the awareness of a lesser force in relation to a greater force.

Consciousness arises in a body that could be incorporated by a greater, more powerful body. This social consciousness only becomes self-consciousness under the influence of the reactive quality of force. The social is unconscious in relation to the ego, but ego is always self-consciousness in relation to the social insofar as it is dominated by *ressentiment*. The person who resents the power of the institution misunderstands its *raison d'etre*: [t]he institution exists to provide the oblique means for the satisfaction of desire (cf. Chapter 3). So long as the nature of the institution and the organization is misconceived

[26] 'Spinoza suggested a new direction for the sciences and philosophy. He said that we do not even know what a body *can do* [cf. Spinoza *Ethics* III 2 Proof], we talk about consciousness and spirit and chatter on about it all, but we do not know what a body is capable of, what forces belong to it or what they are preparing for. Nietzsche knew that the hour had come, "[w]e are in the phases of modesty of consciousness" ([...] *Will to Power*, 676). To remind consciousness of its necessary modesty is to take it for what it is: a symptom; nothing but the symptom of a deeper transformation and the activities of entirely non-spiritual forces' [*NP* 39].

[27] 'Consciousness usually only appears when a whole wants to subordinate itself to a superior whole. ... Consciousness is born in relation to a being of which we could be a function' [*VP* II 227].

policing the expression and satisfaction of desire, both individual and institution will be separated from what they can do. To explain Nietzsche's positive conception of desire and its relation to his critique of consciousness we need to further elaborate the relationship between Hegel's lord and bondsman.

5.8 The path to self-consciousness in Hegel: Labour, desire and consumption

Hegel explains how only the bondsman succeeds in achieving an authentic consciousness of being through his relationship with his lord. There are two stages to the bondsman's 'education': first, he confronts death, 'the absolute Lord'; in death the bondsman perceives the absolute negation of all material existence: '[b]ut this pure universal movement, the absolute melting away of everything, is the simple, essential nature of self-consciousness, absolute negativity, *pure being-for-self* which is *implicit* in this consciousness' [Hegel, 1977: 194]. The bondsman's self-consciousness arises from his contemplation of death as the absolute negation of life.

The bondsman's self-consciousness is a residual idea of the passage of life into death. This captures the partial negation of the dialectic which always leaves something behind, it is a negation 'which supersedes in such a way as to preserve and maintain what is superseded' [*PS* 188].

This is an abstract start but Hegel finds a more concrete development in the bondsman's relation to his lord: '[t]his moment of pure being-for-self is also *explicit* for the bondsman, for in the lord it exists for him as his *object*. Furthermore, his consciousness is not this dissolution of everything stable merely in principle; in his service he *actually* brings this about' [*PS* 194]. The bondsman's abstract encounter with death becomes concrete in his relationship with the lord he serves. The bondsman is locked into a relation of unequal forces, a hierarchy; he is *formally* negated by the independent consciousness of his lord and he is *actively* negated in his relation to his labour. These two negations complete the bondsman's 'education'.

The bondsman's domination by his lord does not constitute recognition, it merely provides 'the beginning of wisdom'. It is the bondsman's relation to his labour that reveals his essential nature and allows him to become 'conscious of what he truly is' [*PS* 195]. By projecting himself onto the object of his labour, he negates himself in order to affirm himself in the thing; then by transforming (negating) the thing by his labour he recognizes his own essential nature (*GD* 40).

Lord and bondsman subsist in a relation of unequal dependency: [t]he consciousness of each mediated with itself through the consciousness of the other, 'a consciousness that is bound up with the independence of things. "Things" of the material world, nature, are the objects of desire' [Game, 1991: 71]. Having power over both the bondsman's consciousness and things, the lord dominates the relation: 'he holds the other in subjection' [*PS* 190]. The lord has an immediate relation to things because he does not need to transform them by labour: things present no resistance to his desire to consume them; in his enjoyment of the thing he annihilates it completely (*PS* 190). By this analysis, the lord's desire is absolutely negative, his consumption entirely destructive, negation without recuperation; in Marxian terms, unproductive consumption (Game, 1991: 71).

The bondsman has a very different relation to the thing. Whereas the objects of the master's desire are transitory and provide only fleeting satisfaction, the object of the slave's labour resists his negation and appears to be permanent and independent (*GD* 40). Hegel identifies consciousness with work: '[w]ork ... is desire held in check, fleetingness staved off' [*PS* 195]. Thus the bondsman's relation of labour provides solid grounds for his self-consciousness. The lord's relation of immediate consumption meets no resistance because he has no need to work; he is therefore unable to realize his essential nature, a 'certain *being-for-self* as the truth of himself' [*PS* 192]. The lord's penalty for his unrestricted consumption is his own continued negation: the bondsman's reward is that, in the partial satisfaction of labour, both the object and desire are preserved. The lord's relation to the thing is like death's relation to life, a total negation which leaves nothing behind: the bondsman's relation is one of partial negation, a dialectical relation which recuperates and preserves a part of what it destroys.

Hegel's allegory makes an important moral connection between work, self-consciousness and the restraint of desire. The bondsman's dependency on his lord is transformed through labour into a moral superiority over the lord; while the lord appears to be merely a cipher of unrestrained desire and consumption, dissipating his energies rather than preserving them in the artefacts of labour. Thus, Hegel's analysis places a high moral value on work, a valuation shared by capitalist and Marxist doctrines.[28] This enables the capitalist and Marxist state alike to extol the moral value of work and to condemn the lord's life of unfettered, unconscious consumption – rhetorically.

[28] Anthony makes this point strongly in *The Ideology of Work* (1977).

5.9 Nietzsche on labour, desire and consumption

Let us now revise Hegel's lord and bondsman relation using the terms of Nietzsche's master and slave logic. Nietzsche and Hegel are very close in their analysis of the relation between lord/master and bondsman/slave, but their conclusions are diametrically opposed. The lord's absolute negation is equivalent to Nietzsche's total critique, destruction taken to its limit, a force inseparable from its manifestation (*GD* 42). The bondsman's partial negation is Nietzsche's destructive force 'held in check'; it is desire, active force or indeed critique, separated from what it can do by *ressentiment*. In Nietzsche, morality is what occurs in the interval between a force and its manifestation: in Hegel, morality is equivalent to work. Hence Hegel's moral evaluation of work is the 'fiction' of Nietzsche's reactive force: force is separated from its manifestation by morality; desire is separated from consumption by labour. Nietzsche recognizes the slave's reflective moment of self-consciousness as the interiorization of force, an active force falsified, deprived of its conditions of operation and separated from what it can do: '[b]eing interiorised, being turned back against itself – this is the way in which active force becomes truly reactive' [*NP* 128]. Hegel and Nietzsche both locate essence in the movement of being, but whereas Hegel discovers a force reflected back onto itself to form a self-conscious interiority, Nietzsche discloses a force that exteriorizes itself inexorably as the will to power (*GD* 42). Hegel's lord of unrestrained desire is Nietzsche's master of active power; Hegel's bondsman, whose 'education' is completed by his realization of self-consciousness, is Nietzsche's slave of *ressentiment* and bad conscience. Viewed from a Nietzschean perspective, Hegel's critical project falls victim to its own dialectical method: what is recuperated is the being of the slave, the consciousness of the slave, the reactive quality of a force which rebounds upon itself, desire partially frustrated. Hegel's analysis serves to support the value placed on work by the established order: an ideology of work already enshrined in the state. For, as Mark Twain wrote, if work was really so great the rich would have hogged it all years ago.

To be creative one must destroy established values, including the value of work as a moral burden. The master who consumes the object consumes his desire, no debt of self-consciousness alights to weigh down a life of continuous affirmation and becoming. By contrast, the slave who does not discharge his desires takes them on as a burden, retains their unsatisfied residue and, in his formation of self-consciousness, he becomes that residue. From a Hegelian view, self-consciousness is essentially internalized desire; from a Nietzschean view, it is interiorized force, a burden, a debt of experience, that grows heavier and more constraining, until action becomes impossible (*NP* 116).

5.10 Labour as human essence

Hegel claims that the slave's essence is not particular to the slave, but is the very essence of being. Consciousness is desire held in check by the obligation to transform the object of desire, to *work*. Hegel's logic turns on the slave's unequal relation to the master, which means the essence of being is closely involved with his servitude (*GD* 43). This reading of Hegel presented a dilemma for Marxism claiming to critique Hegel's idealist state philosophy, while retaining his dialectical method to exalt the working classes: if what is preserved and purified by the slave's critical education is his servitude, then the Stakhanovite 'dignity' of labour (*GD* 44) could not escape the taint of slavery, for the essence of labour as human essence only emerges from the unequal relation between slave and master. The inference is clear: there can be no workers without masters, since the self-consciousness of the worker only arises in the context of this hierarchical relationship. In fact Marx does not dispute Hegel's definition of the worker's servitude, what he disputes is Hegel's claim that this *constitutes his essence*. Marx presents an analogous argument concerning the state: 'Hegel is not to be blamed because he describes the existence of the Modern State such as it is, but because he passes off what it is as the *essence of the State*' [Marx and Engels, 1978: 63].

Marx exposes the fundamental error leading Hegel to affirm established values as essences and, therefore, as the only possible values. Neither Marx nor Nietzsche dispense with essence as such, both rather conceive it in materialist terms as creative force. A positive conception of work as creative force presents work as self-transformation: to be truly creative work cannot confine itself to the terms of an established order, its creativity must begin with the destruction of order as the preliminary movement of creative organization. This allows us to assert analogously that the reactive institutions we *have* do not represent the active force of constitution that we are; and that the process of organization that we know as reactive and conservative is not representative of essential organization. As Hume and Bergson say, laws are not natural to Man, what is natural to him is the propensity to create laws. The challenge, therefore, is to learn how to make laws adequate to their legislators; that do not immediately decay into order.

A proliferation of laws gives the impression that their essence is itself more lawful than creative. This is why a partial critique will not suffice.

A total critique, *pars destruens, pars construens* must destroy even and *especially* the false essence as the locus of a transcendental order. 'If the worker is to reach a point of genuine affirmation, of self-valorization, the attack has to be directed at the "essence", at those values which define the worker as such – against servitude, against work' [*GD* 44].

A total critique turns its destructive force back upon itself in order to purge any trace of authenticity. This is partly what Nietzsche means by the Man who wants to perish and to be overcome (*NP* 178). A similar perception is evident in Tronti's (1966) description of the worker's struggle against capital: '[i]n order to struggle against capital, the working class must struggle against itself inasmuch as it is capital. ... Worker's struggle against work, struggle of the worker against himself inasmuch as worker'.[29] Tronti grasps the position of the worker as a 'standing negation' [Taylor, 1975], who must go to the limit of critique by negating the part of himself that is worker and thereby destroying his *ressentiment*. To exalt himself as worker is to react against the system which defines him as such, but by preserving the terms of that definition, he falls victim to the dialectic, the partial critique, producing only reform, not revolution, and a 'new' legitimation of compliance.

Tronti sees the true relation between labour and capital: labour is the capitalist relation of reactive forces embodied in the worker *as worker*. Here we see the historical incorporation of *ressentiment* in relations between corporeal and corporate organization. The liberal conception of the *individual* arises specifically from the embodiment of capitalist relations. Hume's original social atom, the partial interest of the family or tribe, is fragmented into the individual as a unit of capitalist labour. Capital [L. *capitalis*] refers to value *per capita*, the value of the head. The true consciousness of the slave is an expression of this abstract individuation.

Yet even the destruction of capital is not adequate to Nietzsche's total critique. Capital is but one historical manifestation of the embodiment of *ressentiment* and bad conscience. Hegel did not see that a speculative analysis of being is only the precursor to the destruction of the values it exposes, and that this destruction is itself but the first moment in the creative organizational process. The movement of organization is completed by the affirmation of newly created values, by a newly created Man, Nietzsche's Overman.

Nietzsche cannot be understood without grasping his radical pluralism or perspectivism: 'pluralism (otherwise known as empiricism) ... is the properly philosophical way of thinking, the one invented by

[29] Tronti (1966) *Operai e capitale*, quoted in *GD* 44.

philosophy ... the only principle of a violent atheism. The Gods are dead but they have died from laughing, on hearing one God claim to be the only one' [*NP* 4]. This statement conveys the force of Deleuze's critique of Hegel, who wanted to ridicule pluralism (*NP* 4): the dialectic is not only negative and abstract, from a materialist viewpoint *it is not even philosophy*: it is monotheism masked as philosophy; God is presupposed from the start. This is why Deleuze claims that pluralism is the dialectic's most ferocious and only profound enemy (*NP* 8): 'Nietzsche's "yes" is opposed to the dialectical "no"; affirmation to dialectical negation; difference to dialectical contradiction; joy, enjoyment, to dialectical labour; lightness, dance, to dialectical responsibilities' [*NP* 9].

5.11 Nietzsche's dicethrow: Will to power and eternal return

A question remains as to how a philosophy of efficient difference and impersonal forces, can account for the *constitutive* process of organization. How do corporeal and corporate bodies come into being; how is anything constituted in the given? We can begin to answer this by reference to Nietzsche's invocation of chance and necessity in being, as the game of dice which the gods play at their table, the earth.[30] The game has two moments: the dicethrow and the dicefall; the affirmation of becoming and the affirmation of the being of becoming; will to power and eternal return, respectively (*NP* 25). The dicethrow is the movement of chance and multiplicity generated by the efficient difference of becoming. The dice falling back is the moment of necessity, unity and being. The combination shown on the dicefall is not the realization of a preformed possibility, it is rather the affirmation of chance in the dicethrow. The specific combination is unforeseeable: Nietzsche's dice are blank until they are thrown, this is what he means by the affirmation of chance. It is the same as Bergson's virtual which creates its own terms of actualization: not only the specific combination, the specific terms of the given are created in the dicethrow.

The dicefall is the moment of organization, forming a unity, but also affirming the creative multiplicity of that unity. An institution is not a combination which confirms a preformed expression of desire: *the institution as the dicefall* affirms the differentiation of desires even as it forms oblique means for their satisfaction. As Man continually creates

[30] 'For the earth is a table of the gods, and trembling with creative words and the dice throws of the gods' [*Thus Spoke Zarathustra* III 'The Seven Seals' 3, p. 245].

his culture, so he creates his own nature as the material terms of that cultural creation. We must listen carefully to the nuances of Deleuze's reading: Nietzsche's dicethrow is not a repetition of a probability, nor is the result of the throw an affirmation of chance in the throw.[31] 'The dice which are thrown once are the affirmation of *chance*, the combination which they form on falling is the affirmation of *necessity*' [*NP* 26]. The dicefall necessarily affirms the number or destiny that brings the dice back.[32] In this sense the second moment of the game is also the two moments together or the player who comprehends the whole. The eternal return is the result of the dicethrow, the affirmation of necessity which composes the fragments of chance. Thus, it is also the *reaffirmation* of chance itself (*NP* 27–8).

The eternal return is the moment of organization, bringing elements actualized in the dicethrow into a coherent unity (*GD* 48). Nietzsche (1968) expresses this relation between chance and destiny, dicethrow and dicefall, in terms of chaos and cycle, elements often presented as fundamentally opposed forces. For Plato, the chaos of becoming is unlimited and only forced into a circular relation with itself by the application of an external law.[33] With the exception of Heraclitus, Nietzsche does not find his idea of eternal return in antiquity. The ancients rather saw the being of becoming as a subjugation of becoming; they did not perceive the cycle of being as internal to the movement of becoming.[34] 'There was not first of all chaos, then little by little a regular and circular movement of all the forms: on the contrary, all this is eternal, removed from becoming; if there ever was a chaos of forces the chaos was eternal and has reappeared in every cycle. *Circular movement* has not come into being, it is the original law, in the same way as the mass of force is the original law without exception or possible infraction. All becoming happens inside of the cycle and the *mass of force*' [*VP* II 325].[35]

[31] 'It is not that a large number of throws produce the repetition of a combination but rather the number of the combination which produces the repetition of the dicethrow' [*NP* 25–6].
[32] 'There are many numbers with increasing or decreasing probabilities, but only one number of chance as such, one fatal number which reunites all the fragments of chance' [*NP* 26].
[33] 'This is how becoming or chaos are transferred to the side of an obscure mechanical causality and the cycle is referred to a kind of finality which is imposed from the outside' [*NP* 28].
[34] '[T]he presence of the law in becoming and of play in necessity' [*NP* 29].
[35] Cf. Burrell (1992) on circular versus linear versions of organizational time.

All of which is profoundly relevant to organization theory. To oppose a cultural law of organization to a natural state of disorganization or chaos would, from a Nietzschean perspective, be fundamentally mistaken as it implies that organization is external to nature, to becoming and to force. The argument for rejecting this view is found in Deleuze's critique of transcendentalism. Materialism admits no origin, no locus for organizational movement external to the concrete forces of nature. If we consider organization as embodied, this embodiment is not a subjugation of the given, it is the effect of the constitutive principle of the eternal return immanent to the given. A body is *organized* in the sense that organization is nature's counterpoint to its internal difference. The first moment of the game, the moment of becoming (differentiation, multiplicity) implies the second moment, the moment of being (unification) and this second moment is the return or affirmation of the first.

The virtual does not actualize itself randomly. It is informed by the immanent principle of its return: chaos and the cycle, chance and destiny, differentiation and organization, these are irreducible moments but they are also the essential and inseparable moments of a non-dialectical synthesis. The expansive movement of becoming implies the circular motion of its return. The moment of chance, the dicethrow, is the moment of total critique, when the table of values is shattered and the whole of chance affirmed unreservedly. The moment of destiny, the dicefall, is the moment of total affirmation and the creation of new forms and new values; the affirmation of chance is reaffirmed in the being of becoming.[36] The eternal return signifies the coming together of a plurality of forces to compose an organized corporeal or corporate body.

5.12 Organization: Will to power and eternal return

What distinguishes Nietzsche's game of dice from a purely ontological description is that the eternal return is *willed*. Every throw must fall back but only those willed affirmatively fall back eternally. What determines the quality of a destiny is the quality of will willing its return. This is the remarkable feature of Nietzsche's ontology, *being is always willed* – which is why we do not ask the Platonic question, '[w]hat is being?' As Hegel's dialetic demonstrates, a concept of being abstracted from

[36] 'The two moments imply one another as a series of shattering and gathering, as a centripetal moment, and a centrifugal moment, as emanation and constitution' [*GD* 48–9].

concrete beings is equivalent to nothingness. The question, '[w]ho wills being?' translates a speculative enquiry into a practical study of forces and values.

What is the relation of this will to Nietzsche's will to power? We can begin to understand will to power by recalling the internal nature of Bergson's efficient difference as the internal movement of being. Bergson's critique of the dialectic is that it mobilizes the cause of difference as external to the effect. Efficient difference, by contrast, invokes difference as the internal motor of being. Nietzsche's concept of will to power is similar: will to power is internal to force. Force is not willed by any agency external to itself, nor does force 'will' anything other than itself.[37] Nietzsche's will to power is equivalent to Bergson's efficient difference, with the distinction that Nietzschean becoming does not occur spontaneously as an unlimited expansive movement: it is willed by a will internal to becoming, *internal to difference,* the differential and genetic element, the internal dynamic of differentiation. Thus, will to power is in no way anthropomorphic (*NP* 51).

Whereas force is distinguished by *active* and *reactive* qualities, *affirmative* and *negative* designate the primordial qualities of the will to power (*NP* 53–4). Whatever is willed negatively occurs only once whereas whatever is willed affirmatively returns eternally (*NP* 54). Thus, the eternal return is the principle of an ethics, it provides the will with a practical rule: '*whatever you will, will it in such a way that you also will its eternal return*' [*NP* 68]. This is the meaning of affirmation: to will whatever you will with your whole being.[38] Affirmation is not an effort or a quantity of the will to power, it is a quality of selection, and the principle which guides this selection is the thought of the eternal return.

What is the practical relation between the will to power and the eternal return? The eternal return is the being of becoming, the moment of the dicefall, the moment of destiny. 'But becoming is double: becoming active and becoming reactive, becoming-active of reactive forces and becoming-reactive of active forces. But *only becoming-active has being*' [*NP* 71, emphasis added]. The dicethrow is the becoming of being: the dicefall the being of becoming. Defining becoming active as contingent on the affirmative quality of the will to power, Nietzsche transforms

[37] 'The *victorious* concept "force", by means of which our physicists have created God and the world, still needs to be *completed*: an *inner* will must be *ascribed* to it, which I designate as "will to power"' [*WP* 619].

[38] 'If, in all that you will you begin by asking yourself: is it certain that I will to do it an infinite number of times? This should be your most solid centre of gravity' [*VP* IV 242].

ontology into ethics; by making the will to power internal to force he destroys the transcendental sphere of morality. If will is internal to force, there is no space for morality; only a practical selection of the will to be, 'a selective ontology' [*NP* 72], an ethics.

5.13 Organization: Burden or relief?

Nietzsche raises affirmation to its highest power, but only on the site of a total negation: real affirmation is always preceded by a terrible negation and destruction. 'The lion becomes a child but the child's "holy yes" must be preceded by the lion's "holy no"' [*NP* 177]. This is not the hollow 'Yes' of the pragmatist or the fool, the type of Nietzsche's ass, whose 'Yes' is a false affirmation, a yes that is incapable of saying 'No' (*NP* 178). Conversely, one who can only say 'No' has no power of affirmation, not even the power of real negation. For Nietzsche, negation is only a preliminary destruction prior to creation. To be selective, to be ethical, one must have the power both to destroy and to create. Only one who can affirm understands that the power of negation is linked to creation, *pars destruens, pars construens*. The ass's affirmation is unthinking; 'acquiescing in the real as it is, taking reality as it is upon oneself' [*NP* 181]. As a beast of burden, the ass feels the weight of the real on its back. It knows only how to bear loads and interprets life solely in those terms: '[t]he idea of the real in itself is an ass's idea' [*NP* 181].

If Man's vestigial instincts provide his special burden of world-openness, his active relief is the institution. How foolish to constitute and bear this relief as a new burden, yet this is the prevailing negative idea and feeling of the institution. In feeling the institution as a burden, Man is like Nietzsche's ass which 'only ever grasps consequences separated from their premises, products separated from the spirit which animates them' [*NP* 181]. A negative theory of organization does not grasp the essence of the institution as relief from our world-openness because it does not properly comprehend the nature of Man. We construct the institutions we deserve, given our incomprehension. We think of institutions as solid and permanent, thereby reproducing the problem in the solution. As relief, the institution should be *enlightening* in a sense that has less to do with illumination and more to do with *leavening* (L. *levamen* relief), making being light, flexible and mobile: to affirm becoming, to become active. This activeness implies lightness and dexterity, dancing, not trudging or marching to a monotonous beat. But when we negate becoming we negate active force by dividing it from what it can do, and this is a becoming reactive of active force. The dancing is weighed down by the burden of the negative and can proceed only painfully with a bent back.[39]

The eternal return is all about the lightness of being, the science of the cycle, bearing the burden of chaos in such ways that it can hardly alight on one's back. To face the real does not mean we need to bear it. The 'men of the present' – the free thinkers, whom Nietzsche accuses of accepting everything at face value – still labour under an old delusion: that all heavy things are real and positive, and that he who carries them is real and affirmative. 'But this reality which unites the camel and its burden to the point of confusing them in a single mirage is only the desert, the reality of the desert, nihilism' [*NP* 182]. Nothing returns in this 'Land of Culture', everything is too heavy for that, everything that becomes is negative and dies: '[y]ou are half-open doors at which grave-diggers wait. And this is *your* reality: "[e]verything is worthy of perishing" ... what do I care if beetles and dragonflies sit themselves on my bundle! Truly, it shall not become heavier on that account!' [*Z* 'Of the Land of Culture', 143]. Nietzsche teaches how to say 'No' to Man's negative culture, to nihilism, to a culture of asses, camels, slaves. When nihilism speaks it offers us the burden of the present, the established order; all that is acknowledged as real. It speaks the language of the ass, who always brays 'Yes'. To truly say 'No', the no of a total critique, is to say 'No' to all values. Only this 'holy no' prepares the ground for real affirmation.

5.14 Nietzsche and organization: Affirmation of affirmation

If Man is, or can become an ethical animal, it is not due to any intrinsically *human* quality; but because the will to power occurs in Man with a special intensity. Each species in nature is the answer to a question posed by its environment. Man is one answer to his world-openness but not the only answer and, from Nietzsche's viewpoint, certainly not the best, because we do not properly understand the question: who wills human being? Who wills sociality and organization? This '[w]ho?' does not refer to any person or institution directly, it refers to the affirmative or negative qualities of the will to power (hence '[w]*hich one* wills it?') manifested in human and social embodiment.

[39] In Kafka's imagery, with a bowed head (cf. Deleuze and Guattari, 1986).

Man must overcome himself by affirming difference in life, affirming life itself in its chance becoming.[40] This affirmation is still an evaluation, but from the perspective of a will that enjoys its own difference in life. For Nietzsche, there was no possibility for this affirmation to be achieved by Man, who is too much the product of his own spirit of *ressentiment* and bad conscience. Culture is the social historical embodiment of the negative will and reactive forces. Thus, a total critique takes the negative so far as to will its own destruction, clearing the ground ready for the affirmation of the Overman. Man can raise negation to a power of affirmation but *'affirming in its full power, affirming affirmation itself – this is beyond man's strength'* [*NP* 185].

The Overman is not Man reformed, or reborn; he is certainly not Man crucified and resurrected: Nietzsche sees in the Paulian interpretation of Christ only a distant anticipation of the false dialectical synthesis (*NP* 156). We can grasp what Nietzsche means by affirmation in its full power by his allegory of Dionysus and Ariadne. Dionysus is affirmation taken to the highest power, a pure affirmation of becoming; but Nietzsche is still not satisfied, he requires a further step to eliminate even the remotest possibility of counter-negation. Dionysian affirmation of becoming requires confirmation in the affirmation of being. Ariadne provides that affirmation in her love for Dionysus, sealing the eternal return in a double affirmation. *'Eternal affirmation of being, eternally I am your affirmation'* [*NP* 187].

Ariadne is the eternal return, the selective principle of being. Her affirmation of Dionysus is the affirmation of multiplicity, becoming and chance; and it is also the affirmation of unity in multiplicity, being in becoming, the necessity of chance. If Dionysus is the dicethrow, Ariadne is the dice falling back.

In organizational terms, becoming is the production of the given, explaining fan wise; and being is the composition of that multiplicity into the organism, the constitutive moment of embodiment bringing different elements under a greater, more powerful relation. From this perspective the organizing principle is internal to being – to suppose that it can be imposed by any external agency would be to slide back into transcendentalism. The moment of composition, the eternal return, is the moment of organization as the affirmation of affirmation: the Dionysian affirmation of becoming and Ariadne's love which returns affirmation to itself as a form, a composition. A materialist philosophy

[40] 'Destruction as the active destruction of the Man who wants to perish and to be overcome announces the creator' [*NP* 177–178].

of organization cannot separate these but for ease of expression: Ariadne transforms the affirmative given into an affirmative nature (*NP* 189). An affirmative theory of organization cannot properly be designated as either Dionysian or Ariadnean, therefore; it refers to both, to their infinitely affirmative relation, to their unity as affirmation of affirmation.

Deleuze reads Nietzsche as a philosopher of affirmation, joy and practice, against Hegel's dialectical philosophy of negation, pessimism and speculation (*NP* 195). By affirming an active over a reactive type of force, Nietzsche longs to replace the sad hierarchy of human culture, in which slave logic rules over master logic, with a joyful hierarchy of being as the becoming active of all forces. This is a philosophy of practice, not of consciousness. 'Nietzsche's practical teaching is that difference is happy; that multiplicity, becoming and chance are adequate objects of joy by themselves and that only joy returns' [*NP* 190]. But Nietzsche gives little guidance as to how his teaching could be realized. 'Who wills the eternal return, who wills affirmation, who wills joy, who wills practice?' To answer these questions in a personalist way, to locate them on a human scale instead of upon the distant peaks of Zarathustra's dominion, we must turn to Spinoza, whom Nietzsche recognized as his sole philosophical predecessor.

6
Organization as Joyful Practice

> It was on Spinoza that I worked the most seriously according to the norms of the history of philosophy – but it was Spinoza more than any other that gave me the feeling of a gust of air that pushes you on the back each time you read him, a witches broomstick that he mounts you atop. We have not yet begun to understand Spinoza, and I myself no more than others.
>
> —*Deleuze, Dialogues 15*[1]

6.1 Spinoza's materialism: Substance, attributes and modes

This is the hardest pitch. The reader should be prepared for a steep ascent into Spinoza's philosophy. The terminology is Scholastic and may be unfamiliar. The climb will, however, be rewarding as the view from Spinoza's plateaus are unlike any others, so I encourage the reader to persevere, and not to give up.

Deleuze reads the opening of Spinoza's *Ethics* as an ontological meditation on the real distinction in being, contrasting it with the earlier, Cartesian tradition. Cartesian scholars proposed three distinctions in being; a *real* distinction between two or more *substances*; a *modal* distinction between a substance and a mode that it implies

[1] Nietzsche felt a similar exhilaration when he discovered Spinoza's works, late in his life: 'I am utterly amazed, utterly enchanted. I have a precursor, and what a precursor! I hardly knew Spinoza: that I should have turned to him just now, was inspired by "instinct." ... My lonesomeness, which, as on very high mountains, often made it hard for me to breathe and made my blood rush out, is now at least a twosomeness' [Postcard to Overbeck, 30 July, *The Portable Nietzsche*, 92].

and a *reasonable* distinction (*distinction de raison*) between a substance and an *attribute* (*EPS* 29).[2] According to Spinoza the first distinction is impossible because it postulates more than one substance: it is merely a *quantitative* distinction. In Spinoza, *real* distinctions are necessarily *qualitative*: numerical distinctions are not real (*E* IP 1–P8) and real distinctions are not numerical (*E* IP 9–P11).[3] Spinoza recognizes but one cosmic substance, and *real* distinctions are therefore qualifications of that substance. Numerical distinctions by contrast are insubstantial and refer to an external cause.[4]

God or substance is the internal differential cause of itself (*causa sui*) and of all things (*effects*).[5] A real distinction is always a differential quality of substance, which Spinoza terms an *attribute*. The attributes are defined as '[w]hat the intellect perceives of substance, as constituting its essence' [*E* IDef. 4]. Each attribute is absolutely different to every other: '[e]ach attribute is conceived through itself and in itself' [*Letter to Oldenburg* II]. The attributes are really distinct: no attribute needs any other in order to be conceived, so that each expresses an absolutely simple quality of substance (*SPP* 51–2). According to the principle of univocity, however, 'all the essences, distinct in the attributes, *are as one in the substance*' [*SPP* 51, emphasis added]. Thus, Spinoza presents a universal substance ('God') as the efficient internal cause of its own different qualities, each of which is expressed in a unique attribute. The attributes are heterogeneous in themselves but univocal in substance.

Substance is composed of an infinite number of attributes of which Man knows only two, *thought* and *extension*. Thought and extension are the infinite qualities (essences) involved in human existence, inasmuch

[2] The meanings of the terms, substance, attribute and mode will become clearer as we proceed.

[3] I have adopted the conventional notation for Spinoza's works. The *Ethics* comprises axioms (A), corollaries (C), demonstrations (D), definitions (Def.) and scholia (S). The five parts of the *Ethics* are denoted by Roman numerals; the propositions, scholia, etc., are numbered with Arabic numerals. Thus '(*E* IP 9–11)' refers to *Ethics*, Part I, Propositions 9–11.

[4] 'Whatever is of such a nature that there can be many individuals of that nature must ... have an external cause to exist.' [*E* IP 8S2]

[5] It was apparently inconceivable for a seventeenth-century philosopher to address nature without presupposing its Creator. In the materialist tradition, however, God is positively conceived as the universal substance: '[t]heology and philosophy of science were intertwined, spectacularly in the theories of Spinoza and Malebranche, less obtrusively, but still firmly, in the doctrines of Locke' [Ayers (1975), in George Berkeley, *Philosophical Works* p. xvi].

as we are composed of mind and body (*E* IIP 1, 2). Although our existence is composed only of these two, we know there is an infinity of other attributes because God's absolute power of existing cannot be exhausted by the attributes of thought and extension (*SPP* 52). The more attributes are expressed in a thing, the greater its reality (*E* IP 9) and the more existence it has (*E* IP 11). Being composed of an infinite number of real distinctions (attributes), God's existence is both absolutely real and absolutely different in itself; God complicates all distinctions in (his) being.

Spinoza's conceptions of substance and real distinctions (attributes) propose a *positive ontology of difference* contrasting with Cartesian and Hegelian negative conceptions. Descartes' real distinction is relative: *x* is distinct from *y*, but *x* and *y* are not distinct in themselves (*GD* 61). This is a negative and external conception of difference; nothing is different except in a negative relation to another thing. Spinoza eliminates negation from the analysis: x and y are different in themselves.

Univocity means that the attributes are expressed in existing *modes, effects* and *bodies* in the same way that they constitute the universal substance (*SPP* 52). Spinoza therefore rejects the principles of eminence, equivocity or analogy, according to which God possesses the perfections in a superior form. Spinoza's attributes are immanent and univocal: 'the same attributes are affirmed of the substance they compose and of the modes they contain' [*SPP* 52]. The attributes of extension and thought compose Man in exactly the same way that they constitute God – except that in Man they constitute our entire being, whereas in God they are but two of an infinite number of other attributes.

Univocity is composed of three 'figures', the first being that the attributes are the same in the substance and in the modes; the second is that all the attributes are immanent to a single common cause in substance and the third is that the relation between the substance and the modes, via the attributes, is *necessary*, not accidental, that is, all the modes are attributable to substance.[6]

Spinoza's conception of substance as *causa sui* is of '*a cause of itself, in itself and through itself*' (*EPS* 162).[7] The source of real distinction in being is God/substance, whose power of differentiation is absolutely internal to his nature. Thus Spinoza's real distinction refers to the positive

[6] For further explanations of *cause* and *necessity* cf. *SPP* 53–4 and 93–4, respectively.

[7] 'By cause of itself I understand that whose essence involves existence; or that whose nature cannot be conceived except as existing' [*E* I Def. 1].

movement of differentiation that constitutes the universal substance.[8] There is no room for negative thinking in Spinoza's philosophy. Hegel's dialectic is pre-empted by the first definition of the *Ethics*; a dialectical opposition finds no anchorage in material difference. Hegel's logic is itself founded on his explicit negation of Spinoza's thought, but what is the practical contribution of a philosophy that reacts against the substantial distinction in being, compared to a philosophy that begins and never falters in its affirmation of that distinction? The answer is that the former promotes sadness and diminishes the power to act, while the latter promotes joy and increases the power of action. This is the practical distinction between Hegel's negative idealism and Spinoza's affirmative materialism and joyful practice. I shall argue that the Hegelian inspired philosophy of sad passions and inhibited action prevails in organizational theory and practice, and should be rejected in favour of a Spinozian philosophy of joyful passion and creative action.

Organization is practical in gathering elements under a more powerful relation. By power we do not imply a capacity to act that may or may not be realized according to will. As Nietzsche says, the only rigorous definition of power is actual force; there is will only insofar as it is internal to force itself. If the only attributes known to mankind are thought and extension, then these are also the only attributes known to organization. It follows that what distinguishes corporeal from corporate existence is not a *qualitative* difference in their power but a *quantitative* difference: in their power of thinking and of acting and, therefore, in their power of existing. The organization embodies a greater power to exist than the individual even though the essence of both involves the same attributes. But it embodies a greater power of existing only if it is real, active and joyful. Many, perhaps most, organizations fail to meet these criteria: the organizations that we have actually diminish the force of their participants.

6.2 Spinoza's expressivism and organization

Comprising an infinite number of attributes, Spinoza's substance has an absolute power to exist and to *express* existence. The attributes express the essence of substance univocally: each attribute absolutely distinct in itself but each 'spoken in the same voice'. This means that all effects are expressions of substance as the universal cause. God

[8] 'By substance I understand what is in itself and is conceived through itself, that is, that whose concept does not require the concept of another thing from which it must be formed' [*E* IDef. 3].

expresses, or produces the existence of things (effects) in the same sense that he causes his own existence (*E* IP 25S; *SPP* 53). Spinoza invokes the Scholastic couple *explicare-implicare*, explicate-implicate. 'Explain is a "strong" term in Spinoza that does not signify an operation of the intellect external to the thing, but an operation of the thing internal to the intellect' [*SPP* 68]. An adequate logical demonstration discloses a substantial movement in the thing itself; it does not impute such a movement speculatively: '[e]xplication is always a self-explication, a development, an unfolding, a dynamism: the thing *explains itself*' [*SPP* 68]. Thus, substance is explained in the attributes; the attributes explain substance and the attributes in turn are explained in the modes, which explain the attributes.

We should not think that implication is in any sense opposed to explanation: they rather coexist as two fundamental movements in nature: 'that which explains thereby implies, that which develops involves. ... Nature is the common order of explications and implications' [*SPP* 68]. The couple explain-imply is completed by the term *comprehend* – that which explains also implies its comprehension. Similarly, explication-implication is completed by *complication* – that which explicates itself implies the complication within itself: 'Spinoza thus rediscovers a whole tradition of the Middle Ages and the Renaissance, which defined God through "complicatio": God complicates all things, while each thing explains and implies God' [*SPP* 68]. The link between complication and comprehension invokes a parallelism between body and intellect to which we shall return later. Spinozian substance is both perfectly immanent and expressive: 'God is the universal complication, in the sense that everything is in it; and the universal explication in the sense that it is in everything' [*EPS* 175].

In organization theory, *explication* can be applied to flows of material goods, personnel, waste, etc., generated by a production process. This expansive movement also *implies* an impression or recording of these flows constituting the organization's administrative structure, and more fully, its mode of being.[9] The organization comprehends (comprises) its productive power, while the latter comprehends all of *its* material products. But according to Spinoza's *explicare-implicare*, that which develops also envelops. Development is usually conceived as a purely expansive movement of design and evolution, but a more rigorous, materialist approach

[9] A theory of a *production* which is also a *recording* and *consumption* is elaborated in Deleuze and Guattari's (1983) conceptions of desire and the body-without-organs.

is possible. Spinozian organizational development refers to the devolution of organization in the sense of that which it materially expresses (goods, personnel, waste, etc.). This devolution *involves* a certain recording of its expression. That which is produced implies a mode or structure of production: as the organization produces or develops, so it envelops the traces of that production into its structure. In a similar fashion, responsibility devolved from higher to lower levels necessarily *involves* a recorded chain of accountability. The point is that any kind of *expression* automatically entails an *impression*. This accords with an empirical analysis of sensation in the corporeal body but it applies just as strongly to the corporate body. A production implies an accounting, broadly defined, and the adequacy of these twin powers determines the organization's comprehension of itself as a cause of effects.

6.3 Spinoza's analysis of power: Organization, a power to affect and to be affected

Spinozian attributes constitute the essential qualities of all bodies, but they do not explain the behaviour of bodies.[10] For this Spinoza requires a materialist analysis of *power*. The power of the absolute and the power of the existing body are related univocally: '[d]ivine power is twofold: an absolute power of existing, which entails a power of producing all things; an absolute power of thinking, hence of self-comprehension, which entails the power of comprehending all that is produced. The two powers are like two halves of the Absolute' [*SPP* 98].

The two powers should not be confused with the two attributes of thought and extension. The attribute of extension cannot exhaust the power of existing, which is as we have seen, composed of an infinity of attributes: the power of existing is 'an unconditioned totality which possesses a priori all the attributes as formal conditions' [*SPP* 98]. The attribute of thought cannot exhaust the power of thinking for a different reason: although all ideas formally exist in it, the attribute of thought has another aspect as the absolute power of thinking. 'The important thing is not to confuse the strict equality of the attributes

[10] 'Historians have never been interested in what has really happened to human bodies – what bodies have *felt*. Yet until we have succeeded in reconstructing the development of our bodies in history, we will remain strangers to ourselves – confined to a haunted, subjugated nature, unable to experience other bodies as equals, incapable of the physical (more than simply sexual) experience of communism' [Theweleit 1987, *Male Fantasies*, Minneapolis: University of Minnesota].

relative to the power of acting, and the strict equality of the two powers relative to absolute essence' [*SPP* 98].

We shall return to this distinction in due course, for the present we note that Spinoza's two powers are consistent with an empiricist view of relations between thought and extension: '[t]he intellect has no more power to think than its objects have to exist; the power to think and know cannot be greater than a necessarily correlative power of existing' [*EPS* 86].[11] As with Nietzschean power, Spinozian power is immediate, it has nothing to do with separating force from its manifestation, will from action, cause from effect. Thus, Spinoza identifies power as the active essence of being: 'The identity of power and essence means: power is always act or, at least, in action [*en act*] (*EPS* 93).

Thus we can say that an organization, to the extent it can be designated as a distinct entity, is identical with its power of existing and its power of comprehending existence. As a productive being, the organization's power of existing is equivalent to its power of producing; while its power of comprehension refers to its comprehension of its own nature as a cause of effects, including products and *their* effects. By focusing squarely on what the organization actually produces and on its own level of comprehension of the causality involved in that production, we can begin to redefine the fundamental terms of organization theory. This redefinition begins by rejecting all notions of power that separate a force from what it can do. A materialist approach to organization theory is not primarily concerned with a fictional power to act dependent on an external will: it is chiefly interested in what actually happens, with power en acte, with what is actually done.

The question now becomes '[h]ow much power, how much existence and comprehension can a body have?' And since from this view power always refers to efficient or effective power, the question can be rephrased in terms equally meaningful on personal and organizational levels: '[h]ow *effective* is a given body or organization, and how effective can it become?' Spinoza's conception of efficient power allows the problem of personal and organizational effectiveness to be conceived in new way, because Spinozian power is both a principle of *action* and a principle of *affection*: a power to act implies both a *productivity* and a *sensibility*: '[a]ll power bears with it a corresponding and inseparable power to be affected' [*EPS* 93].

Spinoza affirms God or substance as both the absolute power to affect and the absolute power to be affected. In accordance with the principle of univocity, all things expressed by God are instantiations of his power.

[11] Modified translation (*GD* 71).

But Spinoza is not introducing a third power of affectivity (in addition to the powers of thought and existence), he rather defines the power of existence as having two indivisible parts: the power to effect and the power to be affected (*GD* 72). On the basis of this analysis we can hypothesize that an organization's effectiveness, its power of action, which is a power of production, is equivalent to its power to be affected.

This hypothesis involves our definition of organization as *embodied*, an identity to be apprehended by reference to Spinoza's definition of all existing things or bodies in *modes*. A mode refers to '[t]he affections of a substance; that is, that which is in something else and is conceived through something else' [*E* IDef. 5]. This definition invokes the second term of what *is*: the first term is God as *causa sui*, that which is in itself; the second term is that which is in something else (*E* IA 1; *SPP* 91). The relation between the substance and the mode is univocal. Modes (bodies of all kinds) are distinct from substance in essence and existence, yet are produced in the same attributes that constitute the essence of substance. God produces an infinity of things in an infinity of modes' [*E* IP 16]. This means that God's effects are real bodies in modes with an essence and existence of their own, but they have no essence or existence apart from the attributes in which they are produced (*SPP* 91).

The power to exist (in substance and in mode) is thus defined by the power to be affected. Deleuze presents three nuances of affection, each referring to a distinct level of being. At the level of substance, the affections (*affectio*) are the attributes and the modes of substance. In a second nuance the affections denote what happens to the mode, its modifications, the effects of other modes on it. At this level the affections are (1) corporeal traces or *images* and (2) their *ideas* which involve the nature of the affecting external body and that of the affected body (*SPP* 48).[12] These ideas, in a third nuance, constitute a state of body and mind in relation to preceding and succeeding states, so that an affection is felt as a passage or duration from one state of perfection to another. These continual variations are experienced as 'affects' or feelings (*affectus*) (*SPP* 48–9). In practical terms Spinoza distinguishes between the affection (*affectio*) which involves the presence and the nature of the affecting body as an image or trace in the affected body, and the feeling-affect (*affectus*) which involves an increase or decrease of the power of acting of the affected body (*E* III Def. 3).

[12]'The affections of the human body whose ideas present external bodies as present in us, we shall call images of things. ... And when the mind regards bodies in this way, we shall say that it imagines" [*E* IIP 16], Spinoza's affinity with Hobbes (cf. *Leviathan* pp. 87–94) and Hume is evident here.

An existing mode, effect, thing, body or organization, is defined by Spinoza as a certain power to be affected (*SPP* 49–50). When my body encounters another, it can happen that this other body is *good* for mine in the sense that it enters into composition with it and thereby increases its power of acting (e.g., a food, a loved being, an ally), or that it is *bad* for it in that it decomposes it and diminishes its power (a poison, a hated being, an enemy). In the first case, the power of the other body combines with the first, making it stronger; in the second case the other body reduces my power, leaving me weaker. The passage of composition and its increase of the power of acting are called *joy*; the passage of decomposition and its reduction of the power of acting are called *sadness*. Thus the power of acting varies with the joy or sadness evoked by encounters with external causes. The feeling-affects of joy or sadness follow from the image affection or idea of the body that agrees or does not agree with mine. When that feeling-affect comes back upon the idea from which it followed, then joy becomes *love*, and sadness *hatred* (*SPP* 50). Thus, through manifold external encounters and under variable conditions, the affects continually fulfil the body's power to be affected (*SPP* 50).

Feelings-affects (*affectus*) caused by encounters with external bodies always spring from a confused idea of that body and our own; such an idea is *inadequate* since it does not clearly comprehend its cause. Since we are not their adequate cause, these affects are *passions* (*SPP* 50). Even when our power of acting is increased by joy this is still a passion 'insofar as a Man's power of acting is not increased to the point where he conceives himself and his actions adequately' (*E* IVP 59D).

The distinction between sad and joyful passions in Spinoza leads to a more fundamental distinction between *passions* and *actions*. If the idea of the affecting body is *adequate*, if it is a clear rather than a confused image affection, if it grasps the essence of the affecting body and does not involve it in our own state, if it is the idea of an internal cause that expresses the essential agreement between ourself, others and God, then this idea adequately comprehends its cause, and the affects it produces are not passions but *actions* (*SPP* 50–1). Action, in Spinoza's sense, arises from an adequate comprehension of one's own power to act; only when I gain full possession of my power through adequate ideas of the cause of my affections is joyful action possible. Joyful action (action is always joyful in Spinoza) – as opposed to joyful passion – does not denote an increase in our power to act but rather the formal active possession of that power (*SPP* 51).

A body's power is always fulfilled by a combination of *passive* affections (*passions*) produced by external bodies in our own body, and *active*

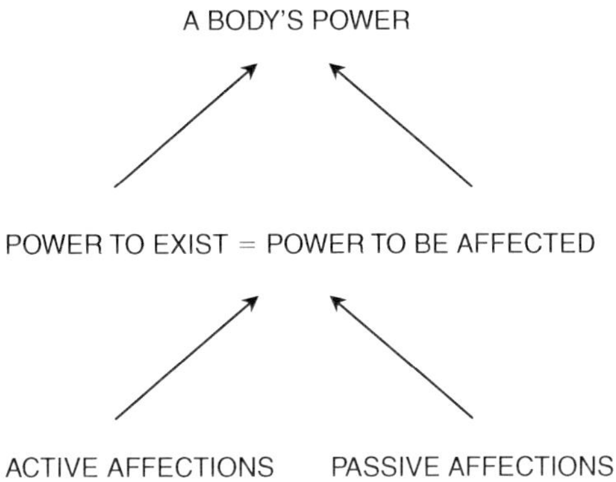

Figure 6.1 A body's internal structure of power (Adapted from *GD* 73)

affections (*actions*) produced by the body's own essence (*EPS* 93). Hardt (*GD* 73) presents this analysis figuratively (Figure 6.1).

6.4 Spinoza's corporeal philosophy

Spinoza's *Ethics* is a philosophy of the body; his materialism consists in establishing the body's internal structure of affections. He warns us against expending too much effort on philosophizing about consciousness when *we do not even know what a body can do* (*SPP* 18). Nietzsche sees this too: we are fascinated by consciousness but the really surprising thing is *the body* (*SPP* 18). Consciousness is the locus of *effects* not of *causes*.[13]

Spinoza's active affections refer to body and mind in a parallel relation, where any action in the body is also an action in the mind; any passion in the body is also a passion in the mind (*E* IIIP 2S; IIP 13S). As thought and extension are absolutely distinct attributes, there is no causality between mind and body and no primacy in the series of mental over physical actions or vice versa (*SPP* 18). According to Descartes, when the body acts the mind is acted upon and when the mind acts the body is acted upon. But in Spinoza's *Ethics* body and mind are equal, as all attributes are equal relative to substance as their univocal cause. A modification is necessarily a modification *in all attributes simultaneously*. Spinoza shows how our empirical experience of the body is

[13] This is why Deleuze (1991: 21–36), after Hume and Comte, warns against 'impossible psychologies': how can mind be a proper object of science when it is purely a site of effects?

surpassed by the body and that our conscious experience of the mind is likewise surpassed by the mind. This is similar to Hume's invocation of the principles of association which transcend the given; it is what Bergson is saying in his ontological principle of efficient difference; it is what Nietzsche is saying when he invokes the will to power and the eternal return; and it is what Spinoza is saying when he claims that we do not even know what a body is capable of: each of these philosophers comprehends the profound mistake in granting sovereignty to consciousness. We must therefore discover the powers of the body in order to disclose, *in a parallel fashion*, the powers of mind surpassing consciousness, thus to *compare* the two powers. By adopting the model of the body, Spinoza implies no devaluation of thought relative to extension, 'but ... a devaluation of consciousness in relation to thought: a discovery of the unconscious, of an *unconscious of thought* just as profound as *the unknown of the body*' [*SPP* 18–19]. Spinoza shows us that to understand mind we must first understand the body.

Consciousness is by nature the locus of inadequate ideas because it registers effects while remaining ignorant of causes. Causality is defined by the series of causes and the series of effects.[14] The series of causes is defined in terms of encounters between existing relations: 'each body in extension, each idea or each mind in thought are constituted by the characteristic relations that subsume the parts of that body, the parts of that idea. When a body "encounters" another body, or an idea another idea, it happens that the two relations sometimes combine to form a more powerful whole, and sometimes one decomposes the other, destroying the cohesion of its parts. And this is what is prodigious in the body and the mind alike, these sets of living parts that enter into composition with and decompose one another according to complex laws' [*SPP* 19].

The series of causes is the order of composition and decomposition of relations in nature. We can think of these as the relations of *organization* and *disorganization*, respectively. As conscious beings we only ever observe and feel the *effects* of these modifications, the effects of organization and disorganization: when we encounter a body that composes with our own we experience joy; and when we encounter a body that decomposes our own we experience sadness. Our natural condition is such that we experience only what happens to our body, what happens to our mind; we take in only the effect of a body on our own body,

[14] Deleuze's (1990) *Logic of Sense* addresses a related conception of causality inspired by Stoic philosophy.

the effect of an idea on our own idea or mind. But we know nothing of the rules according to which all these relations compound with and decompose one another (*SPP* 19). Thus, the natural conditions of our knowledge of things and our consciousness of ourselves lead us to have only *inadequate ideas*, ideas which are confused effects separated from their real causes (*SPP* 19).

6.5 Implications of Spinoza's corporeal philosophy for organization theory

Insofar as the body is an organic collection of parts subsumed under a characteristic relation, and an organization is a larger body than our own but equally constituted by an organic relation of parts, we see no obstacle to treating the body and the organization as homologous in terms of the actions of cause and effect. Body and organization both refer to heterogeneous elements set into a common, unifying motion – this is the meaning of organ common to both terms. A body or organization exists as a certain power to act and to be acted upon, to effect and be affected. Spinoza's critique is that we experience our bodies and minds only on the level of effects, in ignorance of their causes. Applied to organization theory this critique is potentially devastating: our 'empirical' studies of organization are not at all empirical in the rigorous sense established through Hume's, Nietzsche's and Spinoza's philosophies. Ours is a naive version of empiricism, an empiricism of effects which, in the absence of any knowledge of causes, is analogous to a primitive animism. Spinoza shows us that we have hardly begun to understand positivism as a science of causes in the natural, still less the social world. To seek this understanding we must adopt the model of the body, since unconscious physical encounters between bodies are the fundamental causality of mind, knowledge and consciousness, as embodied effects.

Spinoza's model of the body discloses a way of defining organization in terms of *corporate affectivity*. This will yield a view of the organization as a heterogeneous set of coherent relations between parts, which encounter other heterogeneous sets of coherent relations of parts (other organizations, other bodies) and is subject to compositive and decompositive effects on its power accordingly. *The power of organization as a process is the power of compositive relations per se*. The power of an organization is the power of a body, that is, a certain power of existing as defined by its characteristic capacity to act and to be acted upon, to affect and to be affected. This power is always actual, always fulfilled by active and passive affects. Depending on the balance of that fulfilment, a given organization is predominantly active or passive: the *passive organization* is characterized by its inadequate comprehension of the affective causes of its own composition or decomposition as a power to exist. Its ability to apprehend only effects, *what happens* to it in its own terms, while remaining ignorant of the causes, leads to an excessive valuation of consciousness. The *active organization*, by contrast, is characterized by its comprehension of the causes of fluctuations in its power and is therefore an organization that has brought its power under its own control.

The natural conditions of organizational perception are similar to those of other bodies, which means that there are no wholly *active* organizations in Spinoza's sense. As in the case of corporeal bodies, so the affective capacities of corporate bodies will be dominated by passive affects. This means that the vast majority of bodies are passive. Passivity means that a body's constitutive relations are formed by its inadequate comprehension of its external encounters with other bodies. Such encounters can either compose or decompose the body's power of acting, its force of existing. The *passage* of composition is a feeling of joy, of decomposition a feeling of sadness. Therefore we must propose the existence of joyful and sad *corporate* passions.

What are corporate joy and sadness like? They are feelings-effects (*affectus*) felt throughout the corporate body and mind (culture). As in the case of our own body, the corporation suffers passions systemically, each organ of the body suffering decrease or increase in its power of action which affects the organized socio-technical body as a whole. The organs of the corporate body are its human and machinic elements combining to compose its socio-technical motion. Therefore the sad and joyful passions experienced by the corporation are distributed throughout its human organs, both in their individual internal relations and in their extrinsic relations with each other.[15]

6.6 The passive and the active body/organization

The precise expressions of passive effects in the body are less important than their relation to its power of action. In this sense the passions are symptomatic of a more profound passage. An encounter which composes

[15] One may see here a partial anticipation of the desiring machines in Deleuze and Guattari's *Anti-Oedipus*: there the distinction between bodies and machines is abandoned.

the body's relations and causes a feeling of joy involves an *increase in its power of action*, while an encounter which decomposes its relations, causing a feeling of sadness, *diminishes its power of action*. Spinoza is interested in the active power of bodies from two perspectives: from a speculative-analytical perspective he anatomizes this power; and from a practical-constitutive perspective he explains how a body can move from a state of weakness to a more powerful state by harnessing that analysis; how a body can transform its predominant experience of sad passive encounters, into joyfully active encounters.

The passive organization has only inadequate ideas of its encounters with other bodies; the active organization has adequate ideas of its encounters. Applied to the corporate mind (culture), ideas refer to those ideas that form relations between its human parts in the attribute of thought: the ideas that occur to personal minds as a function of their organizational *membership*.[16] In Spinoza's analysis, an idea is a modification in the attribute of thought and every modification occurs in every attribute simultaneously; therefore, a corporate idea always has a correlative corporate action. But only when that idea becomes adequate, only when it's essential relation within the affected body, the affecting body and the Absolute are perfectly apprehended and affirmed, can the passive corporate body begin to take full possession of its power and become active.

All actions and ideas are modifications of attributes originating in God/substance: a modification or body becomes adequate when it perceives this, its essential relation to substance and its attributes. An adequate idea is one that perceives its empirical origin in the body, in empirical relations between bodies and in the relation between finite bodies and the divine attributes of extension and thought. All of which refers to organization as a complex process of embodiment, of encounters capable of composing or decomposing its constitutive relation, involving joyful or sad passions, premised on adequate or inadequate ideas and leading to action or inaction. There is nothing abstract or idealist in Deleuze's reading of Spinoza: everything in existence takes place in the body as the locus of material thought and extension; nothing is premised on or involves a negation of the sensible.[17, 18]

[16] L. *membrum* limb. Most of us are prosthetic, removed at night; those in total institutions are more permanently attached.

[17] Only things exist. God's existence is not the existence of a thing, it is absolute existence, the absolute power of existing. Insofar as anything exists it is as a degree or instantiation of absolute existence.

[18] Spinozian organization theory addresses organization as a complex process of embodiment; a passionate, thoughtful and active existence. When a corporation

Having analyzed the body, Spinoza explains how that analysis can be transformed into a practical ethics of joyful action. *It is the corporeal equivalence between existence and affectivity that transforms organizational*

---

pollutes a river, for instance, its behaviour is facilitated by its confused idea of the environment as an indifferent exteriority, in contrast to its own differentiated interiority. A clearer idea of relations tells us that environment is neither external nor indifferent: it is nature, ultimate source of all difference in being, radically heterogenous and omnipresent, 'inside' and 'outside' bodies. Environment is equivalent here to Spinoza's substance and the firm is a modification in the attributes of thought and extension, an effect.

A dialectical analysis of relations between the organized body and environment, by contrast, is revealed as a false and negative relation designed to conjure up an ideal interiority of consciousness. It is this separationism (an organizational egoism) which encourages the firm to pollute the elements of its immediate environment. If it adopted a Spinozian perspective the firm could apprehend its pollution as destructive of that from which its own body is constituted. But it fails to comprehend the fundamental nature of its own existence as an affirmation of environment and of all the other bodies constituted in material existence as a whole. It is therefore unable to grasp the nature and significance of its encounters with other bodies including its relation with the river it pollutes.

A river is another kind of body in Spinoza's sense; it denotes a dynamic of parts brought under a unifying relation or flow as a vital ecology. By its poisoning, the firm's encounter with the river decomposes the latter's vital relations. Under those conditions of existence the firm is powerless to prevent this destruction: not only is it ignorant of its role as a cause of the river's decomposition, it is even ignorant of its real effects. As a body, its capacity to act is equivalent to its capacity to be affected and, as it is insensitive to the ecological destruction that it causes, we deduce that its power of action and existence is minimal. The narrowness of its own outlook threatens the firm's existence. Its pollution returns to decompose it in ways it cannot as yet understand: as an increasing cost of the clean water it needs to synthesise its products; as affecting the health of its own employees. If it were sensitive even to its own future, it might effect some improvement to reduce its destructive impact on the environment. But it is actually sensitive to one variable alone, which is short-term profit and loss, which is equivalent to the sensitivity of the tick. Owing to its minimal power to be affected, the firm has an equally minimal power to effect – its weakness is not only a threat to other bodies that it encounters, it is a threat to its own survival. This might be a good thing, the sooner it is destroyed the better in one sense but from a broader, long-term environmental view this would achieve little. Other firms may not be any better. What is needed is a practical revision of organizational conduct. Not a morality, since moral laws are external to bodies and involve the entire negative superstructure of the dialectic that we have sought to abolish from the analysis. What is needed is an organizational *ethics*. A way of acting that does not obey any law external to action itself. But far from an ethics, many firms currently professing to be 'green' merely play with appearances, employ green rhetoric, at best fulfil minimum legal requirements. We are still a very long way from having adequate corporate ideas.

theory into a Spinozian ethics of organized encounters between bodies. Inasmuch as our power to be affected is almost entirely fulfilled by weak, passive affections, the outline of an ethical, practical and joyful project is drawn: how can we experience more joyful and less sad passions; and how can we thereby become less passionate, more active beings?

6.7 The embodied power of organization: The *conatus*

To address these practical questions we return to Spinoza's theory of power. Power is the essence of substance: God is the absolute cause of Himself and of all things, and He is the power of comprehending Himself and all that He produces (*SPP* 98). The existing mode, body or organization is an infinitesimally small degree of this divine power.[19] This is explained by Spinoza's conception of *conatus*. A body comes into existence when an assemblage of extensive parts comes under an organized relation corresponding to the body's essence or degree of power. When this occurs the body's relation is defined as *conatus* (appetite, effort or striving) (*SPP* 98).

The *conatus* as a modal essence is not a possibility but a physical reality which lacks nothing. Once the mode comes into existence, it tends to persevere: the *conatus* envelops an indefinite duration (*SPP* 99). We have seen how a body's power has two equivalent aspects; the power to affect and the power to be affected. The ability to be affected has its weak and its strong aspects: in a body dominated by sad passions the ability to be affected is vulnerability and a weakness. In a body filled with joyful passions and active affects, an ability to be affected becomes a part of that body's power of existing and its strength. The passive body or organization only *suffers* its sensitivity as affects, or passions, while the active body *enjoys* its sensitivity as an increase in its power of action.

A mode's ability to be affected (*aptus*) corresponds to its essence as a degree of divine power (*conatus*).[20] God's capacity for being affected is necessarily filled by active affections, since God is their adequate

[19] 'Man's power, insofar as it is explained through his actual essence, is part of the infinite power of God or Nature' [*E* IVP4S].

[20] *Aptus* is the Latin root of *aptitude*. This forms a interesting connection between Spinoza's philosophy and the Jungian theory underpinning much of 'personality typing' and some 'aptitude testing'. Spinoza's use of *aptus* as an ability to be affected suggests a strong link between Jungian and materialist thought: Both present categories of pre-human types and forces capable of informing a very different theory of aptitude. This would not be a humanistic psychology but rather a somatic science of forces, their expressions and their relations expressed in the different manifestations of the human.

cause. The existing mode's ability to be affected is also fulfilled at every moment, but by affections (*affectio*) and affects (*affectus*) that are passive, as the mode itself is not their adequate cause; they are rather produced in it by other existing modes, and are therefore *imaginations* and *passions*, respectively. The passions (*affectus*) are the figures taken by the *conatus* when it is determined by an affection (*affectio*) that occurs to it (*SPP* 99). The affections that determine the *conatus* are also a cause of consciousness: having become conscious of itself under this or that affect, the *conatus* is called *desire* – which is always a positive desire for something (*SPP* 99). There is no abstract desire. Thus there are two determinations of the *conatus*: on the one hand, it is determined as a degree of power or appetite and, on the other hand, it is *a tendency to maximize the mode's ability to be affected* (*SPP* 9).

In the element of essence all powers are equal as degrees of divine power but, in the element of existence (as bodies), they are not equal and tend to struggle with one another in a contest for greater power. Because it is open to the environment, the existing body is vulnerable to encounters with other bodies capable of decomposing its vital internal relations (*SPP* 100).

As an existing mode, an organization constitutes a *conatus*, or striving; its passions are the figures taken by the *conatus* when it is determined by an affection that occurs to it. An organization that adapts to changing market conditions is an example of such a determination and we can apprehend its passions as the feelings-effects involved in the composition or decomposition of the organization's characteristic relation in response to encounters with other bodies in the market. Sometimes the passion will run slowly through its body as it passes smoothly to a greater or lesser perfection; at other times it might be a sudden spasm of excitement or terror. Corporate passion can be observed in a quickening of the motions of some of its members in response to favourable results, or in the depressed level of activity which greets poor results. This description is not anthropomorphic: we are simply viewing personal activity as connected with something greater than the individual; it is rather *organomorphism*. The affections that determine the corporate *conatus* are a cause of its corporate consciousness; and the corporate *conatus*, having become conscious of itself under affects of joy or sadness, high or low morale, becomes desire.

6.8 Desire is the desire for organization

For Spinoza, desire is embodied. The essence of the mode becomes the *conatus* when it is embodied in a relation between extensive parts; the *conatus* becomes desire when it becomes conscious of its own internal feelings-affects caused by encounters with other bodies. The body is an intensive part of the divine power, as such it is perfect and lacks nothing; even in existence when the body as *conatus* becomes desirous of a greater power of existing, this is not because it lacks anything: it is an effort, a striving or appetite to become more than it is, which means a desire to become organized into a greater, more powerful body; to *overcome itself* by affirming its desire and the desire of other modes. This can involve a total negation in the form of a consumption of the other by decomposing its relation or a total affirmation of the other by composing with it into a new more powerful relation. This is what is meant by organization as *embodiment* and disorganization as *disembodiment*, respectively.

From Deleuze's Spinozist viewpoint, Hegel's dialectic does not reflect what a body can do, nor comprehend its internal structure and the concrete nature of its encounters as the source of original ideas. When a body is decomposed (dies) nothing remains of its essential relation, it is totally consumed without any possible recuperation. Conversely, bodies that compose their *conati* form a greater, more powerful whole or organization in actuality. The individual can fear a loss of its 'authentic' consciousness, identity or ego as a result of its organization with others. Because the individual is an existing mode which envelops an indefinite duration, this is more precisely a fear of losing its memory. As Bergson (Deleuze, 1988, pp. 51–72) says, memory is much greater than the individual; it denotes its whole cultural horizon. To 'lose my identity', therefore, is to have my characteristic relation decomposed, to become disorganized, disembodied. My mind is the idea of my body; therefore 'to lose my mind' involves a loss of my body's relation, even to become a *body-without-organs* (Deleuze and Guattari, 1983). But decomposition is only one option: *composition* involves a whole new experience of embodiment and memory since my fragmentary comprehension of the cultural horizon is conjoined with another fragment. This does not involve a loss of memory but the acquisition of a more adequate memory, a greater comprehension of the whole of which my memory is a part. This is entirely a function of my physical incorporation into a greater physical whole; to become embodied in a larger organization. To affirm identity as cultural embodiment is to affirm the memory that I have, or am, and to be open to encounters that will compose with others. Where is the loss in this? It is the loss only of a liberal ideal that was never founded on concrete relations. Properly understood, individualism has nothing to do with atomism: an individual, corporeal or corporate (all individuals are really both), is always a social organization.

From a Spinozian perspective an organization is a corporate embodiment of power as desire; power conscious of its affective capacity and vicissitudes; and it is also a desire to maintain and increase that power to the ultimate extent when it will cease to be an affective capacity, cease to be subject to vicissitudes and become instead a power of pure action, determined from within as an active organizer of encounters. To achieve this active nature the mode must begin to form *adequate ideas*.

6.9 Spinoza's adequate ideas: Understanding and organization

Thought plays a crucial role in Spinoza's philosophy of the body, one that we need to apprehend properly before we can realize the full implications of Deleuze's Spinozism. Spinoza turns our attention from the true idea to the adequate idea as the proper category of speculation (*GD* 88). A traditional correspondence theory of truth is inadequate because it presents mind as passive, unproductive except insofar as it reproduces a formal reflection of extensive relations (*EPS* 131). Spinoza's conception of the adequate idea is active, a positive production in the attribute of thought and an efficient causality in the power of thought: '[t]he adequate idea is the idea that expresses its own cause and is explained by our own power' [*EPS* 151]. Thus Deleuze finds in Spinoza an epistemology of difference pertaining to the attribute of thought parallel to an ontology of difference pertaining to the attribute of extension. Spinoza's epistemology is ontological inasmuch as it must satisfy the same criteria defined by *causa sui*: a cause of itself, in itself and through itself (*EPS* 162).

The idea is thought's primary mode. An idea represents a state of affairs, while a passion (*affectus*) accompanies the passage from one state of affairs to another. The relation between an idea and a passion is precisely explained in the *Ethics* (*E* IIP 11, 12, 19, 24, 25, 26, 27): a passion presupposes the idea of the body encountered; thus, a feeling of love presupposes an idea of the thing loved, but it is a confused and inadequate idea of the thing. The cause of passion is the inadequate idea. '[t]he only ideas we have under the natural conditions of our perception are the ideas that represent *what happens* to our own body, the effect of another body on ours, that is a mixing of both bodies' [*SPP* 73]. When we speak of imagination or fancy, we refer to the corporeal affections (*affectio*): images are the traces of an external body in our own. Our ideas are reflections of these corporeal images or affections. 'Our ideas are therefore ideas of images or affections that represent a state of things, that is, by which we affirm the presence of the external body so long as our body remains affected in this way' [*SPP* 73–4]. Inadequate ideas indicate the presence (image, trace, *affectio*) of the external body in our own but they do not express the essence of that body as a degree of power.

These traces and the ideas that reflect and affirm them, are connected by memory or habit; if a body is affected by two bodies at the same time, the trace of one prompts the mind to recollect the trace of the other. Hence, the order of ideas in the mind reflects the order of extrinsic fortuitous encounters between bodies; the more arbitrary those encounters, the more inconstant are the images of affection and the association of ideas in the mind; to such an extent that the mind is capable of mixing ideas of diverse bodies to form fantastical figures such as winged horses and abstract categories of things (*SPP* 74). Adequate ideas are very different, they are ideas that we have in the same way that God has the idea that we are. They imply our comprehension of their substantial cause. Adequate ideas are *explained* by our power of knowing and comprehending (formal cause). They *express* another idea as cause, and the idea of God as determining this cause (material cause); they cannot be detached from an autonomous concatenation of ideas in the attribute of thought. This *concatenatio*, uniting formal and material cause, constitutes the intellectual mind as a *spiritual automaton* (*SPP* 74).[21]

As a mere *representation* of a corporeal image (*affectio*) the idea explains nothing about its formal cause in our power of thought, its material cause in other ideas, or God's absolute power of thought. For Spinoza (unlike Descartes), adequate thought is not clear and distinct by virtue of its objective clarity; it is not explained by a superior consciousness but by a logical force (Reason) that surpasses consciousness. The adequate idea explains the ideal material, its expressive content discloses the epistemological cause of the ideal, the internal causality in the attribute of thought and the idea of God as the absolute power of thought (*SPP* 74–5).

Absent from the inadequate idea, therefore, is any development of its formal or material cause. It signals something (the trace of another body) which it does not comprehend. Yet even the *inadequate* idea has a positive value: it affirms the lowest degree of our power of understanding,

[21] Deleuze (1990) discusses the related concept of the 'quasi-autonomous series of ideas' in detail in *The Logic of Sense*.

although it is not explained by it, and it signals its own cause, albeit without expressing it (*SPP* 75). Even if inadequate ideas are all that we have, therefore, our awareness of their inadequacy opens onto the possibility of having adequate ones.

Ideas, adequate or inadequate, are always followed by feelings-affects (*affectus*) and the quality of those feelings (joyful or sad), along with their destiny to become more or less active is determined by the adequacy of their cause in the idea. When the adequate idea is explained by our own power of thought, then we ourselves are the adequate cause of the feelings that result and such feelings are always active. By contrast, when we have inadequate ideas we are not the adequate cause of our feelings and such feelings are always passive. The problem, therefore, is how to form adequate ideas when our natural condition predisposes us to have only inadequate ones.

An increase or decrease in the adequacy of our thoughts denotes a corresponding change in our power. Adequate ideas express the structure and relations of thought and thereby increase our power to think: to express adequate ideas is to explicate the logic of thought, to oneself and others. One adequate idea is therefore a cause of others.[22] Spinoza recognizes that most of our ideas are inadequate and that our power to think is therefore very weak. In this sense, as in others, Deleuze's reading of Spinoza and Nietzsche coincide: '[t]he strategy of the adequate idea makes the question of truth a project of power' [*GD* 90]. The whole movement of Spinoza's philosophy is towards this project: the whole purpose of his analysis of the human condition is to prepare the ground for its practical transformation from a passionate subjection to ideas and affects, caused by confused images of extrinsic encounters with bodies more powerful than ourselves, to an active comprehension of the internal causality of our ideas and our affects. This transforms our power to think from a moral order to an ethical organization. A moral order denotes extrinsic determination by pre-established laws. An ethics, by contrast, involves intrinsic organization of the body's power to sense, to think, to feel and to act. The ethical subject does not obey the law, he makes and remakes the law with every act.

This ethical perspective is a crucial component of Deleuze's practical philosophy. Practice means to produce from the given, not to reproduce images of the given. Spinoza invites us to become adequate, become powerful, become practical. But how can we begin to form

[22] 'Whatever ideas follow in the mind from ideas that are adequate in the mind are also adequate' [*E* IIP 40].

adequate ideas when so many inadequate ideas spoil our power by separating our bodies from what they can do? (*EPS* 148). The answer does not lie in thinking alone: adequacy in Spinoza does not refer only to the attribute of thought but to all attributes equally, since the parallelism of the attributes refers to the identical movement of all the attributes simultaneously. Therefore the argument for an ethics of thought applies also to the attribute of extension; an adequate action in the body is expressive in the same sense as an adequate idea in the mind, it is expressive inasmuch as it explains and envelops its cause.[23]

6.10 Towards a Spinozian ethics of organization

Spinoza's *Ethics* proposes a twofold practical increase in our power of existing: an increase in our power to affect and to be affected. An encounter between two bodies is an encounter between their constitutive relations.[24] They can join together to compose a new more powerful relation, or the constitutive relation of one can decompose the constitutive relation of the other and even bring about its death. Spinoza's ethics is grounded in the universe of bodies and their relations of composition and decomposition. The uncertain and volatile nature of relations between bodies clearly indicates that Spinoza does not address a preformed order of possibility but an open sphere of *organization*.

The passive affections, or passions refer to an inactive, or in Nietzschean terms a *reactive*, response to encounters. They describe an internalization of power that is felt as suffering and which is even the opposite of action.[25] This fits very well with Nietzsche's critique of consciousness. Subjective consciousness is an internalization of passion, an impotence in the field of action, an inability to express the creative power of action; *ressentiment* and bad conscience. Not something acted but something felt (*senti*) (*NP* 111).

Inasmuch as our capacity to be affected is fulfilled by passive affections, it is reduced to its minimal power; insofar as it is fulfilled with active affections its power is increased to its maximum. Our capacity to be affected is minimal because we are dominated by passive affections

[23] '*The adequate is that which discloses the productive dynamic of being*' [*GD* 91, emphasis added].

[24] 'A body's structure is the composition of its relation. What a body can do is the nature and the limits of its power to be affected' [*EPS* 218].

[25] 'Our force of suffering *affirms* nothing, because it *expresses* nothing at all: it "envelops" only our impotence, that is to say, the lowest degree of our capacity to act!' [*EPS* 224].

and by sad passions in particular. God or Substance, as the absolute power of affection, is filled entirely with active affections because it is subject to no other cause than itself and the cause of all affections. We, however, are bound to encounter innumerable bodies more powerful than ourselves that are capable of decomposing our organic relation. Man is supremely vulnerable to decomposing encounters with other bodies.[26] But, as we saw in Gehlen's analysis, the other side of Man's nakedness in the face of nature is his extraordinary world-openness. Man's burden is an affective capacity unregulated by nature; he must therefore invent an art of organizing his encounters with those bodies that are compatible with his own. This is why Spinoza says, '[n]o one has yet determined what the Body can do. ... For no one has yet come to know the structure of the Body so accurately that he could explain all its functions' [*E* IIIP 2S]. Spinoza is not referring to the mechanical body so much as its affective capacity: we do not know what a body can do because we have not yet learned how to organize our encounters with other bodies in order to compose our power with their power. As a practical Spinozian project, organization is the art of selecting encounters with bodies that are composible with our own; and it is the art of increasing our power of existence, which means our power to think and to act adequately. Because we have yet to learn this art of selection, this practical ethics, '*We do not even know of what affections we are capable, nor the extent of our power*. How can we know this in advance?' [*EPS* 226].

Under this definition we have hardly begun to learn the art of organization. Our organizations embody only the minimum of our and their potential power. In this respect Spinoza's analysis discovers an entirely new science of organization, a practical project to transform our pathetic (sad, passive) impotence into a joyfully active practice; a creative practice that is adequate to the affirmative movement of being.

We must begin this ethical practice with the given. Our encounters are indeed *given* in the sense that they occur randomly because we ourselves are not their adequate cause. Consider, for example, the institution of marriage: Spinoza says that we do not comprehend the causes of our passions nor of the ideas which they presuppose. Marriage as we presently know it is therefore the outcome of chance encounters, an expression of our inadequate ideas. We feel love and desire but have no adequate idea as to their real cause except in a confused idea of the presence of the other body as an image in our own. Reconciliation

[26] '[T]he force by which a Man perseveres in existing is limited, and infinitely surpassed by the power of external causes' [*E* IVP 3].

should be no more remarkable than estrangement if our encounters and the relationships we form are such hostages to fortune. The observation that any successful marriage is the fruit of mutual effort is quite compatible with Spinoza's analysis: this mutual effort is a striving to conduct the encounter of marriage under its most favourable aspects. Even where marriage is a more selective institution it tends to be managed on the basis of extrinsic factors such as caste or financial criteria, instead of any adequate comprehension of agreement or disagreement between bodies. The problem, in Spinozian terms, is that while all bodies are marriageable in *essence*, they are all divorced in *existence*. In *essence* all bodies agree and, on that basis our encounters would always result in active affections. In *existence*, however, when bodies become *conatuses*, appetites or strivings, they do not agree. Therefore our actual encounters tend to lead only to passive affections, most of which are sad not joyful.[27] For Spinoza, Man is historically sad and passive: he has little comprehension of his affective structure, and, consequently, little ability to organize his encounters joyfully and actively.

Thus, the terms of Spinoza's practical project of empowerment are presented by his analysis: we are impotent but can become powerful, we are sad but can become joyful and we are passive but can become active. The question remains as to how we can achieve this becoming: '[t]he ethical question falls then, in Spinoza, into two parts: *how can we come to produce active affections*? But first of all: *how can we come to experience a maximum of joyful passions*?; [*EPS* 246]. The answer lies in the *common notions*. Before we address those, we first need to understand how Spinoza reconciles the *conatus* as an intensity of power, with a sense of justice or right. Secondly, we shall need to apprehend the crucial role of reason in Spinoza's practical project of empowerment.

6.11 Spinoza's theory of Right

The *conatus* is an embodiment of power in an organic relation between extensive parts; it is the effort to experience joy, to increase the power of acting and to imagine and find that which destroys the cause of sadness. Spinoza sees no difficulty in reconciling the various definitions of the *conatus*: 'mechanical (preserve, maintain, persevere); dynamic (increase, promote); apparently dialectical (oppose that which opposes, deny that which denies)' [*SPP* 101–2]. Each aspect derives from an

[27] 'Insofar as men are subject to passions, they cannot be said to agree in nature' [*E* IVP 32].

affirmative conception of essence as a degree of power, as an affirmation of essence in God. The *conatus* is the affirmation of essence in existence (*SPP* 102).

'[T]he *conatus* defines the *right* of the existing mode. All that I am determined *to do* in order to continue existing (destroy what doesn't agree with me, what harms me, preserve what is useful to me or suits me) *by means of* given affections (ideas of objects), under determinate affects (joy, sadness, love and hate...) – all this is my natural right' [*SPP* 102]. Thus, Spinoza identifies the power to exist with the right to exist, he sees no room for theoretical rights, theoretical justice; what is right or just is identical with the exercise of power, it is independent of any order of ends or obligations, 'since the *conatus* is the first foundation, the *primum movens*, the efficient and not the final cause' [*SPP* 102]. This right does not exclude aggression, anger, treachery or anything else the appetite may counsel.[28]

What can Spinoza mean by a conception of right that appears identical with the exercise of power, apparently in contradiction to natural justice? His is a materialist critique of abstract and negative theories of right that separate forces from what they can do. It is therefore a critique of morality. What point is there in claiming democratic rights, for example, which exist nowhere in practice; which serve to maintain an elite political class? Material rights exist only in practice, in the power enacted by bodies. The claim that all bodies have equal rights is as absurd as a claim that all have equal power. The question, '[w]hat are people's rights?' is wrongly formed; it should rather be: '[w]*hich one* has the right?' By which we really mean, '[w]*hich one wields power*?'

Spinoza shifts the question of right onto empirical grounds. Unexercised rights, like unexercised powers, are theoretical, whether they apply to a director who does not exercise his or her formal influence at the board; or to an employee who has a legal right to health and safety but is prevented from exercising it (or neglects to). In either case the rights in question are detached from active power and are therefore abstract and void. Such 'rights' may be legally sanctioned, which is quite a different thing from the practical rule. The implications of this critique of right for organizational theory and practice help us to understand the deficit between organizational democracy as an ideal value and as a real process. Indeed, it sets the entire discourse of management in a new perspective. The adage, '[a]ctions speak louder than words' is a telling critique on several levels, but it still mystifies

[28] Spinoza, *Theological – Political Treatise*, chap. 16; *Political Treatise*, chap. 2, 8.

the problem inasmuch as it utilizes a poetic substitution of speech for action.

Spinoza's conception of right is a critique of justice but also its affirmation inasmuch as justice is identical with efficient power. In this sense Spinoza anticipates Nietzsche's total critique of morality that separates the *conatus* from what it can do, from its power to persevere in existing and to strive to increase that power. This is why the *conatus* is the *ethical unit par excellence*; its right is equal to its power of existing and increasing that existence through organization.

6.12 Spinoza's theory of Reason

Each body strives to persevere and to increase its power, and some are more successful than others. Distinguishing the wise from the foolish in this regard is their differing abilities to select encounters involving joyful affects. If it only destroys that which threatens it, an existing mode can strive to persevere in accordance with its natural right, while remaining at the mercy of external encounters with other modes (*SPP* 102). The accidental nature of these encounters always carries a risk of encountering a body powerful enough to destroy it (*SPP* 102–3). Furthermore, whatever joy is experienced by our destruction of other modes is poisoned by the sadness and hatred in which it originates (*SPP* 102). Even in favourable circumstances, their accidental nature will tend to determine our encounters to engage with other modes under their discordant and hostile aspects (*SPP* 102).

The *conatus* will really succeed 'only to the extent that Man strives to *organize* his encounters, that is, among the other modes/bodies, to encounter those which agree with his nature and enter into composition with him, and to encounter them under the very aspects in which they agree and accord with him' [*SPP* 102, emphasis added]. All of which refers to the effort or exercise of Reason. It is Reason that guides our selection of those encounters that will increase our power of acting by experiencing joyful passions, and it is Reason that leads us *to take full possession of that power of action and to experience the joyful actions that proceed from the adequate ideas Reason forms* (*SPP* 103). Wisdom or Virtue in the *Ethics* is nothing more (or less) than this: the *conatus* as a successful effort, as the power of acting exercised under the conditions and encounters favourable to its taking possession of itself as its own efficient cause of active joys. The virtuous Man, the Man of Reason, is *the one who organizes* his encounters successfully, by the ethical selection of adequate ideas and the active affections which follow from them (*SPP* 103).

Taken together, Spinoza's conceptions of Right and Reason present the nucleus of the ethical encounter. Right is always exercised, it affirms the power to act; Reason affirms that right by guiding its exercise in the most favourable directions towards its successful realization through encounters with other modes or bodies.

God's absolute power is twofold: a power of existing and producing, and a power of thinking and comprehending. The power of existing is also twofold in its ability to be affected (affirmed in the attribute of extension) and in its power to have images and ideas (affirmed in the attribute of thought). Since images are impressions of other bodies in our own, it follows that the greater the body's affective power, the more images will appear in the mind (*SPP* 103).[29] Our power of acting varies in turn within our capacity to be affected – so long as the latter power is not yet formally possessed by us. Our power of perceiving and imagining relates to a power of knowing and comprehending which it involves but does not yet formally express. Only under the direction of Reason do our ideas become adequate and our affects active; only when we become causes of our own affects and of our adequate perceptions and ideas does the body take possession of its power of acting and its power of comprehension (*SPP* 103–104)[30]

6.13 The Common notions: Steps towards an organizational ecology

The *conatus* as the embodiment of active power is the *practical unit* of organization; its striving to increase that power through the experience of *joyful affections* is the efficient force of organization. The *conatus* is the ethical dynamic transmuting Spinoza's speculative analysis of the human condition into his practical project of *joyful action*.[31] Joy affirms the composition of being; our increase in power is the constitution of being itself (*GD* 96). Joy and power's increase – these are the internal motors of organization. But how do we embark on this joyful project from our present sad and passive state? There are negative and positive

[29] 'In proportion as a body is more capable than others of perceiving many things at once, or being acted on in many ways at once, so its mind is more capable than others of doing many things at once' [*E* IP 13S].
[30] 'In proportion as the actions of a body depend more on itself alone, and as other bodies concur less in acting, so its mind is more capable of understanding distinctly' [*E* IIP 13S, quoted in *SPP* 104].
[31] 'The sense of joy appears as the properly ethical sense; it is to practice what affirmation itself is to speculation' [*EPS* 272].

approaches to this. The former is determined to devalue the sad passions in favour of joy and to denounce those who cultivate them; this is the practical negation in Spinoza's *Ethics*. Spinoza denounces three types of personages: the Man of sad passions; the Man who exploits them in order to establish his power and the Man who is saddened by the passionate human condition – he may satirize Man's passionate condition, but his is a bad laughter (*EPS* 270; *SPP* 25). The slave, the tyrant and the priest form the moralist trinity, the three figures of sadness.

Since our capacity for affection is always filled, the denunciation of sadness is inseparably linked to the cultivation of joyful passions. But we can only begin to cultivate joy on the basis of a clear apprehension of how it is that certain bodies agree with our own; it is not enough simply to experience that agreement when it occurs: we must seek it out and understand it for what it is. To do this we must come to know the subtle structures of the body, its constitutive individual relation and also the ways in which bodies can compose and decompose one another (*E* IIIP 2S). By determining the variance of constitutive relations between one body and another we will be able to determine their resemblances, however different they might at first appear (*EPS* 278). This investigation into the subtle structures of bodies and their relations seeks to discover and to form *common notions* (*E* IIP 37–40).

'The common notions are so named not because they are common to all minds, but primarily because they represent something common to bodies, either to all bodies (extension, motion and rest), or to some bodies (at least two, mine and another)' [*SPP* 54]. Therefore, the common notions are not *abstract* ideas but *general* ideas. A body is composed of an infinite number of parts under an organized constitutive relation. The parts of the body are characterized by relations of motion and rest which, when they agree with the internal relations of another body, compose with it to form a unity with a greater power of existing. As a combined physical and ideal unit the common notion is the definitive organizational relation.

We should be clear that a common notion is *not* a physical relation per se, it is rather the *idea* of a similarity of composition in two or more existing modes along with the *unity* of that composition (*EPS* 275; SPP 54). Only secondarily are the common notions common to minds, and only to minds whose bodies are affected by the unity of composition in question (*SPP* 54–5). When Deleuze states that the meaning of the common notion is more biological than mathematical – Spinoza gives the example of chyle and lymph as parts of the blood (Letter XXXII to Oldenburg) – he is emphasizing the empirical, organic origins of the common notions as a necessarily adequate idea of a biological unity (*EPS* 2 79; *SPP* 54). Even bodies that do not agree with one another (for example a poisoned body and the poison) have some relations in common: relations of extension, motion and rest. At this general level all bodies are capable of forming common notions, but this is also the level of least utility from a practical perspective. To focus on the most general level would be to risk ignoring their practical function in favour of their speculative sense (*EPS* 281).

Spinoza first introduces the common notions in Book II of the *Ethics* in terms of a speculative order, descending from the most universal (extension, motion and rest) to the least universal. In Book IV he presents them in a different light, as a practically constructive series, ascending from the most specific to the most general. In their practical formation the common notions present the means to understanding the constitutive relations of organized bodies and their active development.

6.14 Forming common notions: A basic organizational principle

When, as we have noted, we encounter a body that agrees with our own (that is, whose constitutive relation agrees with ours, e.g., a nourishing food, a loved being, an ally), we experience a joyful passive affect, although we do not yet adequately know what we have in common. Because this joy increases our power of acting and comprehending, it is the occasional or accidental cause of a common notion (*SPP* 5). To succeed in transforming the occasional and accidental occurrence into a constant and necessary practice we need to be guided by *Reason*: '[r]eason is 1. an effort to select and organize good encounters, that is, encounters of modes that enter into composition with ours and inspire us with joyful passions (feelings that agree with reason); 2. the perception and comprehension of the common notions, that is of relations that enter into this composition, from which one deduces other relations (reasoning) and on the basis of which one experiences new feelings, active ones this time (feelings that *are born* of reason)' [*SPP* 56].

Thus, the experience of joyful passions is only a necessary stage in the formation of the common notions that will replace them with active affects.[32] So long as we are not completely dominated by sad passions

[32] 'We must then, *by the aid of joyful passions*, form the idea of what is common to some external body and our own. For this idea alone, this common notion, is adequate' [*EPS* 283].

we are capable of forming common notions. Our first common notions will be the least general, representing something in common between one's own body and another. From these joyful affects other affects follow, but these are not passive, they are active joys that join with them and then take their place. These first common notions and the active affects they invoke give us the power to form more general common notions, expressing what we have in common even with bodies that disagree with our own and affect it with sadness. From these more general common notions yet more active affects follow to replace the sad passions (*SPP* 56).

Spinoza's practical project begins at the level of the encounter between two bodies, between our own body and another. The turning point between his speculative analysis and his practical ethics is the question of what the individual can do to become adequate, become active, become joyful. Donne's resounding admonition: '[d]o not ask for whom the bell tolls, it tolls for thee" captures the moment of transmutation from the speculative to the practical, the moral to the ethical, the ordered to the organizational and the transcendental to the immanent problem. The answer to the Nietzschean question '[w]ho will's it?' is transmuted into the question '[w]hat do I will?' But this 'I' is not the ego, the false interiority of consciousness, it is the body and all that the body is capable of and can become capable of as an expression of the infinite forces that surpass it.

In order to select adequate encounters we must begin from the inadequate, from where we are: we know that the experience of joy is a sign of agreement between two bodies and that this agreement constitutes an increase in our power; we know that the difference between experiencing this joy as a passive and as an active affection is that the passive effect arises from an external, accidental cause, whereas the active affect arises from an internal, necessary cause. The passage from passive joy to active joy therefore entails substituting an internal for an external cause. The adequate or active encounter differs from the inadequate passive encounter in expressing its internal cause through a clear and distinct idea of the commonality of relations between the encountered body and our own (*GD* 98–9). There is nothing vague or abstract about this procedure: a joyful passion only arises from an external body that is composed of a relationship that agrees with our own. When we form a clear idea of this agreement (a common notion being that idea and the unity formed by that agreement which is its object), then and only then is the joyful affection joined by an active affection which takes its place. The active affect is distinct from the passive feeling from which we began only in its cause. Its cause ceases to be a confused idea of the body that agrees with mine and becomes an adequate idea of what is common to that body and my own (*EPS* 284).[33]

This cumulative ability to become active succeeds only under the tutelage of reason.[34] The common notions refer to the composition of concrete relations between material bodies. They invoke a biological geometry disclosing the unity of composition in Nature as a whole and the modes of variation within that unity (*SPP* 57). On one hand, common notions are adequate ideas because they express their true cause in the substantial relations between bodies: 'representing a unity of composition, they are in the part and the whole alike, and can only be conceived adequately' [*SPP* 55]. On the other hand, common notions are adequate because they express their formal cause in the attribute of thought, they are 'ideas that are formally explained by our power to think and that, materially, express the idea of God as their efficient cause' [*EPS* 279].

6.15 The common notions: An ethical practice of organization

The common notions hold a central place in the *Ethics* as one of its 'fundamental discoveries' [*EPS* 292], (*SPP* 55–6): they disclose how organization, properly defined, is not a process of chance composition but an ethical project driven by desire and guided by reason; chance becomes necessity when the cause of joy is enveloped within the new body itself. The opening definition of the *Ethics*: 'Per *causa sui* intelligo' now reveals its practical meaning: *causa sui* refers to the internal force of organization, a force internal to all bodies in nature (*GD* 99). This is not speculative but ethical; it discloses the principle of becoming adequate, becoming active, becoming more real. This becoming is not a becoming other, nor is it a becoming of the same, it is a becoming different by joining one's own differential relation with the relations of others; an overcoming or transmutation of the body by composing a new more powerful relation with another body.

Spinoza's *mind and body parallelism* differs from other dualist conceptions. It consists of the identity between phenomena in the body and

[33] '[A]n effect which is a passion ceases to be a passion as soon as we form a clear and distinct idea of it' [*E* VP 3].

[34] 'When Spinoza suggests that what agrees with reason may also be born from it, he means that from every passive joy there may arise an active joy distinguished from it only by its cause' [*EPS* 274–5].

phenomena in the mind (*isomorphism*); of the identity of connection between the two series (*isonomy or equivalence* – the connection between two actions in the body is identical to the connection between two thoughts in the mind) and of the identity of being (*isology*) since the same modification is produced in the essential attribute of thought under the existing mode of mind, and in the essential attribute of extension under the existing mode of a body. Body and mind are parallel at the level of the attributes, but at the level of the existing mode they interact to support the success of the *conatus*.

If reason is its guide, the body's internal motor is desire. The *conatus* is the power of the existing mode to exist and to organize that existence by composing with other existing modes. In Spinoza, desire is the embodiment of the power of existing as a *feeling* of power; it is power which has acquired a tendency to joyful passion and action through the affects (feelings). Thus, the formation of a common notion enables the mind to transmute a passion into an action, an inadequate into an adequate idea, imagination into reason. The formation of common notions is therefore the practical constitution of reason (*GD* 101). As ontology is practically constituted and not pre-established, so epistemology is practically constituted as a practical craft of reasoning.

Spinoza presented this practical task redolent in terms of the then infant Industrial Revolution: as the body forms works and tools from raw materials, so the mind forms common notions from inadequate ideas. As these works and tools allow the formation of greater works and tools, so the formation of common notions allows the formation of other, more general common notions: 'and so proceeds by stages, until it reaches the pinnacle of wisdom' [*Emendation of the Intellect* 30–31]. In Chapter 1, the crucial relation between the eye, the hand and the brain was invoked in the context of the embodiment of technology: as the hands explore the tactile world of things, so the mind reflects upon that process; physical and mental techniques develop in a parallel, *isonomous* relation. In the development of technology we can see clear examples of the formation of common notions: when the body forges a ploughshare, a sword,or a manuscript, these objects (the tool and our body) compose a greater unity. The body-plough, body-sword, body-book are more powerful than the body that scratches at the earth with a stick, wields a club or paints scenes on cave walls. When the body succeeds and feels joy in its achievements, and when the mind clearly and distinctly perceives the unity which these technologies have composed, then the unity and the adequate idea of that unity combine to form a common notion. A common notion is the unity of the physical composition joined with the idea of that composition and its cause in the composability of the two bodies. When the body trains its movements in order to manipulate the tool, weapon or manuscript, even though each in a different way is capable of destroying the body (even a book can cause a death sentence to be passed on the author), and when the mind can adequately explain this physical achievement in logical terms, then extension and thought, whether defined as embodied technique and reasoning, practice and theory or desire and reason, become adequate to one another.

Spinoza's materialist conception of the common notions views the development of active joy and reason as equally dependent on sensation and thought. What are given are physical affections (sensations) and mental images (imaginations). Each becomes adequate with the aid of the other: adequate actions depend on the formation of adequate ideas and adequate ideas depend on sensations for the images that they correct and replace. The active joy and the adequate idea are produced by the *conatus* which is the embodiment of power.

Spinoza's philosophy has its transcendental aspects to be sure: substance, the attributes and the two powers of the Absolute; but his practical philosophy is articulated in the passions, actions and ideas of existing bodies. Thus even the transcendental is embodied in the *Ethics*, in the sense that our body, our embodiment as an organism composed of many parts, is presented as the only proper site of our comprehension of existence, knowledge and practical organization.

Spinozism presents a materialist philosophy of organization *par excellence*: it describes the processes by which bodies compose and decompose into greater or lesser organic unities – Spinoza makes no distinction between biological and social organisms. 'Each thing is at once body and mind, thing and idea; it is in this sense that all individuals are *animata* (*E* II13S). The representative power of the idea simply follows from this correspondence'[*SPP* 86]. Organization denotes the selection of joyful encounters between bodies and the transmutation of that joy from passive to active affects by the formation of adequate ideas.

Organization is distinguished from order in that what is given to be organized is the difference in Nature itself; this material difference becomes the stuff of a constitutive effort to find in the given the material causes for accidental compositions and to bring that constitutive power into the possession of the body. The adequate body in Spinoza is *the one that comprehends its own constitutive relations and is capable of selecting encounters to compose with others to form larger, more powerful bodies that surpass it*. Order, by contrast, is the multiplicity determined in its relation by a wholly external, accidental and abstract will. Order denotes a sad passivity (fatalism) and an inability to feel joyful affections or to become active. Yet by the very nature of every thing in existence each body is capable of forming at least one adequate idea, even if it is half-submerged in egoism.

As it is construed in a variety of sciences much of what we call organization falls far short of Spinoza's analytical and practical vision. Many organizations show nothing but ignorance and contempt for bodies and their affective life; they are unaware of the real forces at work in the physical relations that constitute them and which they themselves constitute as a theoretically more powerful force. Spinoza brings a radically new sense to Gouldner's (1969) critique of functionalist organizations in 'The Unemployed Self'. Our experience of organization is often oppressive; conformity, not congruence is demanded; compliance, not creative action is wanted; while passion is actively discouraged as harmful to the ruling order. Such an organization negates difference in the interests of repetition; it desires a homogeneous order rather than a heterogeneous organization. Such an 'organization' denies its substantial being by affirming uniformity to an ideal order which separates the power of efficient difference from what it can do.

6.16 Towards a new conception of organizational effectiveness

According to Spinozism, an organization is a body, an infinite number of parts brought together to form a individual relation or set of relations. The organization's power is constituted by its power of action, which is equal to its power to be affected. This means that *an organization's effectiveness is defined by its power to be affected.* Figure 6.2 shows that the only way for a mode (body, organization) to increase its power to exist is to select encounters with other composable modes which will cause joyful passive affects; and to strive to form common notions that will transmute those passions into actions, thus increasing its power to act joyfully. By following figure 6.2 down the right hand side we read Spinoza's speculative analysis of the human condition; by retracing that movement up the left hand side we discover his practical project to transform that condition: become joyful, become active, become powerful, become *organized.*

We see here a scheme for education and development with a clear organizational theme (*EPS* 288). Deleuze's Spinoza studies disclose an original direction to the perennial search for keys to organizational

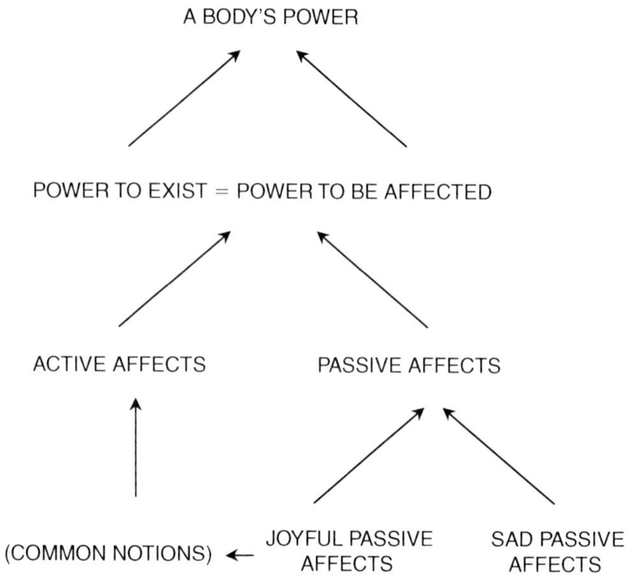

Figure 6.2 From passion to action (Adapted from *GD* 100)

effectiveness. To become more powerful, more practically effective, the organization must embrace its basic constitutive condition as an existing body. Only then will it be able to practically increase its effectiveness *by developing its power to be affected*: intrinsically, by cultivating joyful active relations among its constitutive parts (personnel, technology, administration, etc.); extrinsically, by cultivating joyfully active relations with other bodies in its environment. It has to begin to understand its constitutive corporate relations as the *conatus*, as its embodied desire to preserve and increase its power of existing. This desire is served by striving to form common notions between its own and other bodies. The firm that pollutes could begin with the river it pollutes, by forming a common notion of what it and the river have in common. We cannot expect a sudden conversion in these circumstances, which is why Spinoza articulates a more practical proposition. It is only necessary for the firm to have a very modest idea of its commonality with the river, such as the realization that, due to the increasing burden of purification its own effluent necessitates, its decomposing pollution returns to itself as an increasing cost of the water that it uses. Here, we observe an encounter between ecological and financial systems, mediated through supply and demand.[35] Once the firm forms a common notion of its organic relations with the river and its own financial health, the way is open to form more general common notions, such as that between itself and a local community which may begin to view it in a more positive light: less as a body to be resented because of its destructive contempt for the river and more as a locus of health and enjoyment, as an integral and positive actor in that community.

Too often organizations prove to be unable or unwilling to form an adequate idea of their own role in causing the damage and passions inflamed by pollution; they obfuscate the issue or simply deny responsibility. This is a dialectical response: pollution is a negation of organic relations and the polluter negates that negation by denying its existence or its own accountability. All that is recuperated by this double negation is precisely what Deleuze's reading of Nietzsche describes, nothing but hatred and *ressentiment*, and the bad conscience formed by *ressentiment* which turns back into the body of the community and the body of the firm. To refuse to become active is to deny the causal chain of being, a denial of the possibility of forming common notions, a denial of the physics of bodies, of their power and of that power's increase. Such denial causes only sad passions, the passive sadness of those who believe that action is really impossible. Once we believe so completely in our own impotence we have indeed reached a low point in our existence: we have relinquished the very power to organize.

Not content with having discerned the grand scheme of things, Spinoza is also prescriptive – but he is *realistic*: the sad passivity of the human condition is neither culpable nor irresolvable; it is only its natural condition and any attempt to increase its joyful active aspect must, insofar as it is practical, begin modestly. The grand gesture has little chance of success, being necessarily ignorant of the local situation. Grand gestures are a common curse of organizational life: drives to improve morale, production, participation etc., usually fail because they are empty signifiers that form no common notion with the existing organization. It is better to begin with a common notion of productive relations between two individuals and form more general common notions on that basis, building slowly.

[35] In his Preface to Deleuze's *Spinoza: Practical Philosophy*, Hurley remarks on the connection made between Spinozism and the 'deep' ecology of Norwegian ecophilosopher Arne Naess. As Hurley says, Deleuze's rigorous reading of Spinoza invites a similar ecological interpretation.

Conclusion

The foregoing chapters propose a philosophy of bodies and organizations and of embodiment and organization. In Chapter 1, we began with a discussion of Man as an impossible animal who must organize the conditions of his survival and development, which are termed culture. Culture is comprised by institutions, the collective habits of a community. The true function of institutions is to provide the oblique means for the expression of our desires. Below the level of institutions – though I do not intend this figure of speech to denote a real hierarchy, everything in the real is equivalent and hierarchy is a figure of power – are organizations (noun), and the whole business of culture is termed organization (verb). Culture is man's work. Organization is work informed by certain principles that are the real subject of this treatise.

In Chapter 2 the development of medical technology was proposed as an exemplar of embodiment and organization. In the case of Foucault's history of the hospital we saw that the human body, the teaching hospital and the corpus of medical knowledge and society were all transformed simultaneously, from a medicine of species, which rigorously exclude the patient's body from diagnosis and treatment on both individual and community levels, to a medicine of the body. Almost literally, doctors opened their eyes to the three-dimensional mass of the body. 'Almost' because in quick succession they moved from ignoring the body of the patient, to listening to its diseased noises, through developing a radically new phenomenology of pathology augmented by such instruments as the stethoscope, laryngoscope, ophthalmoscope, X-ray and MRI scanner. By envisaging it as a volume, medicine developed a new theory of the body, which existed and continues to exist as much in the medical imagination as objectively. The renewed interest in epidemiology over the last two or three decades may be seen as an extension of that phenomenology, and as another retreat from the body. Doubtless both perspectives, the objective and phenomenological, are needed.

In Chapter 3 we began what I hope was a painstaking and engaging review of Deleuze's reading of Hume's ideas on human nature. As far as I am aware this was at the time of writing the first attempt to write about Deleuze's Hume study in a systematic way. I expect that some readers of Deleuze would dispute some aspects of my reading, which is to be expected. Deleuze's Hume study laid a new foundation with old stones. Hume's first question was this: how does mind become human nature? Parallel to this is another equally profound enquiry: how is the human socialized? The relevance of these enduring pillars of social philosophy for our purposes lies in Hume's empiricism: everything begins with sensation and their consequential images and ideas. The assemblage of ideas constituting mind are acted upon by principles of association that are not in themselves human. In other words, Man is the involuntary site of physical interactions and ideation acted upon by principles that transcend him. As for the social dimension, the ego thus analysed can never be a unity. To conceive it thus would be akin to pointing to any road intersection and naming it the centre of town. The human individual is no more than a node in a network of families, clans and tribes and it is they, not the sovereign individual, that constitute the natural social unit.

If we characterize Deleuze's Hume study as a philosophical skirmish, his Bergson studies, are declarations of war, and the enemy is Hegel's dialectic. At this point it is appropriate to record that my own experience of reading Deleuze was of a great weight lifted from my mind. I did not know until that moment that the burden I had felt over the preceding years of (abandoned) work on the nature of work and organization, was the dialectical model of argumentation. When, in his Bergson and Nietzsche studies, Deleuze exposed the dialectic as a fallacy, I immediately understood my own frustrations: my despairing intuit that the Hegelian dialectic was a path leading to nowhere was vindicated, indeed articulated: being negatively defined according to a structure of opposition was not a triumphant advance in the history of thought at all; it was exactly what I had felt it to be, a philosophy of resentment, pessimism and intellectual defeatism. Bergson's ontology is, by contrast, optimistic, expansive and exhilarating: Being expands fanwise according to a process of continual transformation or actualization. Being is an unlimited process of becoming.

In Chapter 5 we noted the flaw in Bergson's unconditional love of the élan vital; it could not explain the phenomenon of organization.

Rephrasing the problem in Nietzsche's terms, the dice thrown fall back: that which departs also returns. But whereas every dice-throw must fall back, only some fall back eternally. Only certain 'numbers' carry the conviction of destiny. What distinguishes between the casual dice-throw and the throw that falls back eternally? Nietzsche answers that all force is willed, and it is the quality of that will that determines the outcome of the throw, whether it will fall back only once or for ever. If you will the throw with your whole being, without reserve, only then will it return eternally. If the throw is the becoming of being, the dice falling back is the being of becoming. Taken together these two moments denote the double movement of organization.

In Chapter 6 we took up the problem of will in a more thoroughgoing way. Deleuze's reading of Spinoza finds another double-movement, one of the greatest in the history of Western thought. Spinoza was by trade a lens grinder. Deleuze both held him in awe as a philosopher and admired his moral character, naming him 'the "prince" of philosophers'. In the *Ethics* Spinoza analyses human nature in terms that Nietzsche recognized in the texture of his own thought. Moreover, we know that Hume (1711–76) was one of very few philosophers of his day who were deeply interested in Spinoza (1632–77), or indeed know about him at all. So it is not surprising to find strong resonances between the two. Spinoza analyses the human condition as dominated by destructive interactions between bodies accompanied by sad passions, disempowerment and a lack of constructive action. He then proceeds to describe the remedy: by understanding how my body is affected by another I can begin to choose encounters that increase my power in composition with theirs, and experience more joyful passions leading to action. Congruent with my consistent motif that the corporeal and corporate body are equivalent at every turn of this materialist analysis, I argue that anything Spinoza says about individuals can be applied equally to communities and any other artefact of organization. For many, as I said at the outset, the experience of organizational life is predominantly oppressive. This is painfully ironic when the cultural function of organization is precisely the opposite of this. Organization should relieve, not exacerbate Man's burden of natural indeterminacy. One answer to this problem can be found in Spinoza's ethic of enjoyment.

Glossary

CE	Bergson, Henri (1948) *Creative Evolution*
CM	Bergson, Henri (1946) *The Creative Mind*
B	Deleuze, Gilles (1988) *Bergsonism*
CDB	Deleuze, Gilles (1956) 'La conception de la difference chez Bergson'
ES	Deleuze, Gilles (1991) *Empiricism and Subjectivity*
EPS	Deleuze, Gilles (1990) *Expressionism in Philosophy: Spinoza*
SPP	Deleuze, Gilles (1988) *Spinoza: Practical Philosophy*
F	Deleuze, Gilles (1988) *Foucault*
NP	Deleuze, Gilles (1983) *Nietzsche and Philosophy*
TP	Deleuze, Gilles and Guattari, Felix (1990) *A Thousand Plateaus*
BC	Foucault, Michel (1973) *The Birth of the Clinic*
DP	Foucault, Michel (1977) *Discipline and Punish*
TS	Foucault, Michel (1988) *Technologies of the Self*
M	Gehlen, Alfred (1988) *Man: His Nature and Place in the World*
GD	Hardt, Michael (1993) *Gilles Deleuze: An Apprenticeship in Philosophy*
PS	Hegel G. W. F. (1977) *Hegel's Phenomenology of Spirit*
L	Hobbes, Thomas (1651) *Leviathan*
T	Hume, David (1888) *A Treatise of Human Nature*
GM	Nietzsche F. (1967) *On the Genealogy of Morals*
Z	Nietzsche F. (1961) *Thus Spoke Zarathustra*
AC	Nietzsche F. (1888) *The Antichrist*
VP	Nietzsche F. (1935) *La Volonte de Puissance*
EH	Nietzsche F. (1967) *Ecce Homo*
WP	Nietzsche F. (1968) *The Will to Power*
BGE	Nietzsche, F. (1973) *Beyond Good and Evil*
MRT	Reiser, Stanley Joel (1978) *Medicine and the Reign of Technology*
E	Spinoza, Baruch (1985) *Ethics*
RB	Turner, Bryan S. (1992) *Regulating Bodies*

Bibliography

Anthony, Peter D. (1977) *The Ideology of Work*, London: Tavistock.

Bachat, X. (1801) Anatomie Générale appliquée à la physologie et à médicine, Paris.

Bentham, Jeremy (1843) *Panopticon*, in *The Works of Jeremy Bentham, Published under the Supervision of His Executor, John Bowring*, 11 volumes, Edinburgh: W. Tait.

Bentham, J. (1843) *Panopticon*, in Bowring (ed.) *Works*, IV.

Bergson, Henri (1935 [1932]) *The Two Sources of Morality and Religion* (trans. R. Ashley Audra and Cloudesley Brereton with the assistance of W. Horsfall Carter), New York: Henry Holt & Co.

Bergson, Henri (1941) *La Pensee et le Mouvant*, Paris: Presses Universitaires de France.

Bergson, Henri (1946 [1941]) *La Pensee et le Mouvant, The Creative Mind* [*CM*] (trans. Mabelle Andison), Westport, Connecticut: Greenwood Press.

Bergson, Henri (1944, 1911 [1907]) *Creative Evolution* [*CE*] (trans. Arthur Mitchell), London and New York: Macmillan.

Bergson, Henri (1950 [1889]) *Time and Free Will* (trans. F. L. Pogson), London: Allen and Unwin.

Bergson, Henri (1950a [1896]) *Matter and Memory* (trans. N. M. Paul and W. Scott Palmer), London: George Allen and Unwin.

Berkeley, George (1685–1753) *Philosophical Works*, London: Everyman's Library (1975) David Campbell Ltd.

Bittner, Egon (1965) 'The Concept of Organization', *Social Research*. 32, no. 3, pp. 239–55.

Bogue, Ronald (1989) *Deleuze and Guattari*, London and New York: Routledge.

Bukowski, Charles (1971) *Post Office*, Los Angeles: Black Sparrow Press.

Burrell, Gibson (1992) 'Back to the Future: Time and Organization', in *Rethinking Organization*, Michael Reed and Michael Hughes (eds), London: Sage, pp. 165–83.

Butler, Judith (1987) *Subjects of Desire*, New York: Columbia University Press.

Cervantes Saavedra, Miguel de (1604) *Don Quixote* (trans. J. M. Cohen), London: Penguin.

Comte, Auguste (1853) *The Positive Philosophy of Auguste Comte*; 2 volumes (trans. Harriet Martineau), 2 vols, London: Triibner.

Cooper, Robert (1983) 'The Other: A Model of Human Structuring', in *Beyond Method*, Gareth Morgan (ed.), Beverly Hills: Sage, pp. 202–18.

Cooper, Robert (1989) "Modernism, Postmodernism and Organizational Analysis 3: The Contribution of Jacques Derrida", *Organization Studies*, 10 (4): 479–502.

Darwin, Charles (1872) *The Origin of the Species by Natural Selection*, London: Murray.

Deleuze, Gilles (1953) 'Instincts et Institutions', *Textes et documents philosophiques*, Paris: Hachette.

Deleuze, Gilles (1956) 'Bergson', *Les philosophes celebres*, edited by Maurice Merleau-Ponty, Editions d'Art Lucien Mazenod: Paris, pp. 292–9.

Deleuze, Gilles (1956a) 'La conception de la difference chez Bergson' [*CDB*], *Les etudes bergsoniennes*, no. 4, pp. 77–112.

Deleuze, Gilles (1967) 'Reversing Platonism', *Revue de Metaphysiques et de Morale*, 2. Reproduced in *The Logic of Sense* (1990 [1969] trans. Mark Lester), London: Athlone.

Deleuze, Gilles (1968) *Difference et repetition*, Paris: Presses Universitaires de France.

Deleuze, Gilles (1977) 'Lettre a Michel Cressole', in Michel Cressole, *Deleuze*, Paris: Editions Universitaires.

Deleuze, Gilles (1983 [1962]) *Nietzsche and Philosophy* [*NP*] (trans. Hugh Tomlinson), New York: Columbia University Press.

Deleuze, Gilles (1987) *Dialogues*, with Claire Parnet (trans. Hugh Tomlinson and Barbara Habberjam), New York: Columbia University Press.

Deleuze, Gilles (1988 [1970, 1981]) *Spinoza: Practical Philosophy* [*SPP*] (trans. Robert Hurley), San Francisco: City Lights.

Deleuze, Gilles (1988a [1966]) *Bergsonism* [*B*] (trans. Hugh Tomlinson and Barbara Habberjam), New York: Zone Books.

Deleuze, Gilles (1988b [1986]) *Foucault* [*F*] (trans. Sean Hand), Minneapolis: University of Minnesota Press.

Deleuze, Gilles (1990 [1969]) *The Logic of Sense* (trans. Mark Lester with Charles Stivale; edited by Constantin V. Boundas), London: Athlone.

Deleuze, Gilles (1990a [1968]) *Expressionism in Philosophy: Spinoza* [*EPS*] (trans. Martin Joughin), New York: Zone Books.

Deleuze, Gilles (1991 [1953]) *Empiricism and Subjectivity* [*ES*] (trans. Constantin Boundas), New York: Columbia University Press.

Deleuze, Gilles and Guattari, Felix (1983 [1972]) *Anti-Oedipus* (trans. Robert Hurley, Mark Seem and Helen R. Lane), London: Athlone.

Deleuze, Gilles and Guattari, Felix (1986 [1975]) *Kafka: Toward a Minor Literature* (trans. Dana Polan), Minneapolis: University of Minnesota Press.

Deleuze, Gilles and Guattari, Felix (1987 [1980]) *A Thousand Plateaus* [*TP*] (trans. Brian Massumi), London: Athlone (copyright: University of Minnesota Press, 1987).

Deleuze, Gilles and Guattari, Felix (1994 [1991]) *What is Philosophy?* (trans. Hugh Tomlinson and Graham Burchill), London and New York: Verso.

Derrida, Jacques (1973 [1967]) *Speech and Phenomena* (trans. David B. Allison), Evanston, Illinois: Northwestern University.

Derrida, Jacques (1974 [1967]) *Of Grammatology* (trans. Gayatri Chakravorty Spivak), Baltimore and London: Johns Hopkins.

Derrida, Jacques (1981 [1972]) *Dissemination* (trans. Barbara Johnsone), London: Athlone, pp. 61–171.

Derrida, Jacques (1981a [1972]) *Positions* (trans. Alan Bass), London: Athlone.

Derrida, Jacques (1988) 'Geschlecht II: Heidegger's Hand', in *Deconstruction and Philosophy: The Texts of Jacques Derrida*, John Sallis (ed.), Chicago and London: Chicago University Press, pp. 161–96.

Descartes R. (1986 [1640]) *Meditations on First Philosophy: With Selections from the Objections and Replies* (trans. John Cottingham), Cambridge: Cambridge University.

Elias, Norbert (1987) 'Human Beings and their Emotions', in *The Body: Social Process and Cultural Theory*, Mike Featherstone, Mike Hepworth and Bryan S. Turner (eds), London: Sage.
Emerson, Joan (1970) 'Behaviour in Private Places: Sustaining Definitions of Reality in Gynecological Examinations', in *Recent Sociology*, Hans Peter Dreitzel (ed.), 2, New York: Macmillan, pp. 73–100.
Falk, Pasi (1994) *The Consuming Body*, London: Sage.
Ferdinand, Tonnies (1957) *Community and Society: Gemeinschaft und Gesellschaft*, translated and edited by Charles P. Loomis, The Michigan State University Press.
Foucault, Michel (1965 [1961]) *Madness and Civilization* (trans. Richard Howard), London: Tavistock.
Foucault, Michel (1970) 'Theatrum Philosophicum', *Critique*, in *Language, Counter-Memory, Practice*, Donald F. Bouchard (ed.) (trans. Donald F. Bouchard and Sherry Simon (1977)), Oxford: Blackwell, no. 282, pp. 885–908.
Foucault, Michel (1970a [1966]) *The Order of Things*, London: Tavistock.
Foucault, Michel (1971) 'Orders of Discourse', *Social Science Information* (trans. Rupert Swyer), 10 (2), pp. 7–30.
Foucault, Michel (1973 [1963]) *The Birth of the Clinic* [*BC*] (trans. A. M. Sheridan), London and New York: Routledge.
Foucault, Michel (1977 [1975]) *Discipline and Punish* [*DP*] (trans. Alan Sheridan), London and Harmondsworth: Penguin.
Foucault, Michel (1978 [1976]) *The History of Sexuality, Volume I* (trans. Robert Hurley), London: Penguin.
Foucault, Michel (1980) *Power/Knowledge*, C. Gordon (ed.), Brighton: Harvester Press.
Foucault, Michel (1982) *This is Not a Pipe*, Berkeley: University of California.
Foucault, Michel (1985 [1984]) *The Use of Pleasure: The History of Sexuality, Volume 2* (trans. Robert Hurley), London: Penguin.
Foucault, Michel (1988) *The Care of the Self: The History of Sexuality, Volume 3* (trans. Robert Hurley), London: Penguin.
Foucault, Michel (1988) *Technologies of the Self* [TS], London: Tavistock.
Fox, Alan (1985) *Man Mismanagement*, London: Huchinson.
Fox, Nicholas J. (1993) *Postmodernism, Sociology and Health*, Buckingham: Open University Press.
Freud, Sigmund (1953, 1978), *The Interpretation of Dreams*, in *The Standard Edition of the Complete Psychological Works of Sigmund Freud, vols. IV and V*, London: Hogarth.
Freyer, Hans (1948) *Weltgeschlicht Europas*, vol. 1, Wiesbaden: Dieterich, p. 169.
Game, Ann A. (1991) *Undoing the Social: Toward a Deconstructive Sociology*, Buckingham: Open University.
Gehlen, Alfred (1988) *Man: His Nature and Place in the World* [*M*] (trans. Clare McMillan and Karl Pillemen), New York: Columbia University Press.
Gerth, H. H. and Wright Mills, C. (1948) *From Max Weber*, London: Routledge and Kegan Paul.
Giddens, Anthony (1974) *Positivism and Sociology*, Aldershot: Gower.
Giddens, Anthony (1976) *New Rules of Sociological Method*, London: Hutchinson.
Giddens, Anthony (1984) *The Constitution of Society*, University of California.
Gouldner, Alvin W. (1969) 'The Unemployed Self', in *Work*, vol. II, R. Fraser (ed.), Harmondsworth: Penguin.

Habermas, Jurgen (1987 [1985]) *The Philosophical Discourse of Modernity*, Cambridge: Polity Press.

Hannan, Michael T. and Freeman, John (1979) 'The Population Ecology of Organizations', *American Journal of Sociology*, vol. 82, no. 5, pp. 929–64.

Hardt, Michael (1993) *Gilles Deleuze: An Apprenticeship in Philosophy* [*GD*], London: UCL Press.

Harvey, David (1989) *The Condition of Postmodernity*, Oxford: Blackwell.

Hegel, George Wilhelm Friedrich (1968) *Lectures on the History of Philosophy* (trans. E. S. Haldane and Frances Simpson), London: Routledge & Kegan Paul.

Hegel, George Wilhelm Friedrich (1969) *The Science of Logic* [*SL*] (trans. A. V. Miller), London: Allen and Unwin.

Hegel, George Wilhelm Friedrich (1977) *Hegel's Phenomenology of Spirit* [*PS*] (trans. A. V. Miller), Oxford: Oxford University.

Heidegger, Martin (1982) *Gesamtausgabe, Band 54, Parmenides*, Frankfurt am Main: Vittorio Klostermann.

Heidegger, Martin (2002) "The Origin of the Work of Art" in Heidegger, *Off the Beaten Track*, Cambridge: Cambridge University Press.

Helmholtz, Herman Ludwig Ferdinand von (1916 [1851]) 'Description of an Ophthalmoscope for the Investigation of the Retina of the Living Eye', (trans. Robert Hall), Chicago: Cleveland Press.

Hertz, Robert (1960) *Death and the Right Hand*, London: Cohen & West.

Hobbes, Thomas (1968 [1651]) *Leviathan* [*L*], London: Penguin.

Holub, Robert C. (1991) *Jurgen Habermas*, London and New York: Routledge.

Horkheimer, M and Adorno, T (1973) *The Dialectic of Enlightenment*, London: Verso.

Houlgate, Stephen (1986) *Hegel, Nietzsche and the Criticism of Metaphysics*, Cambridge: Cambridge University Press.

Hume, David (1888 [1738, 1748, 1752]) *A Treatise of Human Nature* [*T*] L. A. Selby-Bigge (ed.), Oxford: Clarendon Press.

Hume, David (1970 [1779]) *Dialogues Concerning Natural Religion*, Nelson Pike (ed.), Indianapolis: Bobbs-Merrill.

Hume, David (2007 [1748]) *An Enguiry Concerning Human Understanding*, Stephen Buckle (ed.), Cambridge: Cambridge University Press.

Hume, David (1957 [1752]) *An Enquiry Concerning the Principles of Morals*, Charles W. Hendel (ed.), Indianapolis: Bobbs-Merrill.

Husserl, Edmund (1962) *Ideas*, New York: Collier.

Irigaray, Luce 1991 [1977]) 'The Poverty of Psychoanalysis', ['Misere de la Psychanalyse', *Critique*, 365] (trans. David Macey), *The Irigaray Reader*, Margaret Whitford (ed.), Oxford and Cambridge, Massachusets: Blackwell, pp. 79–104.

Irigaray, Luce (1991a [1990]) 'Equal or Different?' (trans. David Macey), *The Irigaray Reader*, Margaret Whitford (ed.), Oxford and Cambridge, Massachusets: Blackwell, pp. 30–3.

Irigaray, Luce (1991b) 'Volume Without Contours' (trans. David Macey), *The Irigaray Reader*, Margaret Whitford (ed.), Oxford and Cambridge, MA.: Blackwell, pp. 53–67.

Irigaray, Luce (1991c) 'The Limits of Transference' (trans. David Macey), *The Irigaray Reader*, Margaret Whitford (ed.), Oxford and Cambridge, MA.: Blackwell, pp. 105–17.

Jung, Carl Gustav (1964) *Man and his Symbols*, London: Aldus.

Kamata, Satoshi (1982 [1973, 1980]) *Japan in the Passing Lane: An Insider's Account of Life in a Japanese Auto Factory* (trans. Tatsuru Akimoto), London: Allen and Unwin.

Lacan, Jacques (1977 [1973]) *The Four Fundamental Concepts of Psycho-Analysis* (trans. Alan Sheridan), Harmondsworth: Penguin.

Lacan, Jacques (1977a) *Ecrits: A Selection* (trans. Alan Sheridan), London: Tavistock.

Laënnec, René (1819) *Traite de l'auscultation mediate,* 2 vols, Paris: Brosson & Chaudé.

Laënnec, René (1884) *Traite inedit de l'anatomie patholoaique*, Paris.

Leroi-Gourhan (1964) *Le aeste et la parole, vol. 1, of Technique et langage,* Paris: Albin Michel, p. 161.

Lyotard, Jean-Francois (1984 [1979]) *The Postmodern Condition* (trans. Geoff Bennington and Brian Massumi), Manchester: Manchester University.

Lyotard, Jean-Francois (1988 [1983]) *The Differend* (trans. Georges Van Den Abbeele), Manchester: Manchester University.

Macey, David (1995) 'A Very Active Philosopher' (Obituary for Deleuze), *Guardian*, 7 Nov. 1995.

Marx, Karl (1974) *Capital*, London: Lawrence & Wishart, 3 vols.

Marx, Karl. and Engels, Friedrich (1974) *The German Ideology*, London: Lawrence and Wishart.

Marx, Karl and Engels, Friedrich (1978) 'Critique of Hegel's Philosophy of Right', *The Marx-Engels Reader* Robert Tucker (ed.) New York: Norton.

Mauss, Marcel (1979 [1936]) 'Body Techniques', *Sociology and Psychology* (trans. B. Brewster), London: Routledge & Kegan Paul, pp. 95–123.

Mead, George Herbert (1934) *Mind, Self, and Society*, Charles Morris, (ed.), Chicago and London: University of Chicago.

Merleau-Ponty, Maurice (1962) *Phenomenology of Perception* (trans. C. Smith), London and Henley: Routledge and Kegan Paul.

Miller, D. L. (1984) *George Herbert Mead: Self, Language and the World*, Chicago and London: Chicago University Press.

Morgan, Gareth (1986) *Images of Organization*, Beverly Hills: Sage.

Nietzsche, Friedrich Wilhelm (1888 [1868]) *The Antichrist* [*AC*] (trans. R. J. Hollingdale), Harmondsworth: Penguin.

Nietzsche, Friedrich Wilhelm (1935 [1937]) *La Volonte de Puissance* [*VP*] (trans. G. Bianquis [from the edition of W. Wiirzbach]), Paris: N.R.F. Gallimard.

Nietzsche, Friedrich Wilhelm (1954) *The Portable Nietzsche*, (trans. Walter Kaufmann, ed.), London: Penguin.

Nietzsche, Friedrich Wilhelm (1961, 1969 [1883–92]) *Thus Spoke Zarathustra* [*Z*] (trans. R. J. Hollingdale), Harmondsworth: Penguin.

Nietzsche, Friedrich Wilhelm (1967 [1887]) *On the Genealogy of Morals* [*GM*] (trans. Walter Kaufmann and J. R. Hollingdale), New York: Random House.

Nietzsche, Friedrich Wilhelm (1967 [1888]) *Ecce Homo* [EH] (trans. W. Kaufmann), Random House.

Nietzsche, Friedrich Wilhelm (1968) *The Will to Power* [*WP*] (trans. W. Kaufmann and R. J. Hollingdale), Random House.

Nietzsche, Friedrich (1973 [1886]) *Beyond Good and Evil* [*BGE*] (trans. R. J. Hollingdale), Harmondsworth: Penguin.

Nietzsche, Friedrich Wilhelm (1974 [1882, 1887]) *The Joyful Wisdom* (trans. Walter Kaufmann), New York: Random House.

Nietzsche, Friedrich Wilhelm (1986 [1878, 1886]) *Human, All Too Human* (trans. R. J. Hollingdale), Harmondsworth: Penguin.

Norris, Christopher (1987) *Derrida*, London: Fontana.

O'Gorman (1845) *The Practice of Angling, Particularly as Regards Ireland*, Dublin: William Curry Jun. & Company.

Plato (1979) *Gorgias* (trans. Terence Irwin), Oxford: Clarendon Press.

Plato (1955, 1974, 1987) *The Republic* (trans. Desmond Lee), London: Penguin.

Plessner, Helmut (1976) *Die Frage nach der Conditio humana, aufsatze zur philosophischen Anthropologie*, Frankfurt: Suhrkamp.

Pollock, James E. (1856), 'On a Self-Adjusting Double Stethoscope', *Lancet*, vol. 1, p. 398.

Powell, Walter W and DiMaggio, Paul J. (1991), *The New Institutionalism in Organizational Analysis*, Chicago: University of Chicago.

Readings, Bill (1991) *Introducing Lyotard*, London and New York: Routledge.

Reiser, Stanley Joel (1978) *Medicine and the Reign of Technology* [*MRT*], Cambridge: Cambridge University Press.

Robbe-Grillet, Alain. (1977) 'Order and Disorder in Film and Fiction', *Critical Enquiry*. 4 (1), pp. 1–20.

Rorty, Amelie, ed. (1966) *Pragmatic Philosophy*, New York: Doubleday Anchor.

Rorty, Richard (1991) *Objectivism, Relativism, and Truth: Philosophical Papers*, volume 1, Cambridge: Cambridge University.

Sartre, Jean-Paul (1956) *Being and Nothingness*, New York: Philosophical Library, Part III.

Scheler, Max (1961) *Man's Place in the World*, Boston: Beacon Press.

Singer, Peter (1983) *Hegel*, Oxford: Oxford University Press.

Spinoza, Baruch (1985 [composed 1661–75: published posthumously]) *Ethics* [*E*], in *The Collected Works of Spinoza* (trans. Edwin Curley, ed.), vol. 1, Princeton: Princeton University Press.

Spinoza, Baruch (1985) *Theological – Political Treatise*, in *The Collected Works of Spinoza* (trans. Edwin Curley, ed.), vol. 1., Princeton: Princeton University Press.

Spinoza, Baruch (1985) *Political Treatise*, in *The Collected Works of Spinoza* (trans. Edwin Curley, ed.), vol. 1., Princeton: Princeton University Press.

Taylor, Charles (1975) *Hegel*, Cambridge: Cambridge University Press.

Theweleit, Klaus (1987) *Male Fantasies*, Minneapolis: University of Minnesota.

Thomas, K. (1964) 'Work and Leisure in Pre-Industrial Society', *Past and Present*, no. 29, pp. 50–66.

Thomas, Mark (1972) *Spinoza's Theory of Truth*, New York: Columbia University Press.

Tronti, Mario (1966) *Operai e capital*, Turin: Einaudi.

Turner, Bryan S. (1987) *The Body and Society*, London and New York: Routledge.

Turner, Bryan S. (1991) 'Missing Bodies, toward a Sociology of Embodiment', *Sociology of Health and Illness*, vol. 13 (2), pp. 265–72.

Turner, Bryan S. (1991) 'Recent Developments in the Theory of the Body", in *The Body: Social Process and Cultural Theory*, M. Featherstone et al. (eds), London: Sage.

Turner, Bryan S. (1992) *Regulating Bodies* [*RB*], London and New York: Routledge.

Watson, Eben (1865) 'Laryngoscopy and its Revelations', [part 1], *Lancet*, vol. 1, p. 589.
Weinstein, Deena and Weinstein, Michael (1984) 'On the Visual Constitution of Society: The Contributions of Georg Simmel and Jean-Paul Sartre to a Sociology of the Senses', *History of European Ideas*, vol. 5, no.4, pp. 349–62.
Williams, Raymond (1976) *Keywords; A Vocabulary of Culture and Society* [K], London: Fontana.

Index